VÁCLAV HAVEL
OR
LIVING IN TRUTH

VÁCLAV HAVEL

LIVING IN TRUTH

Twenty-two essays published
on the occasion of the award of
the Erasmus Prize to Václav Havel

Edited by Jan Vladislav

Watkins College
of Art & Design

faber and faber
LONDON · BOSTON

First published in The Netherlands in 1986 by
Meulenhoff Amsterdam in association with Faber and Faber
First published in Great Britain in 1987 by
Faber and Faber Limited
3 Queen Square London WC1N 3AU
This paperback edition first published in 1989
Reprinted 1990 (three times)

Printed in Great Britain by
Richard Clay Ltd, Bungay, Suffolk
All rights reserved

British Library Cataloguing in Publication Data

Havel, Václav
Václav Havel or Living in truth.
I. Title   II. Vladislav, Jan
087'.86   PG5039.18.A9

ISBN 0-571-14440-3

Published with the financial support of
the Praemium Erasmianum Foundation

Contents

CONTENTS

Foreword

The award of the 1986 Erasmus Prize to Václav Havel seemed the appropriate occasion to draw the attention of a larger public to the work of this Czech playwright and essayist. Well known to students of Czech literature and those sympathetic to dissident movements in eastern Europe, Václav Havel gives evidence in his works of ideas and an attitude to life that transcend these two aspects. It is the search for truth in its purest form that drives him; a truth which is inseparable from a desire for impartiality and which should be looked for primarily within oneself. Havel has made it clear that, in principle, every human being needs an area of personal privacy in which he or she can be authentic, and that to philosophers, historians, legal experts, scientists, artists, writers and journalists – in short those to whom impartiality is of special importance – this authenticity is a *sine qua non*. He is therefore right to point out that, by its nature, the search for truth does not admit any compromise for external reasons. He bases his view on the fact that one should look at life honestly and realistically and that one must take account of man with all his weaknesses and imperfections.

It is a mark of the great distance and the stature of Havel's work that in his criticism he makes clear that this tendency does not only exist in his own surroundings, but that it could also be found in the West. This aspect makes him more than a critic of certain political systems and it is for this reason that Havel should be an example to all.

It is the wish of the Praemium Erasmianum Foundation that by publishing this volume a larger public will learn of the

writings of Václav Havel. It is our hope that these essays b
the laureate and his friends will contribute to a bett
understanding of man and his capabilities. The contributio
by other writers, collected by the editor, are proof of t
interest and importance that Havel's work arouses.

Last but not least, we want to thank Jan Vladislav for all t
work he has done and for compiling a book which more tha
meets our expectations.

G. A. Wagner, preside
H. R. Hoetink, direct

Acknowledgements

Václav Havel's six essays which make up Part One of this volume are here published together for the first time. This was made possible thanks to the kind agreement of the author and his publisher Rowohlt Verlag. I wish to thank also the publishers and journals where these essays have been published in English for the first time: *Survey* for the 'Letter to Dr Gustáv Husák'; Palach Press and Hutchinson and Co. for 'The power of the powerless'; the Charta 77 Foundation for 'Six asides about culture' and 'An anatomy of reticence'; the *Salisbury Review* for 'Politics and conscience'; the *Idler* for 'Thriller'. Thanks are also due to the translators of Havel's essays, namely Erazim Kohák, Roger Scruton and Paul Wilson for their kind co-operation. Most translations have been revised for this edition.

Editing Part Two was made considerably easier by the helpful understanding of all contributors from Czechoslovakia and abroad. I wish to thank in particular Samuel Beckett and his publishers, Faber and Faber, for permission to use *Catastrophe*; the Lamuv Verlag for H. Böll's 'Courtesy towards God'; T. Garton Ash and *Granta* for 'Prague – a poem, not disappearing'; Pavel Kohout and the University of British Columbia Press for 'The chaste centaur'; Milan Kundera for 'Candide had to be destroyed'; Arthur Miller for 'I think about you a great deal'; Tom Stoppard and Grove Press for 'Introduction' (to *The Memorandum*).

Special thanks are due to the authors who contributed original essays to this collection, namely Jiří Gruša, Ladislav Hejdánek, Harry Järv, Iva Kotrlá, Zdena Salivarová, Milan

Šimečka, Josef Škvorecký, Zdenek Urbánek and Ludvík Vaculík – as well as to the translators of essays in Part Two: J. R. Littelboy, D. Armour, D. Viney, M. Pomichalek and A. Mozga, K. Seigneurie, A. G. Brain, and G. Theiner. Last but not least, I wish to thank the Document Centre for the Promotion of Independent Czechoslovak Literature (Hanover) and especially its Executive Director/Curator, Dr Vilém Prečan, for his most friendly help.

Jan Vladislav

a all my writings,' Václav Havel explicitly recalled not long o, 'my starting point has always been what I know, my wn experience of this world I live in, my experience of yself. In short, I have always written about what matters to e in this life: what I see, what interests me, what arouses y concern – I shouldn't think I could find any other place to art from. However, it has always been my hope in my riting that, by bearing witness to certain specific experi- ces of the world, I will be able to disclose something *iversally human*, specific experience only being a way and a eans of saying something about being in general, about •ople in today's world, about the crisis of modern-day amanity – in other words, those matters that concern us all.'

When Václav Havel wrote these lines, he particularly had mind his writings for the theatre and was addressing mself above all to future producers of his new play *Largo* *solato*. But he is not solely *e* playwright, and despite his sclaimers and his efforts on different occasions to stress that • is no philosopher, and that it is not his ambition to onstruct a conceptually fixed system', there can be no doubt at Václav Havel has become an exponent of unofficial :ech thinking: thinking based on the specific, personal perience of someone who has opted for that most deman- ng of freedoms – the freedom to live in one's own country d think as one likes. Thus his remarks about the fun- mental starting point of his writing not only sum up the iderlying characteristic of his theatrical works but also what a highly personal feature of the other half of his *oeuvre*: his

essays, the number of which is growing all the time, alo
with their importance.

In the case of an author writing for the theatre like Vác
Havel, and living in a country like Czechoslovakia, suck
development is only to be expected. In a world where thea
– the social art *par excellence* – has been unable for yea
decades even, to fulfil its prime function of universal a
constantly renewed catharsis, the very *raison d'être* of
playwright's work is also severely jeopardized, and Ha
became aware of this danger very early on in his car
through his own, very bitter personal experience. He
long realized at first hand, not only that 'theatre, of all
artistic genres, is the most closely tied to a particular time a
place', but also that playwrights without a theatre
'something like a bird without a nest; they are cut off fr
their true home, from the lifeblood of a given social "here a
now" which is the source and destination of their writing,
place where their work first comes to life and becomes its
from which it draws its life, and without which it could w
lose all sense and meaning.'

There are countries at the present time, including Hav
own homeland, where, in order to defend the imperil
meaning of their writing and their very *raison d'être*, as well
to face up to the difficulties of being silenced artists -
situation which is all the more arduous for dramatists in vi
of the nature of their art – playwrights are being obliged
find other outlets, other ways of speaking out, so as to av
being confined entirely to their own particular, though a
precarious, instrument – the writing of plays. This
undoubtedly one of the reasons why, for years now, Vác
Havel also has repeatedly turned to the free, open a
flexible form of the essay as a means of speaking directly
his public, above all in the circles of Czech and Slov
unofficial culture, but also outside them, and international
He is thereby able to side-track the complex and precari
mechanism which theatre, in common with all the offici
administered, controlled and censored mass media, rep
sents under many regimes.

Certainly, this does not mean that Havel is in any way turning his back on the theatre. His recent plays, the tragi-comic *Largo Desolato* and the Faustian *Temptation*, prove that the opposite is true, and that, for him, drama continues to be not simply the focus of interest in his life, but his preferred medium for testifying to those matters which, in one way or another, 'concern us all'. Neither is it true to say that Havel's use of the essay is a recent phenomenon. He exploited the form most successfully as early as the sixties, at the time he was writing his first plays. What is without doubt, however, is that the number and significance of his essays rose sharply in the seventies and eighties, as 'normalization' rolled on. This was also a time when he was gaining increasing experience of the new regime and its unavowed – though increasingly thorough and menacing – endeavours to erase the individual and national identity of the Czechs and Slovaks.

It was in that context that a number of Havel's essays acquired a new dimension – often assuming manifesto form. His *Open letter to President Husák* of 1975 (concerning the country's political entropy) represented an undoubted milestone in the history of the Czech spiritual resistance of the seventies and prefigured its culmination in the *Declaration of Charter 77*. And it was only natural that Václav Havel should have been one of the initiators of that declaration and one of Charter 77's first spokesmen. This too was a natural consequence of his standpoint as someone who endeavours, through his thinking and writing, through his plays and essays alike, to reflect consistently on his own specific and personal experience of the world and of himself.

Experience in this sense is not something passive or something that comes about of its own accord; neither is it something solely to do with *consciousness*. It is also, and possibly above all, something we call down on ourselves; something which, to a great extent, we ourselves prepare for by accepting or rejecting the world we live in. It is something that commits our *conscience*. Václav Havel treats this theme in detail in his next important essay, *The power of the powerless*, in

1978. At the heart of this wide-ranging paper he places the question of *living in the truth* and the *higher responsibility* of all individuals wherever they are, but above all in those parts of the world where the human identity is most at risk, not only from those in power, but from individual human beings themselves. Even in these realms, this is not just another case of abstract speculation on a well-worn theme. Above all, it is an urgent testimony to a specific experience of the world – the sort that almost everyone in Czechoslovakia in the seventies lived through – and continues to live through today. All the author of *The power of the powerless* did was to describe and summarize it, in order to show where it was leading, and in certain cases, what it was committing people to – not just those who lived through it, but everyone else too. Again, the form chosen is the 'essay', in the sense of an endeavour, with the help of personal witness, to disclose 'something *universally human*' and say something 'about being in general, about people in today's world, and about the crisis of modern-day humanity'.

Specific experience of the world and specific witness to it are bought at a price, though. This is confirmed also by a glance at Václav Havel's curriculum vitae: ostracized as a child for his 'class origins' so that he was deprived of a proper chance to study, years of harassment which turned into direct persecution in the course of normalization, two trials on charges brought by the regime, and a sentence of four and a half years' imprisonment of which he served three years and eight months before being paroled, seriously ill, in March 1983. In countries like present-day Czechoslovakia, such stories tend to be commonplace rather than the exeption and are mainly important for the victim. In Václav Havel's case, however, they have not only deeply marked his life, but also and above all, his work. This is because they have served, again and again, to renew the author's specific experience of the world and of himself. It is this experience that has ensured that the starting point – and goal – of all his writing (and here I have his essays particularly in mind) is never merely speculative or abstract. On the contrary, even though they are not purely autobiographical, his essays are always very tightly bound up with his personal experience and they make no bones about it: suffice it to read his *Politics and conscience* or *Thriller*. Though anything but rhetorical, Havel's essays respond in an exceptionally eloquent and urgent, though always specific, fashion to the no less specific, urgent, and eloquent challenges of the times we live in.

In the part of the world where Václav Havel lives, all such challenges and the responses to them inevitably acquire political overtones. It would be wrong, however, to reduce his essays to this chance and incidental element. Although they understandably have their origins in the specific circumstances of a particular time and place, and although they naturally react to specific situations whose existence is contingent on a particular regime, Havel's reflections have a much wider significance and their intention is much more profound. In this sense, one could apply to them something that Havel recently wrote about his plays: 'Were my plays regarded solely as a description of a particular social or political system, I would feel I had failed as an author; were, on the other hand, they regarded simply as a portrayal of humankind or of the world, I would feel I had succeeded.'

Basically, the same goes for his essays. Not even in them does the author offer us 'solely a description of a particular social or political system'. The essays also consist, above all, of his continuing reflections 'on the burden of being; on people's arduous struggle to protect their own identity from impersonal power which seeks to take it away from them; on the strange contradiction between people's actual capacities and the role they are obliged to play by reason of their environment, their destiny and their own work; on how easy it is in theory to know how to live one's life, but how difficult it is to do so in practice; on the tragic incapacity of people to understand each other, even when they wish each other the best; on human loneliness, fear and cowardice, etc. etc. – and finally, of course, (and most importantly) on the tragi-comic and absurd dimensions of all these themes.' Were we not aware that these comments were written in 1984 for producers of his play, *Largo Desolato*, we might easily take them as a commentary on certain of his essays, such as *Politics and conscience* written at the beginning of that year.

There is a sense in which Havel's plays and essays constitute two aspects of one and the same 'entity'. Whereas in the plays these main themes are viewed and treated 'from within' as it were, and constitute what the author himself has called 'a sort of *musical reflection* on the burden of being', in the essays, these themes are viewed and analysed in a more 'external' manner on the lines of a *clinical report*, which constitutes, at the same time, an urgent call for moral renewal, for 'living in the truth', which he writes about in *The power of the powerless*, or again, for 'people to retrieve their humanity and resume their responsibility for the world' and assert 'politics as morality in practice', which he deals with in *Politics and conscience*.

It is possible that the appeals that emerge from Havel's reflections may appear to some to be naive, unrealistic and illusory faced with the state of today's world as so poignantly depicted in his essay, *Thriller*. In all events, the nature of these appeals is such that they could scarcely have visible results in the foreseeable future, let alone political success. The author of *Politics and conscience* is fully aware of this fact, and says as much himself. At the same time though, he recalls another proven reality that is of outstanding importance, namely, that even in the world as it is now, 'those apparently powerless individuals who have the courage to speak the truth out loud and stand by what they say body and soul, and are prepared to pay dearly for doing so, have – astonishingly enough – greater power – however formally disfranchised they are – than thousands of anonymous electors in others circumstances.'

Toward the end of that essay, Havel cites two such examples: Alexander Solzhenitsyn and Jan Patočka. Other names could easily be added to the list, including Havel's own, without a doubt.

Of course, Václav Havel neither is, nor seeks to be a philosopher, constructing 'a conceptually fixed system'. However, he is, without doubt, an author whose thinking and actions are marked by what I would sooner call 'iron logic' were it not of such a lively, organic and spiritual kind. But however we describe it, it is clearly something extremely demanding, if not actually implacable. It is something that goads him, again and again, on the basis of his own specific experience of the world and himself, to engage in specific, personal reflection about it all and to voice his own specific, personal assent or protest; to act, in other words, according to his own specific, personal conscience. Broadly speaking, this is how these main themes are linked together in Havel's thinking: at the end of the chain we find the theme of specific, personal responsibility, which people bear, but also choose (to their own cost) as their destiny.

Responsibility as fate is possibly one of the most typical, individual and – apparently – personal themes of Havel's thinking. It was explicitly advanced in the essay in which Havel introduces the Western reader to the last novel by Ludvík Vaculík, another of those to have chosen that most demanding of freedoms. It is this very freedom to live and think as one likes in one's own country which is the main – albeit unnamed – protagonist of Vaculík's novel, *The Czech Dreambook*. This provides the basis for the portrait that Havel paints of his friend. However, every portrait, we know, is also a self-portrait, and this is just as true about Havel's sketch of Vaculík. Though it was certainly not his intention, there can be no doubt that he laid particular stress on those traits that characterize also, if not above all, his own life story:

> From this viewpoint, *The Czech Dreambook* appears as a novel about responsibility, will and fate; about responsibility that is – if one may so put it – stronger than the will; about the tragedy of fate stemming from responsibility; about the futility of all human endeavours to break out of the role that responsibility has imposed; about responsibility as destiny.

Responsibility as destiny; we could hardly find a better motto for Václav Havel.

Jan Vladislav

PART ONE

SIX TEXTS BY VÁCLAV HAVEL

Letter to Dr Gustáv Husák, General Secretary of the Czechoslovak Communist Party

Dear Dr Husák,

In our offices and factories work goes on, discipline prevails. The efforts of our citizens are yielding visible results in a slowly rising standard of living: people build houses, buy cars, have children, amuse themselves, live their lives.

All this, of course, amounts to very little as a criterion for the success or failure of your policy. After every social upheaval, people invariably come back in the end to their daily labours, for the simple reason that they want to stay alive; they do so for their own sake, after all, not for the sake of this or that team of political leaders.

Not that going to work, doing the shopping and living their own lives is by any means all that people do. They do much more than that: they commit themselves to numerous output norms which they then fulfil and over-fulfil; they vote as one man and unanimously elect the candidates proposed to them; they are active in various political organizations; they attend meetings and demonstrations; they declare their support for everything they are supposed to. Nowhere can any sign of dissent be seen from anything that the government does.

These facts, of course, are not to be made light of. One must ask seriously, at this point, whether all this does not confirm your success in achieving the tasks your team set itself – those of winning the public's support and consolidating the situation in the country?

The answer must depend on what we mean by consolidation.

In so far as it is to be measured solely by statistical returns of various kinds, by official statements and police accounts of the public's political involvement, and so forth, then we can certainly hardly feel any doubt that consolidation has been achieved.

But what if we take consolidation to mean something more, a genuine state of mind in society? Supposing we start to inquire after more durable, perhaps subtler and more imponderable, but none the less significant factors, i.e. what lies hidden behind all the figures by way of genuine personal, human experience? Supposing we ask, for example, what has been done for the moral and spiritual revival of society, for the enhancement of the truly human dimensions of life, for the elevation of man to a higher degree of dignity, for his truly free and authentic assertion in this world? What do we find when we thus turn our attention from the mere set of outward manifestations to their inner causes and consequences, their connections and meanings, in a word, to that less obvious plane of reality where those manifestations might actually acquire a general human meaning? Can we, even then, consider our society 'consolidated'?

I make so bold as to answer, No; to assert that, for all the outwardly appealing facts, inwardly our society, far from being a consolidated one, is, on the contrary, plunging ever deeper into a crisis more dangerous, in some respects, than any we can recall in our recent history.

I shall try to justify this assertion.

The basic question one must ask is this: *why* are people in fact behaving in the way they do? Why do they do all these things that, taken together, form the impressive image of a totally united society giving total support to its government? For any unprejudiced observer, the answer is, I think, self-evident: they are driven to it by *fear*.

For fear of losing his job, the schoolteacher teaches things he does not believe; fearing for his future, the pupil repeats them after him; for fear of not being allowed to continue his studies, the young man joins the Youth League and participates in whatever of its activities are necessary; fear that, under the monstrous system of political credits, his son or daughter will not acquire the necessary total of points for enrolment at a school leads the father to take on all manner of responsibilities and 'voluntarily' to do everything required. Fear of the consequences of refusal leads people to take part in elections, to vote for the proposed candidates and to pretend that they regard such ceremonies as genuine elections; out of fear for their livelihood, position or prospects, they go to meetings, vote for every resolution they have to, or at least keep silent: it is fear that carries them through sundry humiliating acts of self-criticism and penitence and the dishonest filling out of a mass of degrading questionnaires; fear that someone might inform against them prevents them from giving public, and often even private, expression to their true opinions. It is the fear of suffering financial reverses and the effort to better themselves and ingratiate themselves with the authorities that in most cases makes working men put their names to 'work commitments'; indeed, the same motives often lie behind the establishment of Socialist Labour brigades, in the clear realization that their chief function is to be mentioned in the appropriate reports to higher levels. Fear causes people to attend all those official celebrations, demonstrations and marches. Fear of being prevented from contiuing their work leads many scientists and artists to give allegiance to ideas they do not in fact accept, to write things they do not agree with or know to be false, to join official organizations or to take part in work of whose value they have the lowest opinion, or to distort and mutilate their own works. In the effort to save themselves, many even report others for doing to them what they themselves have been doing to the people they report.

The fear I am speaking of is not, of course, to be taken in the ordinary psychological sense as a definite, precise emotion. Most of those we see around us are not quaking like aspen leaves: they wear the faces of confident, self-satisfied citizens. We are concerned with fear in a deeper sense, an ethical sense if you will, namely, the more or less conscious participation in the collective awareness of a permanent and

ubiquitous danger; anxiety about what is being, or might b
endangered, becoming gradually used to this threat as
substantive part of the actual world; the increasing degree
which, in an ever more skilful and matter-of-fact way, we g
in for various kinds of external adaptation as the on
effective method of self-defence.

Naturally, fear is not the only building block in the prese
social structure.

None the less, it is the main, the fundamental materia
without which not even that surface uniformity, disciplin
and unanimity on which official documents base the
assertions about the 'consolidated' state of affairs in o
country could be attained.

The question arises, of course, what are people actuall
afraid of? Trials? Torture? Loss of property? Deportation
Executions? Certainly not. The most brutal forms of pressu
exerted by the authorities upon the public are, fortunatel
past history – at least in our circumstances. Today, oppre
sion takes more subtle and choice forms. And even if politic
trials do not take place today – everyone knows how t
authorities manage to manipulate them – they only represe
an extreme threat, while the main thrust has moved into t
sphere of existential pressure. Which, of course, leaves t
core of the matter largely unchanged.

Notoriously, it is not the absolute value of a threat whi
counts, so much as its relative value. It is not so much wha
man objectively loses, as the subjective importance it has f
him on the plane on which he lives, with its own scale
values. Thus, if a man today is afraid, say, of losing t
chance of working in his own field, this may be a fear equal
strong, and productive of the same reactions, as if –
another historical context – he had been threatened with t
confiscation of his property. Indeed, the technique
existential pressure is, in a sense, more universal. For there
no one in our country who is not, in a broad sens
existentially vulnerable. Everyone has something to lose a
so everyone has reason to be afraid. The range of things
man can lose is a very wide one, extending from the manifo

privileges of the ruling caste and all the special opportunities afforded to the powerful – such as the enjoyment of undisturbed work, advancement and earning power, the ability to work at all in one's field, the chance of higher education – down to the mere possibility of living in that limited degree of legal certainty available to other citizens, instead of finding oneself amongst the special class to whom not even those laws which apply to the rest of the public apply, in other words, among the victims of Czechoslovak political apartheid. Yes, everyone has something to lose. The humblest workman's mate can be shifted to an even more lowly and worse paid job. Even he can pay a savage penalty for speaking his mind at a meeting or in the pub.

This system of existential pressure, embracing totally the whole of society and every individual, either as a specific everyday threat or as a general contingency, could not, of course, work effectively if it were not backed up – exactly like the former, more brutal forms of pressure – by its natural hinterland in the power structure, namely, by that force which renders it comprehensive, complex and robust: the ubiquitous, omnipotent state police.

For this is the hideous spider whose invisible web runs right through the whole of society; this is the point at infinity where all the lines of fear ultimately intersect; this is the final and irrefutable proof that no citizen can hope to challenge the power of the state. And even if most of the people, most of the time, cannot see this web with their own eyes, nor touch its fibres, even the simplest citizen is well aware of its existence, assumes its silent presence at every moment in every place, and behaves accordingly – behaves, that is, so as to ensure the approval of those hidden eyes and ears. And well does he know the importance of that approval. For the spider can intervene in a man's life without any need to have him in his jaws. There is no need at all for a man actually to be interrogated, charged, brought to trial or sentenced. For his superiors are also ensnared in the same web; and at every level where his fate is decided, there are people collaborating or forced to collaborate with the state police. Thus, the very fact that the state police are in a position to intervene at any time in a man's life, without his having any chance of resisting, suffices to rob his life of some of its naturalness and authenticity and to turn it into a kind of endless dissimulation.

If it is fear which lies behind people's defensive attempts to preserve what they have, it becomes increasingly apparent that the chief impulses for their aggressive efforts to win what they do not yet possess are *selfishness* and *careerism*.

Seldom in recent times, it seems, has a social system offered scope so openly and so brazenly to people willing to support anything at any time, as long as it bring them some advantage; to unprincipled and spineless men, prepared to do anything in their craving for power and personal gain; to born lackeys, ready for any humiliation and willing at all times to sacrifice their neighbours' and their own honour for a chance to ingratiate themselves with those in power.

In view of this, it is not surprising that so many public and influential positions are occupied, more than ever before, by notorious careerists, opportunists, charlatans and men of dubious record; in short, by typical collaborators, men, that is, with a special gift for persuading themselves at every turn that their dirty work is a way of rescuing something, or, at least, of preventing still worse men from stepping into their shoes. Nor is it surprising, in these circumstances, that corruption among public employees of all kinds, their willingness quite openly and in any situation to accept bribes and allow themselves shamelessly to be swayed by whatever considerations their various private interests and greed dictate, has reached a level higher than can be recalled during the last decade.

The number of people who sincerely believe everything that the official propaganda says and who selflessly support the government's authority is smaller than it has ever been. But the number of hypocrites rises steadily: up to a point, every citizen is, in fact, forced to be one.

This dispiriting situation has, of course, its logical causes. Seldom in recent times has a regime cared so little for the real attitudes of outwardly loyal citizens or for the sincerity of their statements. It is enough to observe that no one, in the course of ll those self-criticisms and acts of penance, really cares whether people mean what they say, or are only considering their own advantages. In fact, one can safely say that the second assumption is made more or less automatically, without anything immoral being seen in this. Indeed, the prospect of personal advantage is used as the main argument in obtaining such statements. No one tries to convince the penitent that he was in error or acted wrongly, but simply, as a rule, that he must repent in order to save himself. At the same time, the benefits he stands to gain are colourfully magnified, while the bitter taste, which will remain after the act of penance, is played down and treated as an illusion.

And if some eccentric who repented in all sincerity and showed it, for example, by refusing the appropriate reward in principle, should turn up, the regime itself would, in all probability, find him an object of suspicion.

It is fair to say that, in a way, we are all being publicly bribed. If you accept this or that office in your place of work – not, of course, as a means of serving your colleagues, but of serving the management – you will be rewarded with such and such privileges. If you join the Youth League, you will be given the right and access to such and such forms of entertainment. If, as a creative artist, you take part in such and such official functions, you will be rewarded with such and such genuine creative opportunities. Think what you like in private, as long as you agree in public, refrain from making difficulties, suppress your interest in truth and silence your conscience – and the doors will be wide open to you.

If the *principle of outward adaptation* is made the keystone to success in society, what sort of human qualities will be encouraged and what sort of people, one may ask, will come to the fore?

Somewhere between the attitude of timid self-defence *vis-à-vis* the world and that of aggressive eagerness to conquer the world for one's own benefit lies a range of feelings which it would be wrong to overlook, because they, too, play a significant role in forming the moral climate of today's 'united

society': feelings of *indifference* and everything that goes wi
them.

It is as if the shocks of recent history, and the kind
system subsequently established in this country, had le
people to lose any faith in the future, in the possibility
setting public affairs right, in the sense of any struggle f
truth and justice. They shrug off anything that goes beyor
their everyday routine concern for their own livelihood; the
seek all manner of escape routes; they succumb to apath
indifference towards impersonal values and their fellow me
to spiritual passivity and depression.

And everyone who still tries to resist by, for instanc
refusing to adopt the principle of dissimulation as the key
survival, doubting the value of any self-fulfilment purchas
at the cost of self-alienation – such a man appears to his ev
more indifferent neighbours as an eccentric, a fool, a D
Quixote, and in the end is regarded inevitably with son
aversion, like everyone who behaves differently from the re
and in a way which, moreover, threatens to hold up a criti
mirror before their eyes. Or, again, those indifferent neig
bours may expel such a man from their midst or shun him
required, for appearances' sake while sympathizing with hi
in secret or in private, hoping to still their conscience
clandestine approval of a person who acts as they themselv
should, but cannot.

Paradoxically, though, this indifference has become a ve
active social force. For can one deny that it is pla
indifference, rather than fear, that brings many to the voti
booth, to meetings, to membership of official organization
Is not the political support for the regime, which seems to
so successfully supplied, to a large degree a mere matter
routine, of habit, of automatism, of laziness, actually back
by nothing but total resignation? Participation in all t
political rituals which no one believes in is pointless. Still,
least it does ensure a quiet life – and would it be any le
pointless *not* to participate? One would gain nothing, ar
lose the quiet life into the bargain.

Most people are loath to spend their days in ceasele

conflict with authority, especially when it can only end in the defeat of the isolated individual. So why not do what is required of you? It costs you nothing, and in time you cease to bother about it. It is not worth a moment's thought.

Despair leads to apathy, apathy to conformity, conformity to routine performance – which is then quoted as evidence of 'mass political involvement'. All this goes to make up the contemporary concept of 'normal' behaviour – a concept which is, in essence, deeply pessimistic.

The more completely men abandon any hope of general reform, any interest in impersonal goals and values or any chance of exercising influence in an 'outward' direction, the more their energy is diverted in the direction of least resistance, i.e. 'inwards'. People are thinking today far more of themselves, their homes and their families. It is there that they find rest, there that they can forget all the world's folly and freely exercise their creative talents. They fill their homes with all kinds of equipment and pretty things, they try to raise their housing standards, they make life agreeable for themselves, building cottages, looking after their cars, taking more interest in their food and clothing and domestic comfort. In short, they turn their main attention to the material aspects of their private lives.

Clearly, this social orientation has favourable economic results. It encourages improvements in the neglected fields of consumer goods production and public services. It helps to raise the general living standard. Economically regarded, it represents a significant source of dynamic energy, able to succeed, at least partially, in developing society's material wealth, which the inflexible, bureaucratized and unproductive state sector of the economy could hardly ever hope to accomplish. (It is enough to compare state and private house-building as to quantity and quality.)

The authorities welcome and support this spill-over of energy into the private sphere.

But why? Because of its favourable effects as a stimulus to economic growth? Certainly, that is one reason. But the whole spirit of current political propaganda and practice, quietly but systematically applauding this 'inward' orientation as the very essence of human fulfilment on earth, shows only too clearly why the authorities really welcome this transfer of energy. They see it for what it really is in its psychological origins: an escape from the sphere of public activity.

Rightly divining that such surplus energy, if directed 'outward', must sooner or later turn against them – i.e. against the particular forms of power they obstinately cling to – they do not hesitate to represent as human life what is really a desperate substitute for living. In the interest of the smooth management of society, then, society's attention is deliberately diverted from itself, that is, from social concerns. By nailing a man's whole attention to the floor of his mere consumer interests, it is hoped to render him incapable of appreciating the ever-increasing degree of his spiritual, political and moral degradation. Reducing him to a simple vessel for the ideals of a primitive consumer society is supposed to turn him into pliable material for complex manipulation. It is intended to nip in the bud the danger that he might conceive a longing for one of the innumerable, unforeseeable roles which his manhood fits him to play by imprisoning him within the wretched range of parts that he can perform as a consumer, subject to the limitations of a centrally directed market.

All the evidence suggests that the authorities are applying a method quite adequate for dealing with a creature whose only aim is self-preservation. Seeking the path of least resistance, they completely ignore the price that must be paid – the harsh assault on human integrity, the brutal castration of the humanity of men.

Yet these same authorities justify themselves with obsessive insistence by their revolutionary ideology, in which the ideal of man's total liberation has a central place! But what, in fact, has happened to the concept of human personality and its many-sided, harmonious and authentic growth? Of man liberated from the clutches of an alienating social machinery, from a mythical hierarchy of values, formalized freedoms, from the dictatorship of property, the fetish and the might of money? What has happened to the idea that a man should live in full enjoyment of social and legal justice, have a creative share in economic and political power, be raised on high in his human dignity and become truly himself? Instead of free economic decision-sharing, free participation in political life and free intellectual advancement, all he is actually offered is a chance freely to choose which washing machine or refrigerator he wants to buy.

In the foreground, then, stands the imposing façade of great humanistic ideals – and behind it crouches the modest family house of a socialist bourgeois: on the one side, bombastic slogans about the unprecedented increase in every sort of freedom and the unique structural variety of life; on the other side, unprecedented drabness and the squalor of life reduced to a hunt for consumer goods.

Somewhere at the top of the hierarchy of pressures by which man is manipulated into becoming an obedient member of a consumer herd, there stands, as I have hinted, a concealed, omnipotent force: the state police. It is no coincidence, I suppose, that this body should so aptly illustrate the gulf that separates the ideological façade from everyday reality. Anyone who has had the bad luck to experience personally the 'work style' of that institution must be highly amused at the official explanation of its purpose. Does anyone really believe that that shabby swarm of thousands of petty informers, professional narks, complex-ridden, sly, envious, malevolent *petits bourgeois*, and bureaucrats, that malodorous gob of treachery, evasion, fraud, gossip and intrigue 'shows the imprint of the working man, guarding the people's government and its revolutionary achievements against its enemies' designs'? For who would be more hostile to a true workers' government – if everything were not upside down – than your *petit bourgeois*, always ready to oblige and sticking at nothing, soothing his arthritic self-esteem by informing on his fellow citizens, a creature clearly discernible behind the regular procedures of the secret police as the true spiritual author of their 'work style'?

I think it would be hard to explain this whole grotesque contrast between theory and practice, except as a natural consequence of the real mission of the state police today, which is not to protect the free development of man from any assailants, but to protect the assailants from the threat which any real attempt at man's free development poses.

The contrast between the revolutionary teachings about the new man and the new morality and the shoddy concept of life as consumer bliss raises the question of why the authorities actually cling so frantically to their ideology. Clearly, only because their ideology, as a conventionalized system of ritual communications, assures them the appearance of legitimacy, continuity and consistency, and acts as a screen of prestige for their pragmatic practice.

The actual aims of this practice do, of course, leave their traces on the official ideology at every point. From the bowels of that infinite mountain of ideological rhetoric by which the authorities ceaselessly try to sway people's minds, and which – as its communication value is nil – the public, for the most part, scarcely notices, there emerges one specific and meaningful message, one realistic piece of advice: 'Avoid politics if you can; leave it to us! Just do what we tell you, don't try to have deep thoughts, and don't poke your nose into things that don't concern you! Shut up, do your work, look after yourself – and you'll be all right!'

This advice is heeded. That one needs to make a living is, after all, the one point on which a man can rather easily agree with his government. Why not make good use of it then? Especially as you have no other choice anyway.

Where is the whole situation which I have tried to outline here ultimately leading?

What, in other words, is the effect on people of a system based on fear and apathy, a system that drives each man into a foxhole of purely material existence and offers him deceit as the main form of communication with society? To what level is a society reduced by a policy where the only aim is superficial order and general obedience, regardless of by what means and at what price they have been gained?

It needs little imagination to see that such a situation can only lead towards the gradual erosion of all moral standards, the breakdown of all criteria of decency, and the widespread destruction of confidence in the meaning of any such values as truth, adherence to principles, sincerity, altruism, dignity and honour. Life must needs sink to a biological, vegetable level amidst a demoralization 'in depth', stemming from the loss of hope and the loss of the belief that life has a meaning. It can but confront us once more with that tragic aspect of man's status in modern technological civilization marked by a declining awareness of the absolute, and which I propose to call a *crisis of human identity*. For how can the collapse of man's identity be slowed down by a system that so harshly requires a man to be something other than he is?

Order has been established. At the price of a paralysis of the spirit, a deadening of the heart, and devastation of life.

Surface 'consolidation' has been achieved. At the price of a *spiritual and moral crisis in society*.

Unfortunately, the worst feature of this crisis is that it keeps deepening. We only need to raise our sights a little above our limited daily perspective in order to realize with horror how hastily we are all abandoning positions which only yesterday we refused to desert. What social conscience only yesterday regarded as improper is today casually excused; tomorrow it will eventually be thought natural, and the day after be held up as a model of behaviour. What yesterday we declared impossible, or at least averred we would never get accustomed to, today we accept, without astonishment, as a fact of life. And, conversely, things that a little while ago we took for granted we now treat as exceptional: and soon – who knows – we might think of them as unattainable chimeras.

The changes in our assessment of the 'natural' and the 'normal', the shifts in moral attitudes in our society over the past few years have been greater than they might appear at first glance. As our insensitivity has increased, so naturally our ability to discern our own insensitivity has declined.

The malady has spread, as it were, from the fruit and the foliage to the trunk and roots. The most serious grounds for alarm, then, are the prospects which the present state of affairs opens up for the future.

The main route by which society is inwardly enlarged, enriched and cultivated is that of coming to know itself in ever greater depth, range and subtlety.

The main instrument of *society's self-knowledge* is its *culture*: culture as a specific field of human activity, influencing the general state of mind – albeit often very indirectly – and at the same time continually subject to its influence.

Where total control over society completely suppresses its differentiated inner development, the first thing to be suppressed regularly is its culture: not just 'automatically', as a phenomenon intrinsically opposed to the 'spirit' of manipulation, but as a matter of deliberate 'programming' inspired by justified anxiety lest society be alerted to the extent of its own subjugation through that culture which gives it its self-awareness. It is culture that enables a society to enlarge its liberty and to discover truth – so what appeal can it have for the authorities who are basically concerned with suppressing such values? There is only one kind of truth they recognize: the kind they need at the given moment. And only one kind of liberty: to proclaim that 'truth'.

A world where 'truth' flourishes not in a dialectic climate of genuine knowledge, but in a climate of power motives, is a world of mental sterility, petrified dogmas, rigid and unchangeable creeds leading inevitably to creedless despotism.

This is a world of prohibitions and limitations and of orders, a world where cultural policy means primarily the operations of the cultural police force.

Much has been said and written about the peculiar degree of devastation which our contemporary culture has reached: about the hundreds of prohibited books and authors and the dozens of liquidated periodicals; about the carving up of publishers' projects and theatre repertoires and the cutting off of all contact with the intellectual community; about the plundering of exhibition halls; about the grotesque range of persecution discrimination practised in this field; about the breaking up of all the former artistic associations and countless scholarly institutes and their replacement by kinds of dummies run by little gangs of aggressive fanatics, notorious careerists, incorrigible cowards and incompetent upstarts anxious to seize their opportunity in the general void. Rather than describe all these things again, I will offer some reflections on those deeper aspects of this state of affairs which are germane to the subject matter of my letter.

In the first place, however bad the present situation, it still does not mean that culture has ceased to exist altogether. Plays are put on, television programmes go out every day, and even books get published. But this overt and legal cultural activity, taken as a whole, exhibits one basic feature: an overall externalization due to its being estranged in large measure from its proper substance through its *total emasculation as an instrument of human, and so of social, self-awareness*. And whenever, even today, something of incontestably excellent value appears – a superb dramatic performance, let us say, to remain in the sphere of art – then it appears, rather, as a phenomenon to be tolerated because of its subtlety and refinement, and hence, from an official point of view, its relative innocuousness as a contribution to social self-awareness. Yet, even here, no sooner does that contribution begin to be at all keenly perceived than the authorities start instinctively to defend themselves: there are familiar instances where a good actor was banned, by and large, simply for being too good.

But that is not what concerns me at this point. What interests me is how this externalization works in fields where it is possible to describe the human experience of the environment far more explicitly and where the function of promoting social self-awareness is, thus, far more manifestly fulfilled.

I will quote an example. Suppose a literary work, a drama perhaps, undeniably skilful, suggestive, ingenious, meaningful, is published (it does happen from time to time). Whatever the other qualities of the work may be, of one thing we may always be perfectly certain. Whether through censorship or self-censorship, because of the writer's character or his self-deception, as a consequence of resignation or of calculation, it will never stray one inch beyond the taboos of a banal, conventional and, hence, basically fraudulent social consciousness that offers and accepts as genuine experience the mere appearance of experience – a concatenation of smooth, hackneyed, superficial trivia of experience; that is, pallid reflections of such aspects of experience as the social consciousness has long since adopted and domesticated. Despite, or, rather, because of this fact, there will always be people who find such a work entertaining, exciting and interesting, although it sheds no light on anything by any flash of real knowledge revealing what was unknown, expressing what had never been said, or providing new, spontaneous and effective evidence of things hitherto only guessed at. In short, by imitating the real world, such a work in fact, falsifies the real world. As regards the actual forms this externalization takes, it is no accident that the vat most frequently tapped should be the one which, thanks to its proven harmlessness, enjoys the warmest approval of the authorities in our country, whether bourgeois or proletarian. I refer to the *aesthetics of banality*, safely housed within the four walls of good-natured *petit bourgeois* morality; the sentimental philosophy of kitchen-sink country-bumpkin earthiness, and the provincial *Weltanschauung* based on the belief in its general good naturedness. I refer to the aesthetic doctrine whose keystone is the cult of right-thinking mediocrity, bedded in hoary national self-satisfaction, guided by the principle that everything must be slick, trivial and predigested, and culminating in that false optimism which puts the drabbest interpretation on the dictum that 'truth will prevail'.

Of works designed to give literary expression to the government's political ideology, there is today – as you must be aware – an extreme scarcity, and those few are clearly, by professional standards, bad ones. This is not merely because there is no one to write them, but also, I am sure, paradoxical as it may appear, because they would not be particularly welcome. For, from the standpoint of actual contemporary attitudes (those of the consumer society, that is), even if such works were available, proved professionally competent and attracted somebody's interest, they would divert too much attention 'outwards', rub salt into too many old wounds, provoke – through their general and radical political character – too much general and radical political reaction, thus stirring up too many pools that are supposed to be left as stagnant as possible. What far better suits the real interests of the authorities today is what I have called the aesthetics of banality, which misses the truth much more inconspicuously, acceptably and plausibly, and (since it is naturally far more digestible for the conventional mind) is far better calculated to perform the role accorded to culture in the consumer philosophy: not to excite people with the truth, but to reassure them with lies.

It is this kind of artistic output which has naturally always predominated. But in our country, there had always been some chinks at least through which works which could truthfully be said to convey a more genuine kind of human self-awareness reached the public. The road for such works of art was never particularly smooth. They met resistance not only from the authorities, but from easy-going and sluggish conventional attitudes as well. Yet until recently they had always managed in some mysterious way, by devious paths and seldom without delay, to get through to the individual and to society, and so to fulfil the role of culture as the agent of social self-awareness.

This is all that really matters. This is precisely what I take to be really important. And it is also precisely this that the present government – and it can be shown that the achievement is unprecedented since the age of our national revival – has managed to render almost completely impossible, so complete is the present system of bureaucratic control of culture, so perfect the surveillance of every chink through which some major work might see the light of day, so great the fear of government and the fear of art entertained by that little band of men who have deposited in their own pockets the keys of every door.

You will, of course, appreciate that I am speaking at this moment not of the ample indexes, listing the names of all creative artists subject to a total or partial ban, but of a much worse list – of that 'blank index' which includes, a priori, everything which might contain the spark of a slightly original thought, perceptive insight, deeper sincerity, unusual idea or suggestive form; I am speaking of that open warrant for the arrest of anything inwardly free and, therefore, in the deepest sense 'cultural', I am speaking of the warrant against culture issued by your government.

Once more arises the question which I have been posing from the start. What does it all really mean? Where is it leading? What is it going to do to society?

Once more, I take a particular case. Most of the former cultural periodicals, as we know, have ceased to appear in our country. If any have survived, they have been so *gleichgeschaltet* that they are hardly worth considering.

What has been the effect of that?

At first glance, practically none. The wheels of society continue to go round, even without all those literary, artistic, theatrical, philosophical, historical and other magazines whose number, even while they existed, never measured up to the latent needs of society, but which were around and played their part. How many people today still miss those publications? Only the few tens of thousands of people who subscribed to them – a very small fraction of society.

Yet this loss is infinitely deeper and more significant than might appear from the numbers involved. Its real implications are again, of course, hidden, and can hardly be assessed precisely.

The forcible liquidation of such a journal – a theoretical review concerned with the theatre, say – is not just an impoverishment of its particular readers. It is not even merely a severe blow to theatrical culture. It is simultaneously, and above all, the liquidation of a particular organ of society's self-awareness and, hence, an interference, hard to describe in exact terms, in the complex system of circulation, exchange and conversion of nutrients that maintain life in that many-layered organism which is society today; a blow against the natural dynamic of the processes going on within that organism; a disturbance of the balanced interplay of all its various functions, an interplay reflecting the level of complexity reached by society's anatomy. And just as a chronic deficiency of a given vitamin (amounting in quantitative terms only to a negligible fraction of the human diet) can make a man ill, so, in the long run, the loss of a single periodical can cause the social organism much more damage than would appear at first sight. And what if the loss involves not just one periodical, but virtually all?

It is easy to show that the real importance of knowledge, thought and creation is not limited, in the stratified world of a civilized society, to the significance these things have for the particular circle of people who are primarily, directly and, as it were, physically involved with them, whether actively or passively. This is always a small group, especially in the sciences. Yet the knowledge in question, conveyed through however many intermediaries, may in the end affect very profoundly the whole of society, just as politics, including the nuclear threat, physically concerns each one of us, even though most of us have had no experience of the speculations in theoretical physics which led to the manufacture of the atom bomb. That the same holds for non-specific knowledge is shown by many historic instances of an unprecedented cultural, political and moral upsurge throughout society, where the original nucleus of crystallization or catalyst was an act of social self-awareness carried out, and indeed directly and 'physically' perceived, only by a quite small and exclusive circle. Even subsequently, that act may have remained outside the apperception of society at large, yet it was still an indispensable condition of its upsurge. For we never know when some inconspicuous spark of knowledge, struck within range of the few brain cells, as it were, specially adapted for the organism's self-awareness, may suddenly

light up the road for the whole of society, without society
ever realizing, perhaps, how it came to see the road. But that
is far from being the whole story. For even those other
innumerable flashes of knowledge which never illuminate
the path ahead for society as a whole have their deep social
importance, if only through the mere fact that they *happened*;
that they might have cast light; that in their very occurrence
they fulfilled a certain range of society's potentialities – either
its creative powers, or simply its liberties; they, too, help to
make and maintain a climate of civilization without which
none of the more effective flashes could ever occur.

In short, the space within which spiritual self-awareness
operates is *indivisible*; the cutting of a single thread must
injure the coherence of the whole network, and this itself
shows the remarkable interdependence of all those fine
processes in the social organism that I spoke of, the
transcendent importance of each one of them and hence the
transcendent destructiveness wrought by its disturbance.

I would not wish to reduce everything to this single and
still relatively minor aspect of the problem. Still, does it not in
itself confirm the deeply injurious influence on the general
spiritual and moral state of society which the 'warrant against
culture' already has and will have in future, even though its
immediate impact is only on a fairly limited number of heads?

If not a single new Czech novel, of which one could safely
say that it enlarges our experience of the world, has appeared
in recent years in the bookshops, this will certainly have no
public effect. Readers are not going to demonstrate in the
streets and, in the last resort, one finds something to read.
But who will dare assess the real significance of this fact for
Czech society? Who knows how the gap will affect the
spiritual and moral climate of the years to come? How far will
it weaken our ability to 'know ourselves'? How deeply will
such an absence of cultural self-knowledge brand those
whose self-knowing begins only today or tomorrow? What
mounds of mystification, slowly forming in the general
cultural consciousness, will need to be chipped away? How
far back will one need to go? Who can tell which people will

still find the strength to light new fires of truth, when, how and from what resources, once there has been such thorough wastage not only of the fuel, but of the *very feeling that it can be done*?

A few novels of the kind absent from the bookshops do nevertheless exist: they circulate in manuscript. So, in this respect, the situation is not yet hopeless: it follows from everything I have said that if such a novel went around for years, unknown to all but twenty people, the fact of its existence would still be important. It means something that there is such a book, that it could be written at all, that it is alive in at least one tiny area of the cultural consciousness. But what about the fields in which it is impossible to work, except through the so-called legal channels? How can one estimate the actual extent of the damage already done, and still to be done, by the strangling of every interesting development in the stage and cinema whose role as social stimuli is so specific? How much greater still may be the long-term effect of the vacuum in the humanities and in the theory and practice of the social sciences? Who dares measure the consequences of the violent interruption of the long processes of self-knowledge in ontology, ethics and historiography, dependent as they are on access to the normal circulation of information, ideas, discoveries and values, the public crystallization of attitudes?

The overall question, then, is this: what profound intellectual and moral impotence will the nation suffer tomorrow, following the castration of its culture today?

I fear that the baneful effects on society will outlast by many years the particular political interests that gave rise to them. So much the more guilty, in the eyes of history, are those who have sacrificed the country's spiritual future for the sake of their power interests today.

Just as the constant increase of entropy is the basic law of the universe, so it is the basic law of life to be ever more highly structured and to struggle against entropy.

Life rebels against all uniformity and levelling; its aim is not sameness, but variety, the restlessness of transcendence, the adventure of novelty and rebellion against the status quo. An essential condition for its enhancement is the secret constantly made manifest.

On the other hand, the essence of authority (whose aim is reduced to protecting its own permanence by forcibly imposing the uniformity of perpetual consent) consists basically in a distrust of all variety, uniqueness and transcendence; in an aversion to everything unknown, impalpable and currently obscure; in a proclivity for the uniform, the identical and the inert; in deep affection for the status quo. In it, the mechanical spirit prevails over the vital. The order it strives for is no frank quest for ever higher forms of social self-organization, equivalent to its evolving complexity of structure, but, on the contrary, a decline towards that 'state of maximum probability' representing the climax of entropy. Following the direction of *entropy*, it goes *against* the direction of *life*.

In a man's life, as we know, there is a moment when the complexity of structure begins suddenly to decline and his path turns in the direction of entropy. This is the moment when he, too, succumbs to the general law of the universe: the moment of death.

Somewhere at the bottom of every political authority which has chosen the path to entropy (and would like to treat the individual as a computer into which any programme can be fed with the assurance that he will carry it out), there lies hidden the *death principle*. There is an odour of death even in the notion of 'order' which such an authority puts into practice and which sees every manifestation of genuine life, every exceptional deed, individual expression, thought, every unusual idea or wish, as a red light signalling confusion, chaos and anarchy.

The entire political practice of the present regime, as I have tried to outline it here step by step, confirms that those concepts which were always crucial for its programme – order, calm, consolidation, 'guiding the nation out of its crisis', 'halting disruption', 'assuaging hot tempers' and so on

– have finally acquired the same lethal meaning that they have for every regime committed to 'entropy'.

True enough, order prevails: a bureaucratic order of grey monotony that stifles all individuality; of mechanical precision that suppresses everything of unique quality; of musty inertia that excludes the transcendant. What prevails is *order without life*.

True enough, the country is calm. Calm as a morgue or a grave, would you not say?

In a society which is really alive, there is, naturally, always something happening. The interplay of current activities and events, of overt and concealed movement, produces a constant succession of unique situations which provoke further and fresh movement. The mysterious, vital polarity of the continuous and the changing, the regular and the random, the foreseen and the unexpected, has its effect in the *time dimension* and is borne out in the *flow of events*. The more highly structured the life of a society, the more highly structured its time dimension, and the more prominent the element of uniqueness and unrepeatability within the time flow. This, in turn, of course, makes it easier to reflect its sequential character, to represent it, that is, as an irreversible stream of non-interchangeable situations, and so, in retrospect, to understand better whatever is governed by regular laws in society. The richer the life society lives, then, the better it perceives the dimension of social time, the *dimension of history*.

In other words, wherever there is room for social activity, room is created for a social memory as well. Any society that is alive is a society with a *history*.

If the element of continuity and causality is so vitally linked in history with the element of unrepeatability and unpredictability, we may well ask how true history – that inextinguishable source of 'chaos', fountainhead of unrest, and slap in the face for law and order – can ever exist in a world ruled by an 'entropic' regime.

The answer is plain: it cannot. And, indeed, it does not –

on the surface, anyway. Under such a regime, the elimina
tion of life in the proper sense brings social time to a halt, s
that history disappears from its purview.

In our own country, too, one has the impression that fo
some time there has been no history. Slowly but surely, w
are losing the sense of time. We begin to forget what hap
pened when, what came earlier and what later, and th
feeling that it really doesn't matter overwhelms us. A
uniqueness disappears from the flow of events, so does con
tinuity; everything merges into the single grey image of on
and the same cycle and we say, 'There is nothing happen
ing.' Here, too, a deadly order has been imposed: all activit
is completely organized and so completely deadened. Th
deadening of the sense of the time sequence in societ
inevitably kills it in private life as well. No longer backed b
social history or the history of the individual position withi
it, private life declines to a prehistoric level where tim
derives its only rhythm from such events as birth, marriag
and death.

The loss of the sense of social time seems, in every way, t
cast society back into the primeval state where, for thousand
of years, humanity could get no further in measuring it tha
by the cosmic and climatic pattern of endlessly repeate
annual seasons and the religious rites associated with them

The gap left by the disquieting dimension of history has
naturally to be filled. So the disorder of real history i
replaced by the orderliness of *pseudo-history*, whose author i
not the life of society, but an official planner. Instead o
events, we are offered non-events; we live from anniversar
to anniversary, from celebration to celebration, from parad
to parade, from a unanimous congress to unanimous elec
tions and back again; from a Press Day to an Artillery Da
and vice versa. It is no coincidence that, thanks to this sub
stitution for history, we are able to review everything that i
happening in society, past and future, by simply glancing a
the calendar. And the notoriously familiar character of th
recurrent rituals makes such information quite as adequat
as if we had been present at the events themselves.

What we have, then, is perfect order – but at the cost of reverting to prehistory. Even so, we must enter a caveat: whereas for our ancestors the repeated rituals always had a deep existential meaning, for us they are merely a routine performed for its own sake. The government keeps them going to maintain the impression that history is moving. The public goes through the motions to keep out of trouble.

An 'entropic' regime has one means of increasing the general entropy within its own sphere of influence, namely, by tightening its own central control, rendering itself more monolithic and enclosing society in an ever more comprehensive and impermeable straitjacket for unilinear manipulation. But with every step it takes in this direction, it inevitably *increases its own entropy too*.

In an effort to immobilize the world, it immobilizes itself, undermining its own ability to cope with anything new or to resist the natural currents of life. The 'entropic' regime is, thus, essentially doomed to become finally the victim of its own lethal principle, and the most vulnerable victim at that, thanks to the absence of any impulse within its own structure that could, as it were, make it face up to itself. Life, by contrast, with its irrepressible urge to oppose entropy, is able all the more successfully and inventively to resist being violated, the faster the violating authority succumbs to its own sclerosis.

In trying to paralyse life, then, the authorities paralyse themselves and, in the long run, incapacitate themselves for paralysing life.

In other words, life may be subjected to a prolonged and thorough process of violation, enfeeblement and anaesthesia. Yet, in the end, it cannot be permanently halted. Albeit quietly, covertly and slowly, it nevertheless goes on. Though it be estranged from itself a thousand times, it always manages in some way to recuperate; however violently ravished, it always survives, in the end, the power which ravished it. It cannot be otherwise, in view of the profoundly ambivalent nature of every 'entropic' authority, which can only suppress life if there is life to suppress and so, in the last resort, depends for its own existence on life, whereas life in no way depends on it. The only force that can truly destroy life on our planet is the force which knows no compromise: the universal validity of the second law of thermodynamics.

If life cannot be destroyed for good, neither, then, can history be brought entirely to a halt. A secret streamlet trickles on beneath the heavy lid of inertia and pseudo-events, slowly and inconspicuously undercutting it. It may be a long process, but one day it must happen: the lid will no longer hold and will start to crack.

This is the moment when once more something visibly begins to *happen*, something truly new and unique, something unscheduled in the official calendar of 'happenings', something that makes us no longer indifferent to what occurs and when – something truly historic, in the sense that *history* again demands to be heard.

But how, in our particular circumstances, could it come about that history 'demands to be heard'? What does such a prospect really imply?

I am neither historian nor prophet, yet there are some observations touching on the structure of these 'moments' which one cannot avoid making.

Where there is, in some degree, open competition for power as the only real guarantee of public control over its exercise and, in the last resort, the only guarantee of free speech, the political authorities must willy nilly participate in some kind of permanent and overt dialogue with the life of society. They are forced continually to wrestle with all kinds of questions which life puts to them. Where no such competition exists and freedom of speech is, therefore, of necessity sooner or later suppressed – as is the case with every 'entropic' regime – the authorities, instead of adapting themselves to life, try to adapt life to themselves. Instead of coping openly and continually with real conflicts, demands and issues, they simply draw a veil over them. Yet somewhere under the lid, these conflicts and demands continue, grow and multiply, only to burst forth when the moment arrives when the lid can no longer hold them down. That is the moment when the dead weight of inertia crumbles and history steps out again into the arena.

And what happens after that?

The authorities are certainly still strong enough to prevent those vital conflicts from issuing in the shape of open discussion or open rivalry for power. But they have no longer the strength to resist this pressure altogether. So life vents itself where it can – in the secret corridors of power, where it can insist on *secret discussion* and finally on *secret competition*. For this, of course, the authorities are unprepared: any substantive dialogue with life is outside their range of competence. So they panic. Life sows confusion in their council chambers in the shape of personal quarrels, intrigues, snares and confrontations; and even infects, as it were, their own representatives: the death mask of impersonality that their officials wore to identify themselves with the monolith of power is suddenly dropped, revealing live people competing for power in the most 'human' way and struggling in self-defence, one against the other. This is the notorious moment for palace revolutions and putsches, for sudden and outwardly mystifying changes of portfolio and changes of key points in set speeches, the moment when real or construed conspiracies and secret centres are revealed, the moment when real or imaginary crimes are made known and ancient guilt unearthed, the moment for mutual dismissals from office, mutual denigration and perhaps even arrests and trials. Whereas before every man in authority had spoken the same language, used the same clichés, applauded successful fulfilment of the same targets, now suddenly the monolith of power breaks down into distinguishable persons, still speaking the same language, but using it to make personal attacks on one another. And we learn with astonishment that some of them – those, that is, who lost in the secret struggle for power – had never taken their targets seriously and never successfully fulfilled them – far from it – whereas others – the winners – had really meant what they said and are alone capable of achieving their aims.

The more rational the construction of the official calendar of non-events over the years, the more irrational the effect of a sudden irruption of genuine history. All its long-suppressed elements of unrepeatability, uniqueness and incalculability, all its long-denied mysteries, come rushing through the breach. Where for years we had been denied the slightest, most ordinary surprise, life is now one huge surprise – and it is well worth it. The whole disorderliness of history, concealed under artificial order for years, suddenly spurts out.

How well we know all this! How often we have witnessed it in our part of the world! The machine that worked for years to apparent perfection, faultlessly, without a hitch, falls apart overnight. The system that seemed likely to reign unchanged, world without end, since nothing could call its power in question amid all those unanimous votes and elections, is shattered without warning. And, to our amazement, we find that everything was quite otherwise than we had thought.

The moment when such a tornado whirls through the musty edifice of petrified power structures is, of course, far from being just a source of amusement for all of us who are outside the ramparts of authority. For we, too, are always involved, albeit indirectly. Is it not the quiet perennial pressure of life, the ceaselessly resisted, but finally irresistible demands and interests of all society, its conflicts and its tensions, which ever and again shake the foundations of power? No wonder that society continually reawakens at such moments, attaches itself to them, receives them with great alertness, gets excited by them and seeks to exploit them! In almost every case, such tremors provoke hopes or fears of one kind or another, create – or seem to create – scope for the realization of life's various impulses and ambitions and accelerate all kinds of movements within society.

Yet, in almost every case, it is equally true that this situation, owing to the basically unnatural structure of the kind of confrontation with life which such shakeups of power bring about, carries with it many and incalculable risks.

I shall try to illuminate further one such risk.

If every day a man takes orders in silence from an incompetent superior, if every day he solemnly performs ritual acts which he privately finds ridiculous, if he unhesitatingly gives answers to questionnaires which are contrary to his real opinions and is prepared to deny his own self in public, if he sees no difficulty in feigning sympathy or even affection where, in fact, he feels only indifference or aversion, it still does not mean that he has entirely lost the use of one of the basic human senses, namely, the sense of *humiliation*.

On the contrary: even if they never speak of it, people have a very acute appreciation of the price they have paid for outward peace and quiet: the permanent *humiliation of their human dignity*. The less direct resistance they put up to it – comforting themselves by driving it from their mind and deceiving themselves with the thought that it is of no account, or else simply gritting their teeth – the deeper the experience etches itself into their emotional memory. The man who can resist humiliation can quickly forget it; but the man who can long tolerate it must long remember it. In actual fact, then, nothing remains forgotten. All the fear one has endured, the dissimulation one has been forced into, all the painful and degrading buffoonery, and, worst of all, perhaps, the feeling of displayed cowardice – all this settles and accumulates somewhere on the bottom of our social consciousness, quietly fermenting.

Clearly, this is no healthy situation. Left untreated, the abscesses suppurate; the pus cannot escape from the body and the malady spreads throughout the organism. The natural human emotion is denied the process of objectivization and instead, caged up over long periods in the emotional memory, is gradually deformed into a sick cramp, into a toxic substance not unlike the carbon monoxide produced by incomplete combustion.

No wonder, then, that when the crust cracks and the lava of life rolls out, there appear not only well-considered attempts to rectify old wrongs, not only searchings for truth and for reforms matching life's needs, but also symptoms of bilious hatred, vengeful wrath, and a kind of feverish desire for immediate compensation for all the endured degradation. (The impulsive and often wayward forms of this desire may also spring largely from a vague impression that the whole outbreak has come too late, at a time when it has lost its meaning, having no longer any immediate motive and so carrying no immediate risk, when it is actually just an ersatz for something that should have happened in quite a different context.)

No wonder, again, that the men in power, accustomed for years to absolute agreement, unanimous and unreserved support and a total unity of total pretence, are so shocked by the upsurge of suppressed feelings at such a moment that they feel exposed to such an unheard-of threat and, in this mood (assuming themselves to be the sole guarantors of the world's survival), detect such an unprecedented threat to the rest of the world, too, that they do not hesitate to call upon millions of foreign soldiers to save both themselves and the world.

We experienced one such explosion not long ago. Those who had spent years humiliating and insulting people and were then so shocked when those people tried to raise their own voices, now label the whole episode an 'outbreak of passions'. And what, pray, were the passions that broke out? Those who know what protracted and thorough-going humiliations had preceded the explosion, and who understand the psycho-social mechanics of the subsequent reaction to them should be more surprised at the relatively calm, objective and, indeed, loyal form which the 'explosion' took. Yet, as everyone knows, we had to pay a cruel price for that 'moment of truth'.

The authorities in power today are profoundly different from those who ruled prior to that recent explosion. Not only because the latter were, so to speak, the 'original' and their successors a mere formalized imitation, incapable of reflecting the extent to which the 'original' had meanwhile lost its mystique, but primarily for another reason.

For whereas the earlier version rested on a genuine and not inconsiderable social basis derived from the trustful support accorded, though in declining measure, by one part of the population, and on the equally genuine and considerable attractiveness (which also gradually evaporated) of the social benefits it originally promised, today's regime rests solely on the ruling minority's instinct of self-preservation and on the fear of the ruled majority.

In these circumstances, it is hard to foresee all the feasible scenarios for an eventual future 'moment of truth': to foresee how such a complex and undisguised degradation of the whole of society might one day demand restitution. And it is quite impossible to estimate the scope and depth of the tragic consequences which such a moment might inflict, perhaps must inflict, on our two nations.

In this context, it is amazing that a government which advertises itself as the most scientific on record is unable to grasp the elementary rules of its own operations or to learn from its own past.

I have made it clear that I have no fear of life in Czechoslovakia coming to a halt, or of history being suspended for ever with the accession to power of the present leaders. Every situation in history and every epoch have been succeeded by a fresh situation and a new epoch, and for better or worse, the new ones have always been quite remote from the expectations of the organizers and rulers of the preceding period.

What I am afraid of is something else. The whole of this letter is concerned, in fact, with what I really fear – the pointlessly harsh and long-lasting consequences which the present violent abuses will have for our nations. I fear the price we are all bound to pay for the drastic suppression of history, the cruel and needless banishment of life into the underground of society and the depths of the human soul, the new compulsory 'deferment' of every opportunity for society to live in anything like a natural way. And perhaps it is apparent from what I wrote a little way back that I am not

33

only worried about our current payments in terms of everyday bitterness at the spoliation of society and human degradation, or about the heavy tax we shall have to pay in the shape of a long-lasting spiritual and moral decline of society. I am also concerned with the scarcely calculable surcharge which may be imposed on us when the moment next arrives for life and history to demand their due.

The degree of responsibility a political leader bears for the condition of his country must always vary and, obviously, can never be absolute. He never rules alone, and so some portion of responsibility rests on those who surround him. No country exists in a vacuum, so its policies are in some way always influenced by those of other countries. Clearly the previous rulers always have much to answer for, since it was their policies which predetermined the present situation. The public, too, has much to answer for, both individually, through the daily personal decisions of each responsible human being which went to create the total state of affairs, or collectively, as a socio-historic whole, limited by circumstances and in its turn limiting those circumstances.

Despite these qualifications, which naturally apply in our current situation as in any other, your responsibility as a political leader is still a great one. You help to determine the climate in which we all have to live and can therefore directly influence the final size of the bill our society will be paying for today's process of 'consolidation'.

The Czechs and Slovaks, like any other nation, harbour within themselves simultaneously the most disparate potentialities. We have had, still have and will continue to have our heroes, and, equally, our informers and traitors. We are capable of unleashing our imagination and creativity, of rising spiritually and morally to unexpected heights, of fighting for the truth and sacrificing ourselves for others.

But it lies in us equally to succumb to total apathy, to take no interest in anything but our bellies and to spend our time tripping one another up. And though human souls are far from being mere pint pots that anything can be poured into (note the arrogant implications of that dreadful phrase so frequent in official speeches, when it is complained that 'we' – that is, 'the government' – find that such and such ideas are 'being instilled into people's heads'), it depends, nevertheless, very much on the leaders which of these contrary tendencies that slumber in society will be mobilized, which set of potentialities will be given the chance of fulfilment and which will be suppressed.

So far, it is the worst in us which is being systematically activated and enlarged – egotism, hypocrisy, indifference, cowardice, fear, resignation and the desire to escape every personal responsibility, regardless of the general consequences.

Yet even today's national leadership has the opportunity to influence society by its policies in such a way as to encourage not the worse side of us, but the better.

So far, you and your government have chosen the easy way out for yourselves, and the most dangerous road for society: the path of inner decay for the sake of outward appearances; of deadening life for the sake of increasing uniformity; or deepening the spiritual and moral crisis of our society, and ceaselessly degrading human dignity for the puny sake of protecting your own power.

Yet, even within the given limitations, you have the chance to do much towards at least a relative improvement of the situation. This might be a more strenuous and less gratifying way, whose benefits would not be immediately obvious and which would meet with resistance here and there. But in the light of our society's true interests and prospects, this way would be vastly the more meaningful one.

As a citizen of this country, I hereby request, openly and publicly, that you and the leading representatives of the present regime consider seriously the matters to which I have tried to draw your attention, that you assess in their light the degree of your historic responsibility and act accordingly.

Václav Havel, Writer
8 April 1975

2

The power of the powerless

To the memory of Jan Patočka

I

A spectre is haunting eastern Europe: the spectre of what in the West is called 'dissent'. This spectre has not appeared out of thin air. It is a natural and inevitable consequence of the present historical phase of the system it is haunting. It was born at a time when this system, for a thousand reasons, can no longer base itself on the unadulterated, brutal, and arbitrary application of power, eliminating all expressions of nonconformity. What is more, the system has become so ossified politically that there is practically no way for such nonconformity to be implemented within its official structures.

Who are these so-called 'dissidents'? Where does their point of view come from, and what importance does it have? What is the significance of the 'independent initiatives' in which 'dissidents' collaborate, and what real chances do such initiatives have of success? Is it appropriate to refer to 'dissidents' as an opposition? If so, what exactly is such an opposition within the framework of this system? What does it do? What role does it play in society? What are its hopes and on what are they based? Is it within the power of the 'dissidents' – as a category of sub-citizen outside the power establishment – to have any influence at all on society and the social system? Can they actually change anything?

I think that an examination of these questions – an examination of the potential of the 'powerless' – can only begin with an examination of the nature of power in the circumstances in which these powerless people operate.

II

Our system is most frequently characterized as a dictatorship or, more precisely, as the dictatorship of a political bureaucracy over a society which has undergone economic and social levelling. I am afraid that the term 'dictatorship', regardless of how intelligible it may otherwise be, tends to obscure rather than clarify the real nature of power in this system. We usually associate the term with the notion of a small group of people who take over the government of a given country by force; their power is wielded openly, using the direct instruments of power at their disposal, and they are easily distinguished socially from the majority over whom they rule. One of the essential aspects of this traditional or classical notion of dictatorship is the assumption that it is temporary, ephemeral, lacking historical roots. Its existence seems to be bound up with the lives of those who established it. It is usually local in extent and significance, and regardless of the ideology it utilizes to grant itself legitimacy, its power derives ultimately from the numbers and the armed might of its soldiers and police. The principal threat to its existence is felt to be the possibility that someone better equipped in this sense might appear and overthrow it.

Even this very superficial overview should make it clear that the system in which we live has very little in common with a classical dictatorship. In the first place, our system is not limited in a local, geographical sense; rather it holds sway over a huge power bloc controlled by one of the two superpowers. And although it quite naturally exhibits a number of local and historical variations, the range of these variations is fundamentally circumscribed by a single, unifying framework throughout the power bloc. Not only is the dictatorship everywhere based on the same principles and structured in the same way (that is, in the way evolved by the ruling superpower), but each country has been completely penetrated by a network of manipulatory instruments controlled by the superpower centre and totally subordinated to its interests. In the stalemated world of nuclear parity, of course, that circumstance endows the system with an unprecedented degree of external stability compared with classical dictatorships. Many local crises which, in an isolated state, would lead to a change in the system, can be resolved through direct intervention by the armed forces of the rest of the bloc.

In the second place, if a feature of classical dictatorships is their lack of historical roots (frequently they appear to be no more than historical freaks, the fortuitous consequence of fortuitous social processes or of human and mob tendencies), the same cannot be said so facilely about our system. For even though our dictatorship has long since alienated itself completely from the social movements that gave birth to it, the authenticity of these movements (and I am thinking of the proletarian and socialist movements of the nineteenth century) give it undeniable historicity. These origins provided a solid foundation of sorts on which it could build until it became the utterly new social and political reality it is today, which has become so inextricably a part of the structure of the modern world. A feature of those historical origins was the 'correct understanding' of social conflicts in the period from which those original movements emerged. The fact that at the very core of this 'correct understanding' there was a genetic disposition toward the monstrous alienation characteristic of its subsequent development is not essential here. And in any case, this element also grew organically from the climate of that time and therefore can be said to have its origin there as well.

One legacy of that original 'correct understanding' is a third peculiarity that makes our systems different from other modern dictatorships: it commands an incomparably more precise, logically structured, generally comprehensible and in essence, extremely flexible ideology that, in its elaborateness and completeness, is almost a secularized religion. It offers a ready answer to any question whatsoever; it can scarcely be accepted only in part, and accepting it has profound implications for human life. In an era when metaphysical and existential certainties are in a state of crisis, when people are being uprooted and alienated and are losing their sense of what this world means, this ideology inevitably has a certain hypnotic charm. To wandering humankind it offers an immediately available home: all one has to do is accept it, and suddenly everything becomes clear once more, life takes on new meaning, and all mysteries, unanswered questions, anxiety, and loneliness vanish. Of course, one pays dearly for this low-rent home: the price is abdication of one's own reason, conscience, and responsibility, for an essential aspect of this ideology is the consignment of reason and conscience to a higher authority. The principle involved here is that the centre of power is identical with the centre of truth. (In our case, the connection with Byzantine theocracy is direct: the highest secular authority is identical with the highest spiritual authority.) It is true of course that, all this aside, ideology no longer has any great influence on people, at least within our bloc (with the possible exception of Russia, where the serf mentality, with its blind, fatalistic respect for rulers and its automatic acceptance of all their claims, is still dominant and combined with a superpower patriotism which traditionally places the interests of empire higher than the interests of humanity). But this is not important, because ideology plays its role in our system very well (an issue to which I will return) precisely because it is what it is.

Fourth, the technique of exercising power in traditional dictatorships contains a necessary element of improvisation. The mechanisms for wielding power are for the most part not established firmly, and there is considerable room for accident and for the arbitrary and unregulated application of power. Socially, psychologically, and physically, conditions still exist for the expression of some form of opposition. In short, there are many seams on the surface which can split apart before the entire power structure has managed to stabilize. Our system, on the other hand, has been developing in the Soviet Union for over sixty years, and for approximately thirty years in eastern Europe; moreover, several of its long-established structural features are derived from Czarist absolutism. In terms of the physical aspects of power, this has led to the creation of such intricate and well-developed mechanisms for the direct and indirect manipulation of the entire population that, as a physical power base, it represents something radically new. At the same time, let us not forget that the system is made significantly more effective by state ownership and central direction of all the means of production. This gives the power structure an unprecedented and uncontrollable capacity to invest in itself (in the areas of the bureaucracy and the police, for example) and makes it easier for that structure, as the sole employer, to manipulate the day-to-day existence of all citizens.

Finally, if an atmosphere of revolutionary excitement, heroism, dedication, and boisterous violence on all sides characterizes classical dictatorships, then the last traces of such an atmosphere have vanished from the Soviet bloc. For some time now this bloc has ceased to be a kind of enclave, isolated from the rest of the developed world and immune to processes occurring in it. To the contrary, the Soviet bloc is an integral part of that larger world, and it shares and shapes the world's destiny. This means in concrete terms that the hierarchy of values existing in the developed countries of the West has, in essence, appeared in our society (the long period of coexistence with the West has only hastened this process). In other words, what we have here is simply another form of the consumer and industrial society, with all its concomitant social, intellectual, and psychological consequences. It is impossible to understand the nature of power in our system properly without taking this into account.

The profound difference between our system – in terms of the nature of power – and what we traditionally understand by dictatorship, a difference I hope is clear even from this quite superficial comparison, has caused me to search for some term appropriate for our system, purely for the purposes of this essay. If I refer to it henceforth as a *post-totalitarian* system, I am fully aware that this is perhaps not the most precise term, but I am unable to think of a better one. I do not wish to imply by the prefix 'post-' that the system is no longer totalitarian; on the contrary, I mean that it is totalitarian in a way fundamentally different from classical dictatorships, different from totalitarianism as we usually understand it.

The circumstances I have mentioned, however, form only a circle of conditional factors and a kind of phenomenal framework for the actual composition of power in the post-totalitarian system, several aspects of which I shall now attempt to identify.

III

The manager of a fruit and vegetable shop places in his window, among the onions and carrots, the slogan: 'Workers of the world, unite!' Why does he do it? What is he trying to communicate to the world? Is he genuinely enthusiastic about the idea of unity among the workers of the world? Is his enthusiasm so great that he feels an irrepressible impulse to acquaint the public with his ideals? Has he really given more than a moment's thought to how such a unification might occur and what it would mean?

I think it can safely be assumed that the overwhelming majority of shopkeepers never think about the slogans they put in their windows, nor do they use them to express their real opinions. That poster was delivered to our greengrocer from the enterprise headquarters along with the onions and carrots. He put them all into the window simply because it has been done that way for years, because everyone does it, and because that is the way it has to be. If he were to refuse, there could be trouble. He could be reproached for not having the proper 'decoration' in his window; someone might even accuse him of disloyalty. He does it because these things must be done if one is to get along in life. It is one of the thousands of details that guarantee him a relatively tranquil life 'in harmony with society', as they say.

Obviously the greengrocer is indifferent to the semantic content of the slogan on exhibit; he does not put the slogan in his window from any personal desire to acquaint the public with the ideal it expresses. This, of course, does not mean that his action has no motive or significance at all, or that the

slogan communicates nothing to anyone. The slogan is really
a *sign*, and as such it contains a subliminal but very definite
message. Verbally, it might be expressed this way: 'I, the
greengrocer XY, live here and I know what I must do. I
behave in the manner expected of me. I can be depended
upon and am beyond reproach. I am obedient and therefore I
have the right to be left in peace.' This message, of course,
has an addressee: it is directed above, to the greengrocer's
superior, and at the same time it is a shield that protects the
greengrocer from potential informers. The slogan's real
meaning, therefore, is rooted firmly in the greengrocer's
existence. It reflects his vital interests. But what are those
vital interests?

Let us take note: if the greengrocer had been instructed to
display the slogan, 'I am afraid and therefore unquestion
ingly obedient', he would not be nearly as indifferent to its
semantics, even though the statement would reflect the
truth. The greengrocer would be embarrassed and ashamed
to put such an unequivocal statement of his own degradation
in the shop window, and quite naturally so, for he is a human
being and thus has a sense of his own dignity. To overcome
this complication, his expression of loyalty must take the
form of a sign which, at least on its textual surface, indicates a
level of disinterested conviction. It must allow the green
grocer to say, 'What's wrong with the workers of the world
uniting?' Thus the sign helps the greengrocer to conceal from
himself the low foundations of his obedience, at the same
time concealing the low foundations of power. It hides them
behind the façade of something high. And that something is
ideology.

Ideology is a specious way of relating to the world. It offers
human beings the illusion of an identity, of dignity, and of
morality while making it easier for them to *part* with them. As
the repository of something 'supra-personal' and objective, it
enables people to deceive their conscience and conceal their
true position and their inglorious *modus vivendi*, both from the
world and from themselves. It is a very pragmatic, but at the
same time an apparently dignified, way of legitimizing wha

is above, below, and on either side. It is directed towards people and towards God. It is a veil behind which human beings can hide their own 'fallen existence', their trivialization, and their adaptation to the status quo. It is an excuse that everyone can use, from the greengrocer, who conceals his fear of losing his job behind an alleged interest in the unification of the workers of the world, to the highest functionary, whose interest in staying in power can be cloaked in phrases about service to the working class. The primary excusatory function of ideology, therefore, is to provide people, both as victims and pillars of the post-totalitarian system, with the illusion that the system is in harmony with the human order and the order of the universe.

The smaller a dictatorship and the less stratified by modernization the society under it, the more directly the will of the dictator can be exercised. In other words, the dictator can employ more or less naked discipline, avoiding the complex processes of relating to the world and of self-justification which ideology involves. But the more complex the mechanisms of power become, the larger and more stratified the society they embrace, and the longer they have operated historically, the more individuals must be connected to them from outside, and the greater the importance attached to the ideological excuse. It acts as a kind of bridge between the regime and the people, across which the regime approaches the people and the people approach the regime. This explains why ideology plays such an important role in the post-totalitarian system: that complex machinery of units, hierarchies, transmission belts, and indirect instruments of manipulation which ensure in countless ways the integrity of the regime, leaving nothing to chance, would be quite simply unthinkable without ideology acting as its all-embracing excuse and as the excuse for each of its parts.

IV

Between the aims of the post-totalitarian system and the aims of life there is a yawning abyss: while life, in its essence,

moves towards plurality, diversity, independent self-constitution and self-organization, in short, towards the fulfilment
of its own freedom, the post-totalitarian system demands
conformity, uniformity, and discipline. While life ever strives
to create new and 'improbable' structures, the post-totalitarian system contrives to force life into its most probable
states. The aims of the system reveal its most essential
characteristic to be introversion, a movement towards being
ever more completely and unreservedly *itself*, which means
that the radius of its influence is continually widening as
well. This system serves people only to the extent necessary
to ensure that people will serve it. Anything beyond this, that
is to say, anything which leads people to overstep their
predetermined roles is regarded by the system as an attack
upon itself. And in this respect it is correct: every instance of
such transgression is a genuine denial of the system. It can be
said, therefore, that the inner aim of the post-totalitarian
system is not mere preservation of power in the hands of a
ruling clique, as appears to be the case at first sight. Rather,
the social phenomenon of self-preservation is subordinated
to something higher, to a kind of blind *automatism* which
drives the system. No matter what position individuals hold
in the hierarchy of power, they are not considered by the
system to be worth anything in themselves, but only as
things intended to fuel and serve this automatism. For this
reason, an individual's desire for power is admissible only in
so far as its direction coincides with the direction of the
automatism of the system.

Ideology, in creating a bridge of excuses between the
system and the individual, spans the abyss between the aims
of the system and the aims of life. It pretends that the
requirements of the system derive from the requirements of
life. It is a world of appearances trying to pass for reality.

The post-totalitarian system touches people at every step,
but it does so with its ideological gloves on. This is why life in
the system is so thoroughly permeated with hypocrisy and
lies: government by bureaucracy is called popular government; the working class is enslaved in the name of the

working class; the complete degradation of the individual is presented as his or her ultimate liberation; depriving people of information is called making it available; the use of power to manipulate is called the public control of power, and the arbitrary abuse of power is called observing the legal code; the repression of culture is called its development; the expansion of imperial influence is presented as support for the oppressed; the lack of free expression becomes the highest form of freedom; farcical elections become the highest form of democracy; banning independent thought becomes the most scientific of world views; military occupation becomes fraternal assistance. Because the regime is captive to its own lies, it must falsify everything. It falsifies the past. It falsifies the present, and it falsifies the future. It falsifies statistics. It pretends not to possess an omnipotent and unprincipled police apparatus. It pretends to respect human rights. It pretends to persecute no one. It pretends to fear nothing. It pretends to pretend nothing.

Individuals need not believe all these mystifications, but they must behave as though they did, or they must at least tolerate them in silence, or get along well with those who work with them. For this reason, however, they must *live within a lie*. They need not accept the lie. It is enough for them to have accepted their life with it and in it. For by this very fact, individuals confirm the system, fulfil the system, make the system, *are* the system.

V

We have seen that the real meaning of the greengrocer's slogan has nothing to do with what the text of the slogan actually says. Even so, this real meaning is quite clear and generally comprehensible because the code is so familiar: the greengrocer declares his loyalty (and he can do no other if his declaration is to be accepted) in the only way the regime is capable of hearing; that is, by accepting the prescribed *ritual*, by accepting appearances as reality, by accepting the given rules of the game. In doing so, however, he has himself

45

become a player in the game, thus making it possible for the game to go on, for it to exist in the first place.

If ideology was originally a bridge between the system and the individual as an individual, then the moment he or she steps on to this bridge it becomes at the same time a bridge between the system and the individual as a component of the system. That is, if ideology originally facilitated (by acting outwardly) the constitution of power by serving as a psychological excuse, then from the moment that excuse is accepted, it constitutes power inwardly, becoming an active component of that power. It begins to function as the principal instrument of· ritual communication *within* the system of power.

The whole power structure (and we have already discussed its physical articulation) could not exist at all if there were not a certain 'metaphysical' order binding all its components together, interconnecting them and subordinating them to a uniform method of accountability, supplying the combined operation of all these components with rules of the game, that is, with certain regulations, limitations, and legalities. This metaphysical order is fundamental to, and standard throughout, the entire power structure; it integrates its communication system and makes possible the internal exchange and transfer of information and instructions. It is rather like a collection of traffic signals and directional signs, giving the process shape and structure. This metaphysical order guarantees the inner coherence of the totalitarian power structure. It is the glue holding it together, its binding principle, the instrument of its discipline. Without this glue the structure as a totalitarian structure would vanish; it would disintegrate into individual atoms chaotically colliding with one another in their unregulated particular interests and inclinations. The entire pyramid of totalitarian power, deprived of the element that binds it together, would collapse in upon itself, as it were, in a kind of material implosion.

As the interpretation of reality by the power structure, ideology is always subordinated ultimately to the interests of the structure. Therefore, it has a natural tendency to disengage itself from reality, to create a world of appearances, to become ritual. In societies where there is public competition for power and therefore public control of that power, there also exists quite naturally public control of the way that power legitimates itself ideologically. Consequently, in such conditions there are always certain correctives that effectively prevent ideology from abandoning reality altogether. Under totalitarianism, however, these correctives disappear, and thus there is nothing to prevent ideology from becoming more and more removed from reality, gradually turning into what it has already become in the post-totalitarian system: a world of appearances, a mere ritual, a formalized language deprived of semantic contact with reality and transformed into a system of ritual signs that replace reality with pseudo-reality.

Yet, as we have seen, ideology becomes at the same time an increasingly important component of power, a pillar providing it with both excusatory legitimacy and an inner coherence. As this aspect grows in importance, and as it gradually loses touch with reality, it acquires a peculiar but very real strength. It becomes reality itself, albeit a reality altogether self-contained, one that on certain levels (chiefly inside the power structure) may have even greater weight than reality as such. Increasingly, the virtuosity of the ritual becomes more important than the reality hidden behind it. The significance of phenomena no longer derives from the phenomena themselves, but from their *locus* as concepts in the ideological context. Reality does not shape theory, but rather the reverse. Thus power gradually draws closer to ideology than it does to reality; it draws its strength from theory and becomes entirely dependent on it. This inevitably leads, of course, to a paradoxical result: rather than theory, or rather ideology, serving power, power begins to serve ideology. It is as though ideology had appropriated power from power, as though it had become dictator itself. It then appears that theory itself, ritual itself, ideology itself, makes decisions that affect people, and not the other way around.

If ideology is the principal guarantee of the inner consistency of power, it becomes at the same time an increasingly important guarantee of its *continuity*. Whereas succession to power in classical dictatorships is always a rather complicated affair (the pretenders having nothing to give their claims reasonable legitimacy, thereby forcing them always to resort to confrontations of naked power), in the post-totalitarian system power is passed on from person to person, from clique to clique, and from generation to generation in an essentially more regular fashion. In the selection of pretenders, a new 'king-maker' takes part: it is ritual legitimation, the ability to rely on ritual, to fulfil it and use it, to allow oneself, as it were, to be borne aloft by it. Naturally, power struggles exist in the post-totalitarian system as well, and most of them are far more brutal than in an open society, for the struggle is not open, regulated by democratic rules, and subject to public control, but hidden behind the scenes. (It is difficult to recall a single instance in which the First Secretary of a ruling Communist Party has been replaced without the various military and security forces being placed at least on alert.) This struggle, however, can never (as it can in classical dictatorships) threaten the very essence of the system and its continuity. At most it will shake up the power structure, which will recover quickly precisely because the binding substance – ideology – remains undisturbed. No matter who is replaced by whom, succession is only possible against the backdrop and within the framework of a common ritual. It can never take place by denying that ritual.

Because of this dictatorship of the ritual, however, power becomes clearly *anonymous*. Individuals are almost dissolved in the ritual. They allow themselves to be swept along by it and frequently it seems as though ritual alone carries people from obscurity into the light of power. Is it not characteristic of the post-totalitarian system that, on all levels of the power hierarchy, individuals are increasingly being pushed aside by faceless people, puppets, those uniformed flunkeys of the rituals and routines of power?

The automatic operation of a power structure thus dehumanized and made anonymous is a feature of the fundamental automatism of this system. It would seem that it is precisely the *diktat*s of this automatism which select people lacking individual will for the power structure, that it is precisely the *diktat* of the empty phrase which summons to power people who use empty phrases as the best guarantee that the automatism of the post-totalitarian system will continue.

Western Sovietologists often exaggerate the role of individuals in the post-totalitarian system and overlook the fact that the ruling figures, despite the immense power they possess through the centralized structure of power, are often no more than blind executors of the system's own internal laws – laws they themselves never can, and never do, reflect upon. In any case, experience has taught us again and again that this automatism is far more powerful than the will of any individual; and should someone possess a more independent will, he or she must conceal it behind a ritually anonymous mask in order to have an opportunity to enter the power hierarchy at all. And when the individual finally gains a place there and tries to make his or her will felt within it, that automatism, with its enormous inertia, will triumph sooner or later, and either the individual will be ejected by the power structure like a foreign organism, or he or she will be compelled to resign his or her individuality gradually, once again blending with the automatism and becoming its servant, almost indistinguishable from those who preceded him or her and those who will follow. (Let us recall, for instance, the development of Husák or Gomulka.) The necessity of continually hiding behind and relating to ritual means that even the more enlightened members of the power structure are often obsessed with ideology. They are never able to plunge straight to the bottom of naked reality, and they always confuse it, in the final analysis, with ideological pseudo-reality. (In my opinion, one of the reasons the Dubček leadership lost control of the situation in 1968 was precisely because, in extreme situations and in final questions, its members were never capable of extricating themselves completely from the world of appearances.)

It can be said, therefore, that ideology, as that instrument of internal communication which assures the power structure of inner cohesion is, in the post-totalitarian system, something that transcends the physical aspects of power, something that dominates it to a considerable degree and, therefore, tends to assure its continuity as well. It is one of the pillars of the system's external stability. This pillar, however, is built on a very unstable foundation. It is built on lies. It works only as long as people are willing to live within the lie.

VI

Why in fact did our greengrocer have to put his loyalty on display in the shop window? Had he not already displayed it sufficiently in various internal or semi-public ways? At trade union meetings, after all, he had always voted as he should. He had always taken part in various competitions. He voted in elections like a good citizen. He had even signed the 'anti-Charter'. Why, on top of all that, should he have to declare his loyalty publicly? After all, the people who walk past his window will certainly not stop to read that, in the greengrocer's opinion, the workers of the world ought to unite. The fact of the matter is, they don't read the slogan at all, and it can be fairly assumed they don't even see it. If you were to ask a woman who had stopped in front of his shop what she saw in the window, she could certainly tell whether or not they had tomatoes today, but it is highly unlikely that she noticed the slogan at all, let alone what it said.

It seems senseless to require the greengrocer to declare his loyalty publicly. But it makes sense nevertheless. People ignore his slogan, but they do so because such slogans are also found in other shop windows, on lamp posts, bulletin boards, in apartment windows, and on buildings; they are everywhere, in fact. They form part of the panorama of everyday life. Of course, while they ignore the details, people are very aware of that panorama as a whole. And what else is the greengrocer's slogan but a small component in that huge backdrop to daily life?

The greengrocer had to put the slogan in his window, therefore, not in the hope that someone might read it or be persuaded by it, but to contribute, along with thousands of other slogans, to the panorama that everyone is very much aware of. This panorama, of course, has a subliminal meaning as well: it reminds people where they are living and what is expected of them. It tells them what everyone else is doing, and indicates to them what they must do as well, if they don't want to be excluded, to fall into isolation, alienate themselves from society, break the rules of the game, and risk the loss of their peace and tranquility and security.

The woman who ignored the greengrocer's slogan may well have hung a similar slogan just an hour before in the corridor of the office where she works. She did it more or less without thinking, just as our greengrocer did, and she could do so precisely because she was doing it against the background of the general panorama and with some awareness of it, that is, against the background of the panorama of which the greengrocer's shop window forms a part. When the greengrocer visits her office, he will not notice her slogan either, just as she failed to notice his. Nevertheless their slogans are mutually dependent: both were displayed with some awareness of the general panorama and, we might say, under its *diktat*. Both, however, assist in the creation of that panorama, and therefore they assist in the creation of that *diktat* as well. The greengrocer and the office worker have both adapted to the conditions in which they live, but in doing so, they help to create those conditions. They do what is done, what is to be done, what must be done, but at the same time – by that very token – they confirm that it must be done in fact. They conform to a particular requirement and in so doing they themselves perpetuate that requirement. Metaphysically speaking, without the greengrocer's slogan the office worker's slogan could not exist, and vice versa. Each proposes to the other that something be repeated and each accepts the other's proposal. Their mutual indifference to each other's slogans is only an illusion: in reality, by exhibiting their slogans, each compels the other to accept the rules of the game and to confirm thereby the power that requires the slogans in the first place. Quite simply, each helps the other to be obedient. Both are objects in a system of control, but at the same time they are its subjects as well. They are both victims of the system and its instruments.

If an entire district town is plastered with slogans that no one reads, it is on the one hand a message from the district secretary to the regional secretary, but it is also something more: a small example of the principle of social *auto-totality* at work. Part of the essence of the post-totalitarian system is that it draws everyone into its sphere of power, not so they may realize themselves as human beings, but so they may surrender their human identity in favour of the identity of the system, that is, so they may become agents of the system's general automatism and servants of its self-determined goals, so they may participate in the common responsibility for it, so they may be pulled into and ensnared by it, like Faust with Mephistopheles. More than this: so they may create through their involvement a general norm and, thus, bring pressure to bear on their fellow citizens. And further: so they may learn to be comfortable with their involvement, to identify with it as though it were something natural and inevitable and, ultimately, so they may – with no external urging – come to treat any non-involvement as an abnormality, as arrogance, as an attack on themselves, as a form of dropping out of society. By pulling everyone into its power structure, the post-totalitarian system makes everyone instruments of a mutual totality, the auto-totality of society.

Everyone, however, is in fact involved and enslaved, not only the greengrocers but also the prime ministers. Differing positions in the hierarchy merely establish differing degrees of involvement: the greengrocer is involved only to a minor extent, but he also has very little power. The prime minister, naturally, has greater power, but in return he is far more deeply involved. Both, however, are unfree, each merely in a somewhat different way. The real accomplice in this involvement, therefore, is not another person, but the system itself. Position in the power hierarchy determines the degree of responsibility and guilt, but it gives no one unlimited responsibility and guilt, nor does it completely absolve anyone. Thus the conflict between the aims of life and the aims of the system is not a conflict between two socially defined and separate communities; and only a very generalized view (and even that only approximative) permits us to divide society into the rulers and the ruled. Here, by the way, is one of the most important differences between the post- totalitarian system and classical dictatorships, in which this line of conflict can still be drawn according to social class. In the post-totalitarian system, this line runs *de facto* through each person, for everyone in his or her own way is both a victim and a supporter of the system. What we understand by the system is not, therefore, a social order imposed by one group upon another, but rather something which permeates the entire society and is a factor in shaping it, something which may seem impossible to grasp or define (for it is in the nature of a mere principle), but which is expressed by the entire society as an important feature of its life.

The fact that human beings have created, and daily create, this self-directed system through which they divest themselves of their innermost identity, is not therefore the result of some incomprehensible misunderstanding of history, nor is it history somehow gone off its rails. Neither is it the product of some diabolical higher will which has decided, for reasons unknown, to torment a portion of humanity in this way. It can happen and did happen only because there is obviously in modern humanity a certain tendency towards the creation, or at least the toleration, of such a system. There is obviously something in human beings which responds to this system, something they reflect and accommodate, something within them which paralyses every effort of their better selves to revolt. Human beings are compelled to live within a lie, but they can be compelled to do so only because they are in fact capable of living in this way. Therefore not only does the system alienate humanity, but at the same time alienated humanity supports this system as its own involuntary masterplan, as a degenerate image of its own degeneration, as a record of people's own failure as individuals.

The essential aims of life are present naturally in every person. In everyone there is some longing for humanity's rightful dignity, for moral integrity, for free expression of being and a sense of transcendence over the world of existence. Yet, at the same time, each person is capable, to a greater or lesser degree, of coming to terms with living within the lie. Each person somehow succumbs to a profane trivialization of his or her inherent humanity, and to utilitarianism. In everyone there is some willingness to merge with the anonymous crowd and to flow comfortably along with it down the river of pseudo-life. This is much more than a simple conflict between two identities. It is something far worse: it is a challenge to the very notion of identity itself.

In highly simplified terms, it could be said that the post-totalitarian system has been built on foundations laid by the historical encounter between dictatorship and the consumer society. Is it not true that the far-reaching adaptability to living a lie and the effortless spread of social auto-totality have some connection with the general unwillingness of consumption-oriented people to sacrifice some material certainties for the sake of their own spiritual and moral integrity? With their willingness to surrender higher values when faced with the trivializing temptations of modern civilization? With their vulnerability to the attractions of mass indifference? And in the end, is not the greyness and the emptiness of life in the post-totalitarian system only an inflated caricature of modern life in general? And do we not in fact stand (although in the external measures of civilization, we are far behind) as a kind of warning to the West, revealing to it its own latent tendencies?

VII

Let us now imagine that one day something in our green-grocer snaps and he stops putting up the slogans merely to ingratiate himself. He stops voting in elections he knows are a farce. He begins to say what he really thinks at political meetings. And he even finds the strength in himself to express solidarity with those whom his conscience commands him to support. In this revolt the greengrocer steps out of living within the lie. He rejects the ritual and breaks the rules of the game. He discovers once more his suppressed identity and dignity. He gives his freedom a concrete significance. His revolt is an attempt to *live within the truth*.

The bill is not long in coming. He will be relieved of his post as manager of the shop and transferred to the warehouse. His pay will be reduced. His hopes for a holiday in Bulgaria will evaporate. His children's access to higher education will be threatened. His superiors will harass him and his fellow workers will wonder about him. Most of those who apply these sanctions, however, will not do so from any authentic inner conviction but simply under pressure from conditions, the same conditions that once pressured the greengrocer to display the official slogans. They will persecute the greengrocer either because it is expected of them, or to demonstrate their loyalty, or simply as part of the general panorama, to which belongs an awareness that this is how situations of this sort are dealt with, that this, in fact, is how things are always done, particularly if one is not to become suspect oneself. The executors, therefore, behave essentially like everyone else, to a greater or lesser degree: as components of the post-totalitarian system, as agents of its automatism, as petty instruments of the social auto-totality.

Thus the power structure, though the agency of those who carry out the sanctions, those anonymous components of the system, will spew the greengrocer from its mouth. The system, through its alienating presence in people, will punish him for his rebellion. It must do so because the logic of its automatism and self-defence dictate it. The greengrocer has not committed a simple, individual offence, isolated in its own uniqueness, but something incomparably more serious. By breaking the rules of the game, he has disrupted the game as such. He has exposed it as a mere game. He has shattered the world of appearances, the fundamental pillar of the system. He has upset the power structure by tearing apart what holds it together. He has demonstrated that living a lie is living a lie. He has broken through the exalted façade of the system and exposed the real, base foundations of power. He has said that the emperor is naked. And because the emperor is in fact naked, something extremely dangerous has happened: by his action, the greengrocer has addressed the world. He has enabled everyone to peer behind the curtain. He has shown everyone that it *is* possible to live within the truth. Living within the lie can constitute the system only if it is universal. The principle must embrace and permeate everything. There are no terms whatsoever on which it can coexist with living within the truth, and therefore everyone who steps out of line *denies it in principle and threatens it in its entirety*.

This is understandable: as long as appearance is not confronted with reality, it does not seem to be appearance. As long as living a lie is not confronted with living the truth, the perspective needed to expose its mendacity is lacking. As soon as the alternative appears, however, it threatens the very existence of appearance and living a lie in terms of what they are, both their essence and their all-inclusiveness. And at the same time, it is utterly unimportant how large a space this alternative occupies: its power does not consist in its physical attributes but in the light it casts on those pillars of the system and on its unstable foundations. After all, the greengrocer was a threat to the system not because of any physical or actual power he had, but because his action went beyond itself, because it illuminated its surroundings and, of course because of the incalculable consequences of that illumination. In the post-totalitarian system, therefore, living within the truth has more than a mere existential dimension (returning humanity to its inherent nature), or a noetic dimension (revealing reality as it is), or a moral dimension (setting an example for others). It also has an unambiguous *political* dimension. If the main pillar of the system is living a lie, then it is not surprising that the fundamental threat to it is living the truth. This is why it must be suppressed more severely than anything else.

In the post-totalitarian system, truth in the widest sense of the word has a very special import, one unknown in other contexts. In this system, truth plays a far greater (and above all, a far different) role as a factor of power, or as an outright political force. How does the power of truth operate? How does truth as a factor of power work? How can its power – as power – be realized?

VIII

Individuals can be alienated from themselves only because there is *something* in them to alienate. The terrain of this violation is their authentic existence. Living the truth is thus woven directly into the texture of living a lie. It is the repressed alternative, the authentic aim to which living a lie is an inauthentic response. Only against this background does living a lie make any sense: it exists *because* of that background. In its excusatory, chimerical rootedness in the human order, it is a response to nothing other than the human predisposition to truth. Under the orderly surface of the life of lies, therefore, there slumbers the hidden sphere of life in its real aims, of its hidden openness to truth.

The singular, explosive, incalculable political power of living within the truth resides in the fact that living openly within the truth has an ally, invisible to be sure, but omnipresent: this hidden sphere. It is from this sphere that life lived openly in the truth grows; it is to this sphere that it speaks, and in it that it finds understanding. This is where the potential for communication exists. But this place is hidden and therefore, from the perspective of power, very dangerous. The complex ferment that takes place within it goes on in semi-darkness, and by the time it finally surfaces

into the light of day as an assortment of shocking surprises to
the system, it is usually too late to cover them up in the usual
fashion. Thus they create a situation in which the regime is
confounded, invariably causing panic and driving it to react
in inappropriate ways.

It seems that the primary breeding ground for what might
in the widest possible sense of the word, be understood as an
opposition in the post-totalitarian system is living within the
truth. The confrontation between these opposition forces and
the powers that be, of course, will obviously take a form
essentially different from that typical of an open society or a
classical dictatorship. Initially, this confrontation does not
take place on the level of real, institutionalized, quantifiable
power which relies on the various instruments of power, but
on a different level altogether: the level of human consciousness and conscience, the existential level. The effective range
of this special power cannot be measured in terms of
disciples, voters, or soldiers, because it lies spread out in the
fifth column of social consciousness, in the hidden aims of
life, in human beings' repressed longing for dignity and
fundamental rights, for the realization of their real social and
political interests. Its power, therefore, does not reside in the
strength of definable political or social groups, but chiefly in
the strength of a potential, which is hidden throughout the
whole of society, including the official power structures of
that society. Therefore this power does not rely on soldiers of
its own, but on the soldiers of the enemy as it were – that is to
say, on everyone who is living within the lie and who may be
struck at any moment (in theory, at least) by the force of truth
(or who, out of an instinctive desire to protect their position,
may at least adapt to that force). It is a bacteriological
weapon, so to speak, utilized when conditions are ripe by a
single civilian to disarm an entire division. This power does
not participate in any direct struggle for power; rather it
makes its influence felt in the obscure arena of being itself.
The hidden movements it gives rise to there, however, can
issue forth (when, where, under what circumstances, and to
what extent are difficult to predict) in something visible: a real

political act or event, a social movement, a sudden explosion of civil unrest, a sharp conflict inside an apparently mono-lithic power structure, or simply an irrepressible transforma-tion in the social and intellectual climate. And since all genuine problems and matters of critical importance are hidden beneath a thick crust of lies, it is never quite clear when the proverbial last straw will fall, or what that straw will be. This, too, is why the regime prosecutes, almost as a reflex action preventively, even the most modest attempts to live within the truth.

Why was Solzhenitsyn driven out of his own country? Certainly not because he represented a unit of real power, that is, not because any of the regime's representatives felt he might unseat them and take their place in government. Solzhenitsyn's expulsion was something else: a desperate attempt to plug up the dreadful wellspring of truth, a truth which might cause incalculable transformations in social consciousness, which in turn might one day produce political debacles unpredictable in their consequences. And so the post-totalitarian system behaved in a characteristic way: it defended the integrity of the world of appearances in order to defend itself. For the crust presented by the life of lies is made of strange stuff. As long as it seals off hermetically the entire society, it appears to be made of stone. But the moment someone breaks through in one place, when one person cries out, 'The emperor is naked!' – when a single person breaks the rules of the game, thus exposing it as a game – everything suddenly appears in another light and the whole crust seems then to be made of a tissue on the point of tearing and disintegrating uncontrollably.

When I speak of living within the truth, I naturally do not have in mind only products of conceptual thought, such as a protest or a letter written by a group of intellectuals. It can be any means by which a person or a group revolts against manipulation: anything from a letter by intellectuals to a workers' strike, from a rock concert to a student demonstra-tion, from refusing to vote in the farcical elections, to making an open speech at some official congress, or even a hunger strike, for instance. If the suppression of the aims of life is a complex process, and if it is based on the multifaceted manipulation of all expressions of life then, by the same token, every free expression of life indirectly threatens the post-totalitarian system politically, including forms of expression to which, in other social systems, no one would attribute any potential political significance, not to mention explosive power.

The Prague Spring is usually understood as a clash between two groups on the level of real power: those who wanted to maintain the system as it was and those who wanted to reform it. It is frequently forgotten, however, that this encounter was merely the final act and the inevitable consequence of a long drama originally played out chiefly in the theatre of the spirit and the conscience of society. And that somewhere at the beginning of this drama, there were individuals who were willing to live within the truth, even when things were at their worst. These people had no access to real power, nor did they aspire to it. The sphere in which they were living the truth was not necessarily even that of political thought. They could equally have been poets, painters, musicians, or simply ordinary citizens who were able to maintain their human dignity. Today it is naturally difficult to pinpoint when and through which hidden, winding channel a certain action or attitude influenced a given milieu, and to trace the virus of truth as it slowly spread through the tissue of the life of lies, gradually causing it to disintegrate. One thing, however, seems clear: the attempt at political reform was not the cause of society's reawakening, but rather the final outcome of that reawakening.

I think the present also can be better understood in the light of this experience. The confrontation between 1000 Chartists and the post-totalitarian system would appear to be politically hopeless. This is true, of course, if we look at it through the traditional lens of the open political system, in which, quite naturally, every political force is measured chiefly in terms of the positions it holds on the level of real power. Given that perspective, a mini-party like the Charter would certainly not stand a chance. If, however, this confrontation is seen against the background of what we know about power in the post-totalitarian system, it appears in a fundamentally different light. For the time being, it is impossible to say with any precision what impact the appearance of Charter 77, its existence, and its work has had in the hidden sphere, and how the Charter's attempt to rekindle civic self-awareness and confidence is regarded there. Whether, when, and how this investment will eventually produce dividends in the form of specific political changes is even less possible to predict. But that, of course, is all part of living within the truth. As an existential solution, it takes individuals back to the solid ground of their own identity; as politics it throws them into a game of chance where the stakes are all or nothing. For this reason it is undertaken only by those for whom the former is worth risking the latter, or who have come to the conclusion that there is no other way to conduct real politics in Czechoslovakia today. Which, by the way, is the same thing: this conclusion can be reached only by someone who is unwilling to sacrifice his or her own human identity to politics, or rather who does not believe in a politics that requires such a sacrifice.

The more thoroughly the post-totalitarian system frustrates any rival alternative on the level of real power, as well as any form of politics independent of the laws of its own automatism, the more definitively the centre of gravity of any potential political threat shifts to the area of the existential and the prepolitical: usually without any conscious effort, living within the truth becomes the one natural point of departure for all activities that work against the automatism of the system. And even if such activities ultimately grow beyond the area of living within the truth (which means they are transformed into various parallel structures, movements, institutions, they begin to be regarded as political activity, they bring real pressure to bear on the official structures and begin in fact to have a certain influence on the level of real power), they always carry with them the specific hallmark of their origins. Therefore it seems to me that not even the so-called dissident movements can be properly understood without constantly bearing in mind this special background from which they emerge.

IX

The profound crisis of human identity brought on by living within a lie, a crisis which in turn makes such a life possible, certainly possesses a moral dimension as well; it appears, among other things, as a *deep moral crisis in society*. A person who has been seduced by the consumer value system, whose identity is dissolved in an amalgam of the accoutrements of mass civilization, and who has no roots in the order of being, no sense of responsibility for anything higher than his or her own personal survival, is a *demoralized* person. The system depends on this demoralization, deepens it, is in fact a projection of it into society.

Living within the truth, as humanity's revolt against an enforced position, is, on the contrary, an attempt to regain control over one's own sense of responsibility. In other words, it is clearly a moral act, not only because one must pay so dearly for it, but principally because it is not self-serving: the risk may bring rewards in the form of a general amelioration in the situation, or it may not. In this regard, as I stated previously, it is an all-or-nothing gamble, and it is difficult to imagine a reasonable person embarking on such a course merely because he or she reckons that sacrifice today will bring rewards tomorrow, be it only in the form of general gratitude. (By the way, the representatives of power invariably come to terms with those who live within the truth by persistently ascribing utilitarian motivations to them – a lust for power or fame or wealth – and thus they try, at least, to implicate them in their own world, the world of general demoralization.)

If living within the truth in the post-totalitarian system becomes the chief breeding ground for independent, alternative political ideas, then all considerations about the nature and future prospects of these ideas must necessarily reflect this moral dimension as a political phenomenon. (And if the revolutionary Marxist belief about morality as a product of the 'superstructure' inhibits any of our friends from realizing the full significance of this dimension and, in one way or another, from including it in their view of the world, it is to their own detriment: an anxious fidelity to the postulates of that world view prevents them from properly understanding the mechanisms of their own political influence, thus paradoxically making them precisely what they, as Marxists, so often suspect others of being – victims of 'false consciousness'.) The very special political significance of morality in the post-totalitarian system is a phenomenon that is at the very least unusual in modern political history, a phenomenon that might well have – as I shall soon attempt to show – far-reaching consequences.

X

Undeniably, the most important political event in Czechoslovakia after the advent of the Husák leadership in 1969 was the appearance of Charter 77. The spiritual and intellectual climate surrounding its appearance, however, was not the product of any immediate political event. That climate was created by the trial of some young musicians associated with a rock group called 'The Plastic People of the Universe'. Their trial was not a confrontation of two differing political forces or conceptions, but two differing conceptions of life. On the one hand, there was the sterile puritanism of the post-totalitarian establishment and, on the other hand, unknown young people who wanted no more than to be able to live within the truth, to play the music they enjoyed, to sing songs that were relevant to their lives, and to live freely in dignity and partnership. These people had no past history of political activity. They were not highly motivated members of the opposition with political ambitions, nor were they former politicians expelled from the power structures. They had been given every opportunity to adapt to the status quo, to

63

accept the principles of living within a lie and thus to enjoy life undisturbed by the authorities. Yet they decided on a different course. Despite this, or perhaps precisely because of it, their case had a very special impact on everyone who had not yet given up hope. Moreover, when the trial took place, a new mood had begun to surface after the years of waiting, of apathy and of scepticism towards various forms of resistance. People were 'tired of being tired'; they were fed up with the stagnation, the inactivity, barely hanging on in the hope that things might improve after all. In some ways the trial was the final straw. Many groups of differing tendencies which until then had remained isolated from each other, reluctant to co-operate, or which were committed to forms of action that made co-operation difficult, were suddenly struck with the powerful realization that freedom is indivisible. Everyone understood that an attack on the Czech musical underground was an attack on a most elementary and important thing, something that in fact bound everyone together: it was an attack on the very notion of 'living within the truth', on the real aims of life. The freedom to play rock music was understood as a human freedom and thus as essentially the same as the freedom to engage in philosophical and political reflection, the freedom to write, the freedom to express and defend the various social and political interests of society. People were inspired to feel a genuine sense of solidarity with the young musicians and they came to realize that not standing up for the freedom of others, regardless of how remote their means of creativity or their attitude to life, meant surrendering one's own freedom. (There is no freedom without equality before the law, and there is no equality before the law without freedom; Charter 77 has given this ancient notion a new and characteristic dimension, which has immensely important implications for modern Czech history. What Slábeček, the author of the book *Sixty-eight*, in a brilliant analysis, calls the 'principle of exclusion', lies at the root of all our present-day moral and political misery. This principle was born at the end of the Second World War in that strange collusion of democrats and communists and was subsequently developed further and further, right to the 'bitter end'. For the first time in decades this principle has been overcome, by Charter 77: all those united in the Charter have, for the first time, become equal partners. Charter 77 is not merely a coalition of communists and non-communists – that would be nothing historically new and, from the moral and political point of view, nothing revolutionary – but it is a community that is a priori open to anyone, and no one in it is a priori assigned an inferior position.) This was the climate, then, in which Charter 77 was created. Who could have foreseen that the prosecution of once or two obscure rock groups would have such far-reaching consequences?

I think that the origins of Charter 77 illustrate very well what I have already suggested above : that in the post-totalitarian system, the real background to the movements that gradually assume political significance does not usually consist of overtly political events or confrontations between different forces or concepts that are openly political. These movements for the most part originate elsewhere, in the far broader area of the 'pre-political', where 'living within a lie' confronts 'living within the truth', that is, where the demands of the post-totalitarian system conflict with the real aims of life. These real aims can naturally assume a great many forms. Sometimes they appear as the basic material or social interests of a group or an individual; at other times, they may appear as certain intellectual and spiritual interests; at still other times, they may be the most fundamental of existential demands, such as the simple longing of people to live their own lives in dignity. Such a conflict acquires a political character, then, not because of the elementary political nature of the aims demanding to be heard but simply because, given the complex system of manipulation on which the post-totalitarian system is founded and on which it is also dependent, every free human act or expression, every attempt to live within the truth, must necessarily appear as a threat to the system and, thus, as something which is political *par excellence.* Any eventual political articulation of the movements that grow out of this 'pre-political' hinterland is secondary. It develops and matures as a result of a subse quent confrontation with the system, and not because i started off as a political programme, project or impulse.

Once again, the events of 1968 confirm this. The commun ist politicians who were trying to reform the system cam forward with their programme not because they had sud denly experienced a mystical enlightenment, but becaus they were led to do so by continued and increasing pressur from areas of life that had nothing to do with politics in th traditional sense of the word. In fact they were trying i political ways to solve the social conflicts (which in fact wer confrontations between the aims of the system and the aim of life) that almost every level of society had been experien cing daily, and had been thinking about with increasin openness for years. Backed by this living resonance through out society, scholars and artists had defined the problem in wide variety of ways and students were demanding solu tions.

The genesis of Charter 77 also illustrates the specia political significance of the moral aspect of things that I hav mentioned. Charter 77 would have been unimaginabl without that powerful sense of solidarity among widel differing groups, and without the sudden realization that was impossible to go on waiting any longer, and that th truth had to be spoken loudly and collectively, regardless c the virtual certainty of sanctions and the uncertainty of an tangible results in the immediate future. 'There are som things worth suffering for', Jan Patočka wrote shortly befor his death. I think that Chartists understand this not only a Patočka's legacy, but also as the best explanation of why the do what they do.

Seen from the outside, and chiefly from the vantage poir of the system and its power structure, Charter 77 came as surprise, as a bolt out of the blue. It was not a bolt out of th blue, of course, but that impression is understandable, sinc the ferment that led to it took place in the 'hidden sphere', i that semi-darkness where things are difficult to chart c analyse. The chances of predicting the appearance of th

Charter were just as slight as the chances are now of predicting where it will lead. Once again, it was that shock, so typical of moments when something from the hidden sphere suddenly bursts through the moribund surface of 'living within a lie'. The more one is trapped in the world of appearances, the more surprising it is when something like that happens.

XI

In societies under the post-totalitarian system, all political life in the traditional sense has been eliminated. People have no opportunity to express themselves politically in public, let alone to organize politically. The gap that results is filled by ideological ritual. In such a situation, people's interest in political matters naturally dwindles and independent political thought, in so far as it exists at all, is seen by the majority as unrealistic, far-fetched, a kind of self-indulgent game, hopelessly distant from their everyday concerns; something admirable, perhaps, but quite pointless, because it is on the one hand entirely utopian and on the other hand extraordinarily dangerous, in view of the unusual vigour with which any move in that direction is persecuted by the regime.

Yet even in such societies, individuals and groups of people exist who do not abandon politics as a vocation and who, in one way or another, strive to think independently, to express themselves and in some cases even to organize politically, because that is a part of their attempt to live within the truth.

The fact that these people exist and work is in itself immensely important and worthwhile. Even in the worst of times, they maintain the continuity of political thought. If some genuine political impulse emerges from this or that 'pre-political' confrontation and is properly articulated early enough, thus increasing its chances of relative success, then this is frequently due to these isolated 'generals without an army' who, because they have maintained the continuity of political thought in the face of enormous difficulties, can at the right moment enrich the new impulse with the fruits of their own political thinking. Once again, there is ample evidence for this process in Czechoslovakia. Almost all those who were political prisoners in the early 1970s, who had apparently been made to suffer in vain because of their quixotic efforts to work politically among an utterly apathetic and demoralized society, belong today – inevitably – among the most active Chartists. In Charter 77, the moral legacy of their earlier sacrifices is valued, and they have enriched this movement with their experience and that element of political thinking.

And yet it seems to me that the thought and activity of those friends who have never given up direct political work and who are always ready to assume direct political responsibility very often suffer from one chronic fault: an insufficient understanding of the historical uniqueness of the post-totalitarian system as a social and political reality. They have little understanding of the specific nature of power that is typical for this system and therefore they overestimate the importance of direct political work in the traditional sense. Moreover, they fail to appreciate the political significance of those 'pre-political' events and processes that provide the living humus from which genuine political change usually springs. As political actors – or, rather, as people with political ambitions – they frequently try to pick up where natural political life left off. They maintain models of behaviour that may have been appropriate in more normal political circumstances and thus, without really being aware of it, they bring an outmoded way of thinking, old habits, conceptions, categories and notions to bear on circumstances that are quite new and radically different, without first giving adequate thought to the meaning and substance of such things in the new circumstances, to what politics as such means now, to what sort of thing can have political impact and potential, and in what way. Because such people have been excluded from the structures of power and are no longer able to influence those structures directly (and because they remain faithful to traditional notions of politics established in

68

more or less democratic societies or in classical dictatorships) they frequently, in a sense, lose touch with reality. Why make compromises with reality, they say, when none of our proposals will ever be accepted anyway? Thus they find themselves in a world of genuinely utopian thinking.

As I have already tried to indicate, however, genuinely far-reaching political events do not emerge from the same sources and in the same way in the post-totalitarian system as they do in a democracy. And if a large portion of the public is indifferent to, even sceptical of, alternative political models and programmes and the private establishment of opposition political parties, this is not merely because there is a general feeling of apathy towards public affairs and a loss of that sense of 'higher responsibility'; in other words, it is not just a consequence of the general demoralization. There is also a bit of healthy social instinct at work in this attitude. It is as if people sensed intuitively that 'nothing is what it seems any longer', as the saying goes, and that from now on, therefore, things must be done entirely differently as well.

If some of the most important political impulses in Soviet bloc countries in recent years have come initially – that is, before being felt on the level of actual power – from mathematicians, philosophers, physicians, writers, historians, ordinary workers and so on, more frequently than from politicians, and if the driving force behind the various 'dissident movements' comes from so many people in 'non-political' professions, this is not because these people are more clever than those who see themselves primarily as politicians. It is because those who are not politicians are also not so bound by traditional political thinking and political habits and therefore, paradoxically, they are more aware of genuine political reality and more sensitive to what can and should be done under the circumstances.

There is no way around it: no matter how beautiful an alternative political model may be, it can no longer speak to the 'hidden sphere', inspire people and society, call for real political ferment. The real sphere of potential politics in the post-totalitarian system is elsewhere: in the continuing and cruel tension between the complex demands of that system and the aims of life, that is, the elementary need of human beings to live, to a certain extent at least, in harmony with themselves, that is, to live in a bearable way, not to be humiliated by their superiors and officials, not to be continually watched by the police, to be able to express themselves freely, to find an outlet for their creativity, to enjoy legal security, and so on. Anything that touches this field concretely, anything that relates to this fundamental, omnipresent and living tension, will inevitably speak to people. Abstract projects for an ideal political or economic order do not interest them to anything like the same extent – and rightly so – not only because everyone knows how little chance they have of succeeding, but also because today people feel that the less political policies are derived from a concrete and human 'here and now' and the more they fix their sights on an abstract 'someday', the more easily they can degenerate into new forms of human enslavement. People who live in the post-totalitarian system know only too well that the question of whether one or several political parties are in power, and how these parties define and label themselves, is of far less importance than the question of whether or not it is possible to live like a human being.

To shed the burden of traditional political categories and habits and open oneself up fully to the world of human existence and then to draw political conclusions only after having analysed it: this is not only politically more realistic but at the same time, from the point of view of an 'ideal state of affairs', politically more promising as well. A genuine, profound and lasting change for the better – as I shall attempt to show elsewhere – can no longer result from the victory (were such a victory possible) of any particular traditional political conception, which can ultimately be only external, that is, a structural or systemic conception. More than ever before, such a change will have to derive from human existence, from the fundamental reconstitution of the position of people in the world, their relationships to themselves and to each other, and to the universe. If a better economi and political model is to be created, then perhaps more than ever before it must derive from profound existential and moral changes in society. This is not something that can be designed and introduced like a new car. If it is to be more than just a new variation on the old degeneration, it must above all be an expression of life in the process of transforming itself. A better system will not automatically ensure a better life. In fact the opposite is true: only by creating a better life can a better system be developed.

Once more I repeat that I am not underestimating the importance of political thought and conceptual political work. On the contrary, I think that genuine political thought and genuinely political work is precisely what we continually fail to achieve. If I say 'genuine', however, I have in mind the kind of thought and conceptual work that has freed itself of all the traditional political schemata that have been imported into our circumstances from a world that will never return (and whose return, even were it possible, would provide no permanent solution to the most important problems).

The Second and Fourth Internationals, like many other political powers and organizations, may naturally provide significant political support for various efforts of ours, but neither of them can solve our problems for us. They operate in a different world and are a product of different circumstances. Their theoretical concepts can be interesting and instructive to us but one thing is certain: we cannot solve our problems simply by identifying with these organizations. And the attempt in our country to place what we do in the context of some of the discussions that dominate political life in democratic societies often seems like sheer folly. For example, is it possible to talk seriously about whether we want to change the system or merely reform it? In the circumstances under which we live, this is a pseudo-problem, since for the time being there is simply no way we can accomplish either goal. We are not even clear about where reform ends and change begins. We know from a number of harsh experiences that neither reform nor change is in itself a guarantee of anything. We know that ultimately it is all the same to us whether or not the system in which we live, in the light of a particular doctrine, appears 'changed' or 'reformed'. Our concern is whether we can live with dignity in such a system, whether it serves people rather than people serving it. We are struggling to achieve this with the means available to us, and the means it makes sense to employ. Western journalists, submerged in the political banalities in which they live, may label our approach as overly legalistic, as too risky, revisionist, counter-revolutionary, bourgeois, communist, or as too right-wing or left-wing. But this is the very last thing that interests us.

XII

One concept that is a constant source of confusion chiefly because it has been imported into our circumstances from circumstances that are entirely different, is the concept of an opposition. What exactly is an opposition in the post-totalitarian system?

In democratic societies with a traditional parliamentary system of government, political opposition is understood as a political force on the level of actual power (most frequently a party or coalition of parties) which is not a part of the government. It offers an alternative political programme, it has ambitions to govern, and it is recognized and respected by the government in power as a natural element in the political life of the country. It seeks to spread its influence by political means, and competes for power on the basis of agreed-upon legal regulations.

In addition to this form of opposition, there exists the phenomenon of the 'extra-parliamentary opposition', which again consists of forces organized more or less on the level of actual power, but which operate outside the rules created by the system, and which employ different means than are usual within that framework.

In classical dictatorships, the term opposition is understood to mean the political forces which have also come out with an alternative political programme. They operate either legally or on the outer limits of legality, but in any case they cannot compete for power within the limits of some agreed-upon regulations. Or the term opposition may be applied to forces preparing for a violent confrontation with the ruling power, or who feel themselves to be in this state of confrontation already, such as various guerrilla groups or liberation movements.

An opposition in the post-totalitarian system does not exist in any of these senses. In what way, then, can the term be used?

1 Occasionally the term 'opposition' is applied, mainly by Western journalists, to persons or groups inside the power structure who find themselves in a state of *hidden* conflict with the highest authorities. The reasons for this conflict may be certain differences (not very sharp differences, naturally) of a conceptual nature, but more frequently it is quite simply a longing for power or a personal antipathy to others who represent that power.

2 Opposition here can also be understood as everything that does or can have an indirect political effect in the sense already mentioned, that is, everything the post-totalitarian system feels threatened by, which in fact means everything it is threatened by. In this sense, the opposition is every attempt to live within the truth, from the greengrocer's refusal to put the slogan in his window to a freely written poem; in other words, everything in which the genuine aims of life go beyond the limits placed on them by the aims of the system.

3 More frequently, however, the opposition is usually understood (again, largely by Western journalists) as groups of people who make public their nonconformist stances and critical opinions, who make no secret of their independent thinking and who, to a greater or lesser degree, consider themselves a political force. In this sense, the notion of an 'opposition' more or less overlaps with the notion of 'dissent', although, of course, there are great differences in

the degree to which that label is accepted or rejected. I
depends not only on the extent to which these people
understand their power as a directly political force, and or
whether they have ambitions to participate in actual power
but also on how each of them understands the notion of ar
'opposition'.

Again, here is an example: in its original declaration, Charte
77 emphasized that it was not an opposition because it had n
intention of presenting an alternative political programme. I
sees its mission as something quite different, for it has no
presented such programmes. In fact, if the presenting of ar
alternative programme defines the nature of an opposition ir
post-totalitarian states, then the Charter cannot be consi
dered an opposition.

The Czechoslovak government, however, has considere
Charter 77 as an expressly oppositional association from th
very beginning, and has treated it accordingly. This mean
that the government – and this is only natural – understand
the term 'opposition' more or less as I defined it in point 2
that is, as everything that manages to avoid total manipula
tion and which therefore denies the principle that the system
has an absolute claim on the individual.

If we accept this definition of opposition, then of course w
must, along with the government, consider the Charter
genuine opposition, because it represents a serious challeng
to the integrity of post-totalitarian power, founded as it is or
the universality of 'living with a lie'.

It is a different matter, however, when we look at th
extent to which individual signatories of Charter 77 think c
themselves as an opposition. My impression is that most bas
their understanding of the term opposition on the tradition
meaning of the word as it became established in democrati
societies (or in classical dictatorships); therefore, they under
stand 'opposition', even in Czechoslovakia, as a politicall
defined force which, although it does not operate on the leve
of actual power, and even less within the framework c
certain rules respected by the government, would still nc

74

reject the opportunity to participate in actual power because it has, in a sense, an alternative political programme whose proponents are prepared to accept direct political responsibility for it. Given this notion of an opposition, some Chartists – the great majority – do not see themselves in this way. Others – a minority – do, even though they fully respect the fact that there is no room within Charter 77 for 'oppositional' activity in this sense. At the same time, however, perhaps every Chartist is familiar enough with the specific nature of conditions in the post-totalitarian system to realize that it is not only the struggle for human rights that has its own peculiar political power, but incomparably more 'innocent' activities as well, and therefore they can be understood as an aspect of opposition. No Chartist can really object to being considered an 'opposition' in this sense.

There is another circumstance, however, that considerably complicates matters. For many decades, the power ruling society in the Soviet bloc has used the label 'opposition' as the blackest of indictments, as synonymous with the word 'enemy'. To brand someone 'a member of the opposition' is tantamount to saying he or she is trying to overthrow the government and put an end to socialism (naturally in the pay of the imperialists). There have been times when this label led straight to the gallows, and of course this does not encourage people to apply the same label to themselves. Moreover, it is only a word, and what is actually done is more important than how it is labelled.

The final reason why many reject such a term is because there is something negative about the notion of an 'opposition'. People who so define themselves do so in relation to a prior 'position'. In other words, they relate themselves specifically to the power that rules society and through it, define themselves, deriving their own 'position' from the position of the regime. For people who have simply decided to live within the truth, to say aloud what they think, to express their solidarity with their fellow citizens, to create as they want and simply to live in harmony with their better 'self', it is naturally disagreeable to feel required to define their own, original and positive 'position' negatively, in terms of something else, and to think of themselves primarily as people who are against something, not simply as people who *are* what they are.

Obviously, the only way to avoid misunderstanding is to say clearly – before one starts using them – in what sense the terms 'opposition' and 'member of the opposition' are being used and how they are in fact to be understood in our circumstances.

XIII

If the term 'opposition' has been imported from democratic societies into the post-totalitarian system without general agreement on what the word means in conditions that are so different, then the term 'dissident' was, on the contrary, chosen by Western journalists and is now generally accepted as the label for a phenomenon peculiar to the post-totalitarian system and almost never occurring – at least not in that form – in democratic societies.

Who are these 'dissidents'?

It seems that the term is applied primarily to citizens of the Soviet bloc who have decided to live within the truth and who, in addition, meet the following criteria:

1 They express their nonconformist positions and critical opinions publicly and systematically, within the very strict limits available to them, and because of this, they are known in the West.

2 Despite being unable to publish at home and despite every possible form of persecution by their governments, they have, by virtue of their attitudes, managed to win a certain esteem, both from the public and from their government, and thus they actually enjoy a very limited and very strange degree of indirect, actual power in their own milieu as well. This either protects them from the worst forms of persecution, or at least it ensures that if they are persecuted, it will mean certain political complications for their governments.

3 The horizon of their critical attention and their commitment reaches beyond the narrow context of their immediate surroundings or special interests to embrace more general causes and, thus, their work becomes political in nature, although the degree to which they think of themselves as a directly political force may vary a great deal.

4 They are people who lean towards intellectual pursuits, that is, they are 'writing' people, people for whom the written word is the primary – and often the only – political medium they command, and that can gain them attention, particularly from abroad. Other ways in which they seek to live within the truth are either lost to the foreign observer in the elusive local milieu or – if they reach beyond this local framework – they appear to be only somewhat less visible complements to what they have written.

5 Regardless of their actual vocations, these people are talked about in the West more frequently in terms of their activities as committed citizens, or in terms of the critical, political aspects of their work, than in terms of the 'real' work they do in their own fields. From personal experience, I know that there is an invisible line you cross – without even wanting to or becoming aware of it – beyond which they cease to treat you as a writer who happens to be a concerned citizen and begin talking of you as a 'dissident' who almost incidentally (in his or her spare time, perhaps?) happens to write plays as well.

Unquestionably, there are people who meet all of these criteria. What is debatable is whether we should be using a special term for a group defined in such an essentially accidental way, and specifically, whether they should be called 'dissidents'. It does happen, however, and there is clearly nothing we can do about it. Sometimes, to facilitate communication, we even use the label ourselves, although it is done with distaste, rather ironically, and almost always in quotation marks.

Perhaps it is now appropriate to outline some of the reasons why 'dissidents' themselves are not very happy to be referred to in this way. In the first place, the word is problematic from an etymological point of view. A 'dissident', we are told in our press, means something like 'renegade' or 'backslider'. But dissidents do not consider themselves renegades for the simple reason that they are not primarily denying or rejecting anything. On the contrary, they have tried to affirm their own human identity, and if they reject anything at all, then it is merely what was false and alienating in their lives, that aspect of 'living within a lie'.

But that is not the most important thing. The term 'dissident' frequently implies a special profession, as if, along with the more normal vocations, there were another special one – grumbling about the state of things. In fact, a 'dissident' is simply a physicist, a sociologist, a worker, a poet, individuals who are merely doing what they feel they must and, consequently, who find themselves in open conflict with the regime. This conflict has not come about through any conscious intention on their part, but simply through the inner logic of their thinking, behaviour or work (often confronted with external circumstances more or less beyond their control). They have not, in other words, consciously decided to be professional malcontents, rather as one decides to be a tailor or a blacksmith.

In fact, of course, they do not usually discover they are 'dissidents' until long after they have actually become one. 'Dissent' springs from motivations far different from the desire for titles or fame. In short, they do not decide to become 'dissidents', and even if they were to devote twenty-four hours a day to it, it would still not be a profession, but primarily an existential attitude. Moreover, it is an attitude that is in no way the exclusive property of those who have earned themselves the title of 'dissident' just because they happen to fulfil those accidental external conditions already mentioned. There are thousands of nameless people who try to live within the truth and millions who want to but cannot, perhaps only because to do so in the circumstances in which they live, they would need ten times the courage of those who have already taken the first step. If several dozen are randomly chosen from among all these people and put into a special category, this can utterly distort the general picture. It does so in two different ways. Either it suggests that 'dissidents' are a group of prominent people, a 'protected species' who are permitted to do things others are not and whom the government may even be cultivating as living proof of its generosity; or it lends support to the illusion that since there is no more than a handful of malcontents to whom not very much is really being done, all the rest are therefore content, for were they not so, they would be 'dissidents' too.

But that is not all. This categorization also unintentionally supports the impression that the primary concern of these 'dissidents' is some vested interest that they share as a group, as though their entire argument with the government were no more than a rather abstruse conflict between two opposed groups, a conflict that leaves society out of it altogether. But such an impression profoundly contradicts the real importance of the 'dissident' attitude, which stands or falls on its interest in others, in what ails society as a whole, in other words, on an interest in all those who do not speak up. If 'dissidents' have any kind of authority at all and if they have not been exterminated long ago like exotic insects that have appeared where they have no business being, then this is not because the government holds this exclusive group and their exclusive ideas in such awe, but because it is perfectly aware of the potential political power of 'living within the truth' rooted in the hidden sphere, and well aware too of the kind of world 'dissent' grows out of and the world it addresses: the everyday human world, the world of daily tension between the aims of life and the aims of the system. (Can there be any better evidence of this than the government's action after Charter 77 appeared, when it launched a campaign to compel the entire nation to declare that Charter 77 was wrong? Those millions of signatures proved, among other things, that just the opposite was true.) The political organs and the police do not lavish such enormous attention on 'dissidents' – which may give the impression that the government fears them as they might fear an alternative power clique – because they actually are such a power clique, but because they are ordinary people with ordinary cares, differing from the rest only in that they say aloud what the rest cannot say or are afraid to say. I have already mentioned Solzhenitsyn's political influence: it does not reside in some exclusive political power he possesses as an individual, but in the experience of those millions of Gulag victims which he simply amplified and communicated to millions of other people of good will.

To institutionalize a select category of well-known or prominent 'dissidents' means in fact to deny the most intrinsic moral aspect of their activity. As we have seen, the 'dissident movement' grows out of the principle of equality, founded on the notion that human rights and freedoms are indivisible. After all, did not 'well-known dissidents' unite in KOR to defend unknown workers? And was it not precisely for this reason that they became 'well-known dissidents'? And did not the 'well-known dissidents' unite in Charter 77 after they had been brought together in defence of those unknown musicians, and did they not unite in the Charter precisely *with them*, and did they not become 'well-known dissidents' precisely because of that? It is truly a cruel paradox that the more some citizens stand up in defence of other citizens, the more they are labelled with a word that in effect separates them from those 'other citizens'.

This explanation, I hope, will make clear the significance of the quotation marks I have put around the word 'dissident' throughout this essay.

XIV

At the time when the Czech lands and Slovakia were an integral part of the Austro-Hungarian Empire, and when there existed neither the historical nor the political, psychological or social conditions that would have enabled the Czechs and Slovaks to seek their identity outside the framework of this empire, T. G. Masaryk established a Czechoslovak national programme based on the notion of 'small-scale work' (*drobná práce*). By that he meant honest and responsible work in widely different areas of life but within the existing social

order, work that would stimulate national creativity and national self-confidence. Naturally he placed particular emphasis
on intelligent and enlightened upbringing and education, and
on the moral and humanitarian aspects of life. Masaryk
believed that the only possible starting point for a more
dignified national destiny was humanity itself. Humanity's
first task was to create the conditions for a more human life;
and in Masaryk's view, the task of transforming the stature of
the nation began with the transformation of human beings.

This notion of 'working for the good of the nation' took root
in Czechoslovak society and in many ways it was successful
and is still alive today. Along with those who exploit the
notion as a sophisticated excuse for collaborating with the
regime, there are still many, even today, who genuinely
uphold the ideal and, in some areas at least, can point to
indisputable achievements. It is hard to say how much worse
things would be if there were not many hard-working people
who simply refuse to give up and try constantly to do the best
they can, paying an unavoidable minimum to 'living within a
lie' so that they might give their utmost to the authentic needs
of society. These people assume, correctly, that every piece of
good work is an indirect criticism of bad politics, and that there
are situations where it is worthwhile going this route, even
though it means surrendering one's natural right to make
direct criticisms.

Today, however, there are very clear limitations to this
attitude, even compared to the situation in the 1960s. More
and more frequently, those who attempt to practise the principle of 'small-scale work' come up against the post-totalitarian
system and find themselves facing a dilemma: either one
retreats from that position, dilutes the honesty, responsibility
and consistency on which it is based and simply adapts to
circumstances (the approach taken by the majority), or one
continues on the way begun and inevitably comes into conflict
with the regime (the approach taken by a minority).

If the notion of small-scale work was never intended as an
imperative to survive in the existing social and political structure *at any cost* (in which case individuals who allowed them-

selves to be excluded from that structure would necessarily appear to have given up 'working for the nation') then today it is even less significant. There is no general model of behaviour, that is, no neat, universally valid way of determining the point at which small-scale work ceases to be 'for the good of the nation' and becomes 'detrimental to the nation'. It is more than clear, however, that the danger of such a reversal is becoming more and more acute and that small-scale work, with increasing frequency, is coming up against that limit beyond which avoiding conflict means compromising its very essence.

In 1974, when I was employed in a brewery, my immediate superior was a certain Š, a person well versed in the art of making beer. He was proud of his profession and he wanted our brewery to brew good beer. He spent almost all his time at work, continually thinking up improvements and he frequently made the rest of us feel uncomfortable because he assumed that we loved brewing as much as he did. In the midst of the slovenly indifference to work that socialism encourages, a more constructive worker would be difficult to imagine.

The brewery itself was managed by people who understood their work less and were less fond of it, but who were politically more influential. They were bringing the brewery to ruin and not only did they fail to react to any of Š's suggestions, but they actually became increasingly hostile towards him and tried in every way to thwart his efforts to do a good job. Eventually the situation became so bad that Š felt compelled to write a lengthy letter to the manager's superior, in which he attempted to analyse the brewery's difficulties. He explained why it was the worst in the district and pointed to those responsible.

His voice might have been heard. The manager, who was politically powerful but otherwise ignorant of beer, a man who loathed workers and was given to intrigue, might have been replaced and conditions in the brewery might have been improved on the basis of Š's suggestions. Had this happened, it would have been a perfect example of small-scale work in action. Unfortunately the precise opposite occurred: the manager of the brewery, who was a member of the Communist Party's district committee, had friends in higher places and he saw to it that the situation was resolved in his favour. Š's analysis was described as a 'defamatory document' and Š himself was labelled a 'political saboteur'. He was thrown out of the brewery and shifted to another one where he was given a job requiring no skill. Here the notion of small-scale work had come up against the wall of the post-totalitarian system. By speaking the truth, Š had stepped out of line, broken the rules, cast himself out, and he ended up as a sub-citizen, stigmatized as an enemy. He could now say anything he wanted, but he could never, as a matter of principle, expect to be heard. He had become the 'dissident' of the Eastern Bohemian Brewery.

I think this is a model case which, from another point of view, illustrates what I have already said in the preceding section: you do not become a 'dissident' just because you decide one day to take up this most unusual career. You are thrown into it by your personal sense of responsibility, combined with a complex set of external circumstances. You are cast out of the existing structures and placed in a position of conflict with them. It begins as an attempt to do your work well, and ends with being branded an enemy of society. This is why our situation is not comparable to the Austro-Hungarian Empire, when the Czech nation, in the worst period of Bach's absolutism, had only one real 'dissident', Karel Havliček, who was imprisoned in Brixen. Today, if we are not to be snobbish about it, we must admit that 'dissidents' can be found on every street corner.

To rebuke 'dissidents' for having abandoned 'small-scale work' is simply absurd. 'Dissent' is not an alternative to Masaryk's notion, it is frequently its only possible outcome. I say 'frequently' in order to emphasize that this is not always the case. I am far from believing that the only decent and responsible people are those who find themselves at odds with the existing social and political structures. After all, the brewmaster Š might have won his battle. To condemn those who have kept their positions simply because they have kept them, in other words, for not being 'dissidents', would be just as absurd as to hold them up as an example to the 'dissidents'. In any case, it contradicts the whole 'dissident' attitude – seen as an attempt to live within the truth – if one judges human behaviour not according to what it is and whether it is good or not, but according to the personal circumstances such an attempt has brought one to.

XV

Our greengrocer's attempt to live within the truth may be confined to not doing certain things. He decides not to put flags in his window when his only motive for putting them there in the first place would have been to avoid being reported by the house warden; he does not vote in elections that he considers false; he does not hide his opinions from his superiors. In other words, he may go no further than 'merely' refusing to comply with certain demands made on him by the system (which of course is not an insignificant step to take). This may, however, grow into something more. The greengrocer may begin to do something concrete, something that goes beyond an immediately personal self-defensive reaction against manipulation, something that will manifest his new-found sense of higher responsibility. He may, for example, organize his fellow greengrocers to act together in defence of their interests. He may write letters to various institutions, drawing their attention to instances of disorder and injustice around him. He may seek out unofficial literature, copy it and lend it to his friends.

If what I have called living within the truth is a basic existential (and of course potentially political) starting point for all those 'independent citizens' initiatives' and 'dissident' or 'opposition' movements dealt with in the essays to follow, this does not mean that every attempt to live within the truth automatically belongs in this category. On the contrary, in its most original and broadest sense, living within the truth covers a vast territory whose outer limits are vague and difficult to map, a territory full of modest expressions of human volition, the vast majority of which will remain anonymous and whose political impact will probably never be felt or described any more concretely than simply as a part of a social climate or mood. Most of these expressions remain elementary revolts against manipulation: you simply straighten your backbone and live in greater dignity as an individual.

Here and there – thanks to the nature, the assumptions and the professions of some people, but also thanks to a number of accidental circumstances such as the specific nature of the local milieu, friends, and so on – a more coherent and visible initiative may emerge from this wide and anonymous hinterland, an initiative that transcends 'merely' individual revolt and is transformed into more conscious, structured and purposeful work. The point where living within the truth ceases to be a mere negation of living with a lie and becomes articulate in a particular way, is the point at which something is born that might be called the 'independent spiritual, social and political life of society'. This independent life is not separated from the rest of life ('dependent life') by some sharply defined line. Both types frequently coexist in the same people. Nevertheless, its most important focus is marked by a relatively high degree of inner emancipation. It sails upon the vast ocean of the manipulated life like little boats, tossed by the waves but always bobbing back as visible messengers of living within the truth, articulating the suppressed aims of life.

What is this independent life of society? The spectrum of its expressions and activities is naturally very wide. It includes everything from self-education and thinking about the world, through free creative activity and its communication to others, to the most varied free, civic attitudes, including instances of independent social self-organization. In short, it is an area in which living within the truth becomes articulate and materializes in a visible way.

Thus what will later be referred to as 'citizens' initiatives', 'dissident movements' or even 'oppositions', emerge, like the proverbial one-tenth of the iceberg visible above the water, from that area, from the independent life of society. In other

THE POWER OF THE POWERLESS

words, just as the independent life of society develops out of living within the truth in the widest sense of the word, as the distinct, articulated expression of that life, so 'dissent' gradually emerges from the 'independent life of society'. Yet there is a marked difference: if the independent life of society, externally at least, can be understood as a higher form of living within the truth, it is far less certain that 'dissident movements' are necessarily a higher form of the 'independent life of society'. They are simply one manifestion of it and though they may be the most visible and, at first glance, the most political (and most clearly articulated) expression of it, they are far from necessarily being the most mature or even the most important, not only in the general social sense but even in terms of direct political influence. After all, 'dissent' has been artificially removed from its place of birth by having been given a special name. In fact, however, it is not possible to think of it separated from the whole background out of which it develops, of which it is an integral part, and from which it draws all its vital strength. In any case, it follows from what has already been said about the peculiarities of the post-totalitarian system that what *appears* to be the most political of forces in a given moment, and what thinks of itself in such terms, need not necessarily in fact *be* such a force. The extent to which it is a real political force is due exclusively to its pre-political context.

What follows from this description? Nothing more and nothing less than this: it is impossible to talk about what in fact 'dissidents' do and the effect of their work without first talking about the work of all those who, in one way or another, take part in the independent life of society and who are not necessarily 'dissidents' at all. They may be writers who write as they wish without regard for censorship or official demands and who issue their work – when official publishers refuse to print it – as *samizdat*. They may be philosophers, historians, sociologists and all those who practise independent scholarship and, if it is impossible through official or semi-official channels, who also circulate their work in *samizdat* or who organize private discussions, lectures and seminars. They may be teachers who privately teach young people things that are kept from them in the state schools; clergymen who either in office or, if they are deprived of their charges, outside it, try to carry on a free religious life; painters, musicians and singers who practise their work regardless of how it is looked upon by official institutions; everyone who shares this independent culture and helps to spread it; people who, using the means available to them, try to express and defend the actual social interests of workers, to put real meaning back into trade unions or to form independent ones; people who are not afraid to call the attention of officials to cases of injustice and who strive to see that the laws are observed; and the different groups of young people who try to extricate themselves from manipulation and live in their own way, in the spirit of their own hierarchy of values. The list could go on.

Very few would think of calling all these people 'dissidents'. And yet are not the well-known 'dissidents' simply people like them? Are not all these activities in fact what 'dissidents' do as well? Do they not produce scholarly work and publish it in *samizdat*? Do they not write plays and novels and poems? Do they not lecture to students in private 'universities'? Do they not struggle against various forms of injustice and attempt to ascertain and express the genuine social interests of various sectors of the population?

After having tried to indicate the sources, the inner structure and some aspects of the 'dissident' attitude as such, I have clearly shifted my viewpoint from outside, as it were, to an investigation of what these 'dissidents' *actually* do, how their initiatives are manifested and where they lead.

The first conclusion to be drawn, then, is that the original and most important sphere of activity, one that predetermines all the others, is simply an attempt to create and support the 'independent life of society' as an articulated expression of 'living within the truth'. In other words, serving truth consistently, purposefully and articulately, and organizing this service. This is only natural, after all: if living within the truth is an elementary starting point for every attempt made by people to oppose the alienating pressure of the system, if it is the only meaningful basis of any independent act of political import, and if, ultimately, it is also the most intrinsic existential source of the 'dissident' attitude, then it is difficult to imagine that even manifest 'dissent' could have any other basis than the service of truth, the truthful life and the attempt to make room for the genuine aims of life.

XVI

The post-totalitarian system is mounting a total assault on humans and humans stand against it alone, abandoned and isolated. It is therefore entirely natural that all the 'dissident movements' are explicitly defensive movements: they exist to defend human beings and the genuine aims of life against the aims of the system.

Today the Polish group KOR is called the Committee for Social Self-Defence. The word 'defence' appears in the names of other similar groups in Poland, but even the Soviet Helsinki monitoring group and our own Charter 77 are clearly defensive in nature.

In terms of traditional politics, this programme of defence is understandable, even though it may appear minimal, provisional and ultimately negative. It offers no new conception, model or ideology, and therefore it is not 'politics' in the proper sense of the word, since politics always assumes a 'positive' programme and can scarcely limit itself to defending someone against something.

Such a view, I think, reveals the limitations of the traditionally political way of looking at things. The post-totalitarian system, after all, is not the manifestation of a particular political line followed by a particular government. It is something radically different: it is a complex, profound and long-term violation of society, or rather the self-violation of society. To oppose it merely by establishing a different political line and then striving for a change in government would not only be unrealistic, it would be utterly inadequate, for it would never come near to touching the root of the matter. For some time now, the problem has no longer resided in a political line or programme: it is a problem of life itself.

Thus defending the aims of life, defending humanity, is not only a more realistic approach, since it can begin right now and is potentially more popular because it concerns people's everyday lives; at the same time (and perhaps precisely because of this) it is also an incomparably more consistent approach because it aims at the very essence of things.

There are times when we must sink to the bottom of our misery to understand truth, just as we must descend to the bottom of a well to see the stars in broad daylight. It seems to me that today, this 'provisional', 'minimal' and 'negative' programme – the 'simple' defence of people – is in a particular sense (and not merely in the circumstances in which we live) an optimal and most positive programme because it forces politics to return to its only proper starting point, proper that is, if all the old mistakes are to be avoided: individual people. In democratic societies, where the violence done to human beings is not nearly so obvious and cruel, this fundamental revolution in politics has yet to happen, and some things will probably have to get worse there before the urgent need for that revolution is reflected in politics. In our world, precisely because of the misery in which we find ourselves, it would seem that politics has already undergone that transformation: the central concern of political thought is no longer abstract visions of a self-redeeming, 'positive' model (and of course the opportunistic political practices that are the reverse of the same coin), but rather the people who have so far merely been enslaved by those models and their practices.

Every society, of course, requires some degree of organization. Yet if that organization is to serve people and not the other way around, then people will have to be liberated and space created so that they may organize themselves in meaningful ways. The depravity of the opposite approach, in

which people are first organized in one way or another (by
someone who always knows best 'what the people need') so
they may then allegedly be liberated, is something we have
known on our own skins only too well.

To sum up: most people who are too bound to the traditio
nal political way of thinking see the weaknesses of the 'dissi
dent movements' in their purely defensive character. In con
trast, I see that as their greatest strength. I believe that this is
precisely where these movements supersede the kind of poli
tics from whose point of view their programme can seem so
inadequate.

XVII

In the 'dissident movements' of the Soviet bloc, the defence
of human beings usually takes the form of a defence of
human and civil rights as they are entrenched in various
official documents such as the Universal Declaration of
Human Rights, the International Covenants on Human
Rights, the Final Act of the Helsinki Conference and the
constitutions of individual states. These movements set out
to defend anyone who is being prosecuted for acting in the
spirit of those rights, and they in turn act in the same spirit in
their work, by insisting over and over again that the regime
recognize and respect human and civil rights, and by draw
ing attention to the areas of life where this is not the case.

Their work, therefore, is based on the principle of legality:
they operate publicly and openly, insisting not only that their
activity is in line with the law, but that achieving respect for
the law is one of their main aims. This principle of legality,
which provides both the point of departure and the
framework for their activities, is common to all 'dissident'
groups in the Soviet bloc, even though individual groups
have never worked out any formal agreement on that point.
This circumstance raises an important question: Why, in con
ditions where a widespread and arbitrary abuse of power is
the rule, is there such a general and spontaneous acceptance
of the principle of legality?

On the primary level, this stress on legality is a natural expression of specific conditions that exist in the post-totalitarian system, and the consequence of an elementary understanding of that specificity. If there are in essence only two ways to struggle for a free society – that is, through legal means and through (armed or unarmed) revolt – then it should be obvious at once how inappropriate the latter alternative is in the post-totalitarian system. Revolt is appropriate when conditions are clearly and openly in motion, during a war for example, or in situations where social or political conflicts are coming to a head. It is appropriate in a classical dictatorship that is either just setting itself up or is in a state of collapse. In other words, it is appropriate where social forces of comparable strength (for example, a government of occupation *versus* a nation fighting for its freedom) are confronting each other on the level of actual power, or where there is a clear distinction between the usurpers of power and the subjugated population, or when society finds itself in a state of open crisis. Conditions in the post-totalitarian system – except in extremely explosive situations like the one in Hungary in 1956 – are, of course, precisely the opposite. They are static and stable, and social crises, for the most part, exist only latently (though they run much deeper). Society is not sharply polarized on the level of actual political power, but, as we have seen, the fundamental lines of conflict run right through each person. In this situation, no attempt at revolt could ever hope to set up even a minimum of resonance in the rest of society, because that society is 'soporific', submerged in a consumer rat race and wholly involved in the post-totalitarian system (that is, participating in it and acting as agents of its 'automatism'), and it would simply find anything like revolt unacceptable. It would interpret the revolt as an attack upon itself and, rather than supporting the revolt, it would very probably react by intensifying its bias towards the system, since, in its view, the system can at least guarantee a certain quasi-legality. Add to this the fact that the post-totalitarian system has at its disposal a complex mechanism of direct and indirect surveillance that has no equal in history and it is clear that not only would any attempt to revolt come to a dead end politically, but it would also be almost technically impossible to carry off. Most probably it would be liquidated before it had a chance to translate its intentions into action. Even if revolt were possible, however, it would remain the solitary gesture of a few isolated individuals and they would be opposed not only by a gigantic apparatus of national (and supra-national) power, but also by the very society in whose name they were mounting their revolt in the first place. (This, by the way, is another reason why the regime and its propaganda have been ascribing terroristic aims to the 'dissident movements' and accusing them of illegal and conspiratorial methods.)

All of this, however, is not the main reason why the 'dissident movements' support the principle of legality. That reason lies deeper, in the innermost structure of the 'dissident' attitude. This attitude is and must be fundamentally hostile towards the notion of violent change – simply because it places its faith in violence. (Generally, the 'dissident' attitude can only accept violence as a necessary evil in extreme situations, when direct violence can only be met by violence and where remaining passive would in effect mean supporting violence: let us recall, for example, that the blindness of European pacifism was one of the factors that prepared the ground for the Second World War.) As I have already mentioned, 'dissidents' tend to be sceptical about political thought based on the faith that profound social changes can only be achieved by bringing about (regardless of the method) changes in the system or in the government, and the belief that such changes – because they are considered 'fundamental' – justify the sacrifice of 'less fundamental' things, in other words, human lives. Respect for a theoretical concept here outweighs respect for human life. Yet this is precisely what threatens to enslave humanity all over again.

'Dissident movements', as I have tried to indicate, share exactly the opposite view. They understand systemic change as something superficial, something secondary, something that in itself can guarantee nothing. Thus an attitude that turns away from abstract political visions of the future towards concrete human beings and ways of defending them effectively in the here and now is quite naturally accompanied by an intensified antipathy to all forms of violence carried out in the name of 'a better future', and by a profound belief that a future secured by violence might actually be worse than what exists now; in other words, the future would be fatally stigmatized by the very means used to secure it. At the same time, this attitude is not to be mistaken for political conservatism or political moderation. The 'dissident movements' do not shy away from the idea of violent political overthrow because the idea seems too radical, but on the contrary, because it does not seem radical enough. For them, the problem lies far too deep to be settled through mere systemic changes, either governmental or technological. Some people, faithful to the classical Marxist doctrines of the nineteenth century, understand our system as the hegemony of an exploiting class over an exploited class and, operating from the postulate that exploiters never surrender their power voluntarily, they see the only solution in a revolution to sweep away the exploiters. Naturally, they regard such things as the struggle for human rights as something hopelessly legalistic, illusory, opportunistic and ultimately misleading because it makes the doubtful assumption that you can negotiate in good faith with your exploiters on the basis of a false legality. The problem is that they are unable to find anyone determined enough to carry out this revolution, with the result that they become bitter, sceptical, passive and ultimately apathetic – in other words, they end up precisely where the system wants them to be. This is one example of how far one can be misled by mechanically applying, in post-totalitarian circumstances, ideological models from another world and another time.

Of course, one need not be an advocate of violent revolution to ask whether an appeal to legality makes any sense at all when the laws – and particularly the general laws concerning human rights – are no more than a façade, an aspect of the world of appearances, a mere game behind which lies total manipulation. 'They can ratify anything because they will still go ahead and do whatever they want anyway' – this is an opinion we often encounter. Is it not true that constantly to 'take them at their word', to appeal to laws every child knows are binding only as long as the government wishes, is in the end just a kind of hypocrisy, a Švejkian obstructionism and, finally, just another way of playing the game, another form of self-delusion? In other words, is the legalistic approach at all compatible with the principle of 'living within the truth'?

This question can only be answered by first looking at the wider implications of how the legal code functions in the post-totalitarian system.

In a classical dictatorship, to a far greater extent than in the post-totalitarian system, the will of the ruler is carried out directly, in an unregulated fashion. A dictatorship has no reason to hide its foundations, nor to conceal the real workings of power, and therefore it need not encumber itself to any great extent with a legal code. The post-totalitarian system, on the other hand, is utterly obsessed with the need to bind everything in a single order: life in such a state is thoroughly permeated by a dense network of regulations, proclamations, directives, norms, orders and rules. (It is not called a bureaucratic system without good reason.) A large proportion of those norms function as direct instruments of the complex manipulation of life that is intrinsic to the post-totalitarian system. Individuals are reduced to little more than tiny cogs in an enormous mechanism and their significance is limited to their function in this mechanism. Their job, housing accommodation, movements, social and cultural expressions, everything, in short, must be cosseted together as firmly as possible, predetermined, regulated and controlled. Every aberration from the prescribed course of life is treated as error, licence and anarchy. From the cook in the restaurant who, without hard-to-get permission from the bureaucratic apparatus, cannot cook something special for his customers, to the singer who cannot perform his new song at a concert without bureaucratic approval, everyone, in all aspects of their life, is caught in this regulatory tangle of red tape, the inevitable product of the post-totalitarian system. With ever-increasing consistency, it binds all the expressions and aims of life to the spirit of its own aims: the vested interests of its own smooth, automatic operation.

In a narrower sense the legal code serves the post-totalitarian system in this direct way as well, that is, it too forms a part of the world of regulations and prohibitions. At the same time, however, it performs the same service in another indirect way, one that brings it remarkably closer – depending on which level of the law is involved – to ideology and in some cases making it a direct component of that ideology.

1 Like ideology, the legal code functions as an excuse. It wraps the base exercise of power in the noble apparel of the letter of the law; it creates the pleasing illusion that justice is done, society protected and the exercise of power objectively regulated. All this is done to conceal the real essence of post-totalitarian legal practice: the total manipulation of society. If an outside observer who knew nothing at all about life in Czechoslovakia were to study only its laws, he or she would be utterly incapable of understanding what we were complaining about. The hidden political manipulation of the courts and of public prosecutors, the limitations placed on lawyers' ability to defend their clients, the closed nature, *de facto*, of trials, the arbitrary actions of the security forces, their position of authority over the judiciary, the absurdly broad application of several deliberately vague sections of that code, and of course the state's utter disregard for the positive sections of that code (the rights of citizens): all of this would remain hidden from our outside observer. The only thing he or she would take away would be the impression that our legal code is not much worse than the legal code of other civilized countries, and not much different either, except perhaps for certain curiosities, such as the entrenchment in the constitution of a single political party's eternal rule and

the state's love for a neighbouring superpower. But that is not all: if our observer had the opportunity to study the formal side of the policing and judicial procedures and practices, how they look 'on paper', he or she would discover that for the most part the common rules of criminal procedure are observed: charges are laid within the prescribed period following arrest, and it is the same with detention orders. Indictments are properly delivered, the accused has a lawyer, and so on. In other words, everyone has an excuse: *they have all observed the law*. In reality, however, they have cruelly and pointlessly ruined a young person's life, perhaps for no other reason than because he or she made *samizdat* copies of a novel written by a banned writer, or because the police deliberately falsified their testimony (as everyone knows, from the judge on down to the defendant). Yet all of this somehow remains in the background. The falsified testimony is not necessarily obvious from the trial documents and the section of the criminal code dealing with incitement does not formally exclude the application of that charge to the copying of a banned novel. In other words, the legal code – at least in several areas – is not more than a façade, an aspect of the world of appearances. Then why is it there at all? For exactly the same reason as ideology is there: it provides a bridge of excuses between the system and individuals, making it easier for them to enter the power structure and serve the arbitrary demands of power. The excuse lets individuals fool themselves into thinking they are merely upholding the law and protecting society from criminals. (Without this excuse, how much more difficult it would be to recruit new generations of judges, prosecutors and interrogators!) As an aspect of the world of appearances, however, the legal code deceives not only the conscience of prosecutors, it deceives the public, it deceives foreign observers, and it even deceives history itself.

2 Like ideology, the legal code is an essential instrument of ritual communication outside the power structure. It is the legal code that gives the exercise of power a form, a framework, a set of rules. It is the legal code that enables all components of the system to communicate, to put them-

selves in a good light, to establish their own legitimacy. It provides their whole game with its 'rules' and engineers with their technology. Can the exercise of post-totalitarian power be imagined at all without this universal ritual making it all possible, serving as a common language to bind the relevant sectors of the power structure together? The more important the position occupied by the repressive apparatus in the power structure, the more important that it functions according to some kind of formal code. How, otherwise, could people be so easily and inconspicuously locked up for copying banned books if there were no judges, prosecutors, interrogators, defence lawyers, court stenographers and thick files, and if all this were not held together by some firm order? And above all, without that innocent-looking section 100 on incitement? This could all be done, of course, without a legal code and its accessories, but only in some ephemeral dictatorship run by a Ugandan bandit, not in a system that embraces such a huge portion of civilized humankind and represents an integral, stable and respected part of the modern world. That would not only be unthinkable, it would quite simply be technically impossible. Without the legal code functioning as a ritually cohesive force, the post-totalitarian system could not exist.

The entire role of ritual, façades and excuses appears most eloquently, of course, not in the proscriptive section of the legal code, which sets out what a citizen may not do and what the grounds for prosecution are, but in the section declaring what he or she may do and what his or her rights are. Here there is truly nothing but 'words, words, words'. Yet even that part of the code is of immense importance to the system, for it is here that the system establishes its legitimacy as a whole, before its own citizens, before schoolchildren, before the international public and before history. The system cannot afford to disregard this because it cannot permit itself to cast doubt upon the fundamental postulates of its ideology, which are so essential to its very existence. (We have already seen how the power structure is enslaved by its own ideology and its ideological prestige.) To do this would be to deny everything it tries to present itself as and, thus, one of the main pillars on which the system rests would be undermined: the integrity of the world of appearances.

If the exercise of power circulates through the whole power structure as blood flows through veins, then the legal code can be understood as something that reinforces the walls of those veins. Without it, the blood of power could not circulate in an organized way and the body of society would haemorrhage at random. Order would collapse.

A persistent and never-ending appeal to the laws – not just to the laws concerning human rights, but to all laws – does not mean at all that those who do so have succumbed to the illusion that in our system the law is anything other than what it is. They are well aware of the role it plays. But precisely because they know how desperately the system depends on it – on the 'noble' version of the law, that is – they also know how enormously significant such appeals are. Because the system cannot do without the law, because it is hopelessly tied down by the necessity of pretending the laws are observed, it is compelled to react in some way to such appeals. Demanding that the laws be upheld is thus an act of living within the truth that threatens the whole mendacious structure at its point of maximum mendacity. Over and over again, such appeals make the purely ritualistic nature of the law clear to society and to those who inhabit its power structures. They draw attention to its real material substance and thus, indirectly, compel all those who take refuge behind the law to affirm and make credible this agency of excuses, this means of communication, this reinforcement of the social arteries outside of which their will could not be made to circulate through society. They are compelled to do so for the sake of their own consciences, for the impression they make on outsiders, to maintain themselves in power (as part of the system's own mechanism of self-preservation and its principles of cohesion), or simply out of fear that they will be reproached for being 'clumsy' in handling the ritual. They have no other choice: because they cannot discard the rules of their own game, they can only attend more carefully to those rules. Not to react to challenges means to undermine their own excuse and lose control of their mutual communications system. To assume that the laws are a mere façade, that they have no validity and that therefore it is pointless to appeal to them would mean to go on reinforcing those aspects of the law that create the façade and the ritual. It would mean confirming the law as an aspect of the world of appearances and enabling those who exploit it to rest easy with the cheapest (and therefore the most mendacious) form of their excuse.

I have frequently witnessed policemen, prosecutors or judges – if they were dealing with an experienced Chartist or a courageous lawyer, and if they were exposed to public attention (as individuals with a name, no longer protected by the anonymity of the apparatus) – suddenly and anxiously begin to take particular care that no cracks appear in the ritual. This does not alter the fact that a despotic power is hiding behind that ritual, but the very existence of the officials' anxiety necessarily regulates, limits and slows down the operation of that despotism.

This, of course, is not enough. But an essential part of the 'dissident' attitude is that it comes out of the reality of the human 'here and now'. It places more importance on often repeated and consistent concrete action – even though it may be inadequate and though it may ease only insignificantly the suffering of a single insignificant citizen – than it does in some abstract 'fundamental solution' in an uncertain future. In any case, is not this in fact just another form of 'small-scale work' in the Masarykian sense, with which the 'dissident' attitude seemed at first to be in such sharp contradiction?

This section would be incomplete without stressing certain internal limitations to the policy of 'taking them at their own word'. The point is this: even in the most ideal of cases, the law is only one of several imperfect and more or less external ways of defending what is better in life against what is worse. By itself, the law can never create anything better. Its purpose is to render a service and its meaning does not lie in the law itself. Establishing respect for the law does not automatically ensure a better life for that, after all, is a job for people and not for laws and institutions. It is possible to imagine a society with good laws that are fully respected but in which it is impossible to live. Conversely, one can imagine life being quite bearable even where the laws are imperfect and imperfectly applied. The most important thing is always the quality of that life and whether or not the laws enhance life or repress it, not merely whether they are upheld or not. (Often strict observance of the law could have a disastrous impact on human dignity.) The key to a humane, dignified, rich and happy life does not lie either in the constitution or in the criminal code. These merely establish what may or may not be done and, thus, they can make life easier or more difficult. They limit or permit, they punish, tolerate or defend, but they can never give life substance or meaning. The struggle for what is called 'legality' must constantly keep this legality in perspective against the background of life as it really is. Without keeping one's eyes open to the real dimensions of life's beauty and misery, and without a moral relationship to life, this struggle will sooner or later come to grief on the rocks of some self-justifying system of scholastics. Without really wanting to, one would thus become more and more like the observer who comes to conclusions about our system only on the basis of trial documents and is satisfied if all the appropriate regulations have been observed.

XVIII

If the basic job of the 'dissident movements' is to serve truth, that is, to serve the real aims of life, and if that necessarily develops into a defence of the individual and his or her right to a free and truthful life (that is, a defence of human rights and a struggle to see the laws respected) then another stage of this approach, perhaps the most mature stage so far, is what Václav Benda has called the development of parallel structures.

When those who have decided to live within the truth have

been denied any direct influence on the existing social structures, not to mention the opportunity to participate in them, and when these people begin to create what I have called the independent life of society, this independent life begins, of itself, to become structured in a certain way. Sometimes there are only very embryonic indications of this process of structuring; at other times, the structures are already quite well developed. Their genesis and evolution are inseparable from the phenomenon of 'dissent', even though they reach far beyond the arbitrarily defined area of activity usually indicated by that term.

What are these structures? Ivan Jirous was the first in Czechoslovakia to formulate and apply in practice the concept of a 'second culture'. Although at first he was thinking chiefly of nonconformist rock music and only certain literary, artistic or performance events close to the sensibilities of those nonconformist musical groups, the term 'second culture' very rapidly came to be used for the whole area of independent and repressed culture, that is, not only for art and its various currents but also for the humanities, the social sciences and philosophical thought. This 'second culture', quite naturally, has created elementary organizational forms: *samizdat* editions of books and magazines, private performances and concerts, seminars, exhibitions and so on. (In Poland all of this is vastly more developed: there are independent publishing houses and many more periodicals, even political periodicals; they have means of proliferation other than carbon copies, and so on. In the Soviet Union, *samizdat* has a longer tradition and clearly its forms are quite different.) Culture, therefore, is a sphere in which the 'parallel structures' can be observed in their most highly developed form. Benda, of course, gives thought to potential or embryonic forms of such structures in other spheres as well: from a parallel information network to parallel forms of education (private universities), parallel trade unions, parallel foreign contacts, to a kind of hypothesis on a parallel economy. On the basis of these parallel structures, he then develops the notion of a 'parallel *polis*' or state or, rather, he sees the rudiments of such a *polis* in these structures.

At a certain stage in its development, the independent life of society and the 'dissident movements' cannot avoid a certain amount of organization and institutionalization. This is a natural development and unless this independent life of society is somehow radically suppressed and eliminated, the tendency will grow. Along with it, a parallel political life will also necessarily evolve, and to a certain extent it exist already in Czechoslovakia. Various groupings of a more or less political nature will continue to define themselve politically, to act and confront each other.

These parallel structures, it may be said, represent the most articulated expressions so far of 'living within the truth'. One of the most important tasks the 'dissident movements' have set themselves is to support and develop them. Once again, it confirms the fact that all attempts by society to resist the pressure of the system have their essential beginnings in the pre-political area. For what else are parallel structures than an area where a different life can be lived, a life that is in harmony with its own aims and which in turn structures itself in harmony with those aims? What else are those initial attempts at social self-organization than the efforts of a certain part of society to live – as a society – within the truth, to rid itself of the self-sustaining aspects of totalitarianism and, thus, to extricate itself radically from its involvement in the post-totalitarian system? What else is it but a non-violent attempt by people to negate the system within themselves and to establish their lives on a new basis, that of their own proper identity? And does this tendency not confirm once more the principle of returning the focus to actual individuals? After all, the parallel structures do not grow a priori out of a theoretical vision of systemic changes (there are no political sects involved), but from the aims of life and the authentic needs of real people. In fact, all eventual changes in the system, changes we may observe here in their rudimentary forms, have come about as it were *de facto*, from 'below', because life compelled them to, not because they came before life, somehow directing it or forcing some change on it.

Historical experience teaches us that any genuinely meaningful point of departure in an individual's life usually has an element of universality about it. In other words, it is not something partial, accessible only to a restricted community, and not transferable to any other. On the contrary, it must be potentially accessible to everyone; it must foreshadow a general solution and, thus, it is not just the expression of an introverted, self-contained responsibility that individuals have to and for themselves alone, but responsibility to and for the *world*. Thus it would be quite wrong to understand the parallel structures and the parallel *polis* as a retreat into a ghetto and as an act of isolation, addressing itself only to the welfare of those who had decided on such a course, and who are indifferent to the rest. It would be wrong, in short, to consider it an essentially group solution that has nothing to do with the general situation. Such a concept would, from the start, alienate the notion of living within the truth from its proper point of departure, which is concern for others, transforming it ultimately into just another more sophisticated version of 'living within a lie'. In doing so, of course, it would cease to be a genuine point of departure for individuals and groups and would recall the false notion of 'dissidents' as an exclusive group with exclusive interests, carrying on their own exclusive dialogue with the powers that be. In any case, even the most highly developed forms of life in the parallel structures, even that most mature form of the parallel *polis* can only exist – at least in post-totalitarian circumstances – when the individual is at the same time lodged in the 'first', official structure by a thousand different relationships, even though it may only be the fact that one buys what one needs in their stores, uses their money and obeys their laws. Certainly one can imagine life in its 'baser' aspects flourishing in the parallel *polis*, but would not such a life, lived deliberately that way, as a programme, be merely another version of the schizophrenic life 'within a lie' which everyone else must live in one way or another? Would it not just be further evidence that a point of departure that is not a 'model' solution, that is not applicable to others, cannot be meaningful for an individual either? Patočka used to say that the most interesting thing about responsibility is that we carry it with us everywhere. That means that responsibility is ours, that we must accept it and grasp it *here*, *now*, in this place in time and space where the Lord has set us down, and that we cannot lie our way out of it by moving somewhere else, whether it be to an Indian ashram or to a parallel *polis*. If Western young people so often discover that retreat to an Indian monastery fails them as an individual or group solution, then this is obviously because, and only because, it lacks that element of universality, since not everyone can retire to an ashram. Christianity is an example of an opposite way out: it is a point of departure for me here and now – but only because anyone, anywhere, at any time, may avail themselves of it.

In other words, the parallel *polis* points beyond itself and only makes sense as an act of deepening one's responsibility to and for the whole, as a way of discovering the most appropriate *locus* for this responsibility, not as an escape from it.

XIX

I have already talked about the political potential of living within the truth and of the limitations upon predicting whether, how and when a given expression of that life within the truth can lead to actual changes. I have also mentioned how irrelevant trying to calculate the risks in this regard are, for an essential feature of independent initiatives is that they are always, initially at least, an all-or-nothing gamble.

Nevertheless this outline of some of the work done by 'dissident movements' would be incomplete without considering, if only very generally, some of the different ways this work might actually affect society; in other words, about the ways that responsibility to and for the whole *might* (without necessarily meaning that it must) be realized in practice.

In the first place, it has to be emphasized that the whole sphere comprising the independent life of society and even more so the 'dissident movement' as such, is naturally far from being the only potential factor that might influence the history of countries living under the post-totalitarian system. The latent social crisis in such societies can at any time, independently of these movements, provoke a wide variety of political changes. It may unsettle the power structure and induce or accelerate various hidden confrontations, resulting in personnel, conceptual or at least 'climactic' changes. It may significantly influence the general atmosphere of life, evoke unexpected and unforeseen social unrest and explosions of discontent. Power shifts at the centre of the bloc can influence conditions in the different countries in various ways. Economic factors naturally have an important influence, as do broader trends of global civilization. An extremely important area, which could be a source of radical changes and political upsets, is represented by international politics, the policies adopted by the other superpower and all the other countries, the changing structure of international interests and the positions taken by our bloc. Even the people who end up in the highest positions are not without significance, although as I have already said, one ought not overestimate the importance of leading personalities in the post-totalitarian system. There are many such influences and combinations of influence, and the eventual political impact of the 'dissident movement' is thinkable only against this general background and in the context that background provides. That impact is only one of the many factors (and far from the most important one) that affect political developments, and it differs from the other factors perhaps only in that its essential focus is reflecting upon that political development from the point of view of a defence of people and seeking an immediate application of that reflection.

The primary purpose of the outward direction of these movements is always, as we have seen, to have an impact on society, not to affect the power structure, at least not directly and immediately. Independent initiatives address the hidden sphere; they demonstrate that living within the truth is a human and social alternative and they struggle to expand the space available for that life; they help – even though it is, of course, indirect help – to raise the confidence of citizens; they shatter the world of 'appearances' and unmask the real nature of power. They do not assume a messianic role; they are not a social avant-garde or élite that alone knows best, and whose task it is to 'raise the consciousness' of the 'unconscious' masses (that arrogant self-projection is, once again, intrinsic to an essentially different way of thinking, the kind that feels it has a patent on some 'ideal project' and therefore that it has the right to impose it on society). Nor do they want to lead anyone. They leave it up to each individual to decide what he or she will or will not take from their experience and work. (If official Czechoslovak propaganda described the Chartists as 'self-appointees', it was not in order to emphasize any real avant-garde ambitions on their part, but rather a natural expression of how the regime thinks, its tendency to judge others according to itself, since behind any expression of criticism it automatically sees the desire to cast the mighty from their seats and rule in their places 'in the name of the people', the same pretext the regime itself has used for years.)

These movements, therefore, always affect the power structure as such indirectly, as a part of society as a whole, for they are primarily addressing the hidden spheres of society, since it is not a matter of confronting the regime on the level of actual power.

I have already indicated one of the ways this can work: an awareness of the laws and the responsibility for seeing that they are upheld is indirectly strengthened. That, of course, is only a specific instance of a far broader influence, the indirect pressure felt from living within the truth: the pressure created by free thought, alternative values and 'alternative behaviour', and by independent social self-realization. The power structure, whether it wants to or not, must always react to this pressure to a certain extent. Its response, however, is always limited to two dimensions: repression and adaptation. Sometimes one dominates, sometimes the other. For example, the Polish 'flying university' came under increased persecution and the 'flying teachers' were detained by the police. At the same time, however, professors in existing official universities tried to enrich their own curricula with several subjects hitherto considered taboo and this was a result of indirect pressure exerted by the 'flying university'. The motives for this adaptation may vary from the 'ideal' (the hidden sphere has received the message and conscience and the will to truth are awakened) to the purely utilitarian: the regime's instinct for survival compels it to notice the changing ideas and the changing mental and social climate and react flexibly to them. Which of these motives happens to predominate in a given moment is not essential in terms of the final effect.

Adaptation is the positive dimension of the regime's response, and it can, and usually does, have a wide spectrum of forms and phases. Some circles may try to integrate values or people from the 'parallel world' into the official structures, to appropriate them, to become a little like them while trying to make them a little like themselves, and thus to adjust an obvious and untenable imbalance. In the 1960s, progressive communists began to 'discover' certain unacknowledged cultural values and phenomena. This was a positive step, although not without its dangers, since the 'integrated' or 'appropriated' values lost something of their independence and originality, and having been given a cloak of officiality and conformity, their credibility was somewhat weakened. In a further phase, this adaptation can lead to various attempts on the part of the official structures to reform, both in terms of their ultimate goals and structurally. Such reforms are usually halfway measures; they are attempts to combine and realistically co-ordinate serving life and serving the post-totalitarian 'automatism'. But they cannot be otherwise. They muddy what was originally a clear demarcation line between living within the truth and living with a lie. They cast a smokescreen over the situation, mystify society and make it difficult for people to keep their bearings. This, of course, does not alter the fact that it is always essentially good when it happens because it opens out new spaces. But it does make it more difficult to distinguish between 'admissible' and 'inadmissible' compromises.

Another – and higher – phase of adaptation is a process of internal differentiation that takes place in the official structures. These structures open themselves to more or less institutionalized forms of plurality because the real aims of life demand it. (One example: without changing the centralized and institutional basis of cultural life, new publishing houses, group periodicals, artists' groups, parallel research institutes and workplaces and so on, may appear under pressure from 'below'. Or another example: the single, monolithic youth organization run by the state as a typical post-totalitarian 'transmission belt' disintegrates under the pressure of real needs into a number of more or less independent organizations such as the Union of University Students, the Union of Secondary School Students, the Organization of Working Youth, and so on.) There is a direct relationship between this kind of differentiation, which allows initiatives from below to be felt, and the appearance and constitution of new structures which are already parallel, or rather independent, but which at the same time are respected, or at least tolerated in varying degrees, by official institutions. These new institutions are more than just liberalized official structures adapted to the authentic needs of life; they are a direct expression of those needs, demanding a position in the context of what is already here. In other words, they are genuine expressions of the tendency of society to organize itself. (In Czechoslovakia in 1968 the best known organizations of this type were KAN, the Club of Committed Non-Communists, and K231, an organization of former political prisoners.)

The ultimate phase of this process is the situation in which the official structures – as agencies of the post-totalitarian system, existing only to serve its automatism and constructed in the spirit of that role – simply begin withering away and dying off, to be replaced by new structures that have evolved from 'below' and are put together in a fundamentally different way.

Certainly many other ways may be imagined in which the

aims of life can bring about political transformations in the general organization of things and weaken on all levels the hold that techniques of manipulation have on society. Here I have mentioned only the way in which the general organization of things was in fact changed as we experienced it ourselves in Czechoslovakia around 1968. It must be added that all these concrete instances were part of a specific historical process which ought not be thought of as the only alternative, nor as necessarily repeatable (particularly not in our country), a fact which, of course, takes nothing away from the importance of the general lessons which are still sought and found in it to this day.

While on the subject of 1968 in Czechoslovakia, it may be appropriate to point to some of the characteristic aspects of developments at that time. All the transformations, first in the general 'mood', then conceptually and finally structurally, did not occur under pressure from the kind of parallel structures that are taking shape today. Such structures – which are sharply defined antitheses of the official structures – quite simply did not exist at the time, nor were there any 'dissidents' in the present sense of the word. The changes that took place were simply a consequence of pressures of the most varied sort, some thoroughgoing, some partial. There were spontaneous attempts at freer forms of thinking, independent creation and political articulation. There were long-term, spontaneous and inconspicuous efforts to bring about the interpenetration of the independent life of society with the existing structures, usually beginning with the quiet institutionalization of this life on and around the periphery of the official structures. In other words, it was a gradual process of social awakening, a kind of 'creeping' process in which the hidden spheres gradually opened out. (There is some truth in the official propaganda which talks about a 'creeping counter-revolution' in Czechoslovakia, referring to how the aims of life proceed.) The motive force behind this awakening did not have to come exclusively from the independent life of society, considered as a definable social milieu (although of course it did come from there, a fact that has yet to be fully appreciated). It could also simply have come from the fact that people in the official structures who more or less identified with the official ideology came up against reality as it really was and as it gradually became clear to them through latent social crises and their own bitter experiences with the true nature and operations of power. (I am thinking here mainly of the many 'anti-dogmatic' reform communists who grew to become, over the years, a force inside the official structures.) Neither the proper conditions nor the *raison d'être* existed for those limited, 'self-structuring' independent initiatives familiar from the present era of 'dissident movements' that stand so sharply outside the official structures and are unrecognized by them *en bloc*. At that time, the post-totalitarian system in Czechoslovakia had not yet petrified into the static, sterile and stable forms that exist today, forms that compel people to fall back on their own organizing capabilities. For many historical and social reasons, the regime in 1968 was more open. The power structure, exhausted by Stalinist despotism and helplessly groping about for painless reform, was inevitably rotting from within, quite incapable of offering any intelligent opposition to changes in the mood, to the way its younger members regarded things and to the thousands of authentic expressions of life on the 'pre-political' level that sprang up in that vast political terrain between the official and the unofficial.

From the more general point of view, yet another typical circumstance appears to be important: the social ferment that came to a head in 1968 never – in terms of actual structural changes – went any further than the reform, the differentiation or the replacement of structures that were really only of secondary importance. It did not affect the very essence of the power structure in the post-totalitarian system, which is to say its political model, the fundamental principles of social organization, not even the economic model in which all economic power is subordinated to political power. Nor were any essential structural changes made in the direct instruments of power (the army, the police, the judiciary, etc.). On that level, the issue was never more than a change in the mood, the personnel, the political line and, above all changes in how that power was exercised. Everything else remained at the stage of discussion and planning. The two officially accepted programmes that went furthest in this regard were the April 1968 Action Programme of the Communist Party of Czechoslovakia and the proposal for economic reforms. The Action Programme – it could not have been otherwise – was full of contradictions and halfway measures that left the physical aspects of power untouched. And the economic proposals, while they went a long way to accommodate the aims of life in the economic sphere (they accepted such notions as a plurality of interests and initiatives, dynamic incentives, restrictions upon the economic command system), left untouched the basic pillar of economic power, that is, the principle of state, rather than genuine *social* ownership of the means of production. So there is a gap here which no social movement in the post-totalitarian system has ever been able to bridge, with the possible exception of those few days during the Hungarian uprising.

What other developmental alternative might emerge in the future? Replying to that question would mean entering the realm of pure speculation. For the time being, it can be said that the latent social crisis in the system has always (and there is no reason to believe it will not continue to do so) resulted in a variety of political and social disturbances (Germany in 1953, Hungary, the USSR and Poland in 1956, Czechoslovakia and Poland in 1968, and Poland in 1970 and 1976), all of them very different in their backgrounds, the course of their evolution and their final consequences. If we look at the enormous complex of different factors that led to such disturbances, and at the impossibility of predicting what accidental accumulation of events will cause that fermentation in the hidden sphere to break through to the light of day (the problem of the 'final straw'); and if we consider how impossible it is to guess what the future holds, given such opposing trends as, on the one hand, the increasingly profound integration of the 'bloc' and the expansion of power within it, and on the other hand the prospects of the USSR

disintegrating under pressure from awakening national consciousness in the non-Russian areas (in this regard the Soviet
Union cannot expect to remain forever free of the worldwide
struggle for national liberation), then we must see the
hopelessness of trying to make long-range predictions.

In any case, I do not believe that this type of speculation
has any immediate significance for the 'dissident movements'
since these movements, after all, do not develop from
speculative thinking, and so to establish themselves on that
basis would mean alienating themselves from the very source
of their identity.

As far as prospects for the 'dissident movements' as such
go, there seems to be very little likelihood that future
developments will lead to a lasting coexistence of two
isolated, mutually non-interacting and mutually indifferent
bodies – the main *polis* and the parallel *polis*. As long as it
remains what it is, the practice of living within the truth
cannot fail to be a threat to the system. It is quite impossible
to imagine it continuing to coexist with the practice of living
within a lie without dramatic tension. The relationship of
the post-totalitarian system – as long as it remains what it is –
and the independent life of society – as long as it remains the
locus of a renewed responsibility for the whole and to the
whole – will always be one of either latent or open conflict.

In this situation there are only two possibilities: either the
post-totalitarian system will go on developing (that is, will be
able to go on developing), thus inevitably coming closer to
some dreadful Orwellian vision of a world of absolute
manipulation, while all the more articulate expressions of
living within the truth are definitively snuffed out; or the
independent life of society (the parallel *polis*), including the
'dissident movements', will slowly but surely become a social
phenomenon of growing importance, taking a real part in the
life of society with increasing clarity and influencing the
general situation. Of course this will always be only one of
many factors influencing the situation and it will operate
rather in the background, in concert with the other factors
and in a way appropriate to the background.

Whether it ought to focus on reforming the official structures or on encouraging differentiation, or on replacing them with new structures, whether the intent is to 'ameliorate' the system or, on the contrary, to tear it down: these and similar questions, in so far as they are not pseudo-problems, can be posed by the 'dissident movement' only within the context of a particular situation, when the movement is faced with a concrete task. In other words, it must pose questions, as it were, *ad hoc*, out of a concrete consideration of the authentic needs of life. To reply to such questions abstractly and to formulate a political programme in terms of some hypothetical future would mean, I believe, a return to the spirit and methods of traditional politics, and this would limit and alienate the work of 'dissent' where it is most intrinsically itself and has the most genuine prospects for the future. I have already emphasized several times that these 'dissident movements' do not have their point of departure in the invention of systemic changes but in a real, everyday struggle for a better life 'here and now'. The political and structural systems that life discovers for itself will clearly always be – for some time to come, at least – limited, halfway, unsatisfying and polluted by debilitating tactics. It cannot be otherwise, and we must expect this and not be demoralized by it. It is of great importance that the main thing – the everyday, thankless and never ending struggle of human beings to live more freely, truthfully and in quiet dignity – never imposes any limits on itself, never be half-hearted, inconsistent, never trap itself in political tactics, speculating on the outcome of its actions or entertaining fantasies about the future. The purity of this struggle is the best guarantee of optimum results when it comes to actual interaction with the post-totalitarian structures.

XX

The specific nature of post-totalitarian conditions – with their absence of a normal political life and the fact that any far-reaching political change is utterly unforeseeable – has one positive aspect: it compels us to examine our situation in terms of its deeper coherences and to consider our future in the context of global, long-range prospects of the world of which we are a part. The fact that the most intrinsic and fundamental confrontation between human beings and the system takes place at a level incomparably more profound than that of traditional politics would seem, at the same time, to determine as well the direction such considerations will take.

Our attention, therefore, inevitably turns to the most essential matter: the crisis of contemporary technological society as a whole, the crisis that Heidegger describes as the ineptitude of humanity face to face with the planetary power of technology. Technology – that child of modern science, which in turn is a child of modern metaphysics – is out of humanity's control, has ceased to serve us, has enslaved us and compelled us to participate in the preparation of our own destruction. And humanity can find no way out: we have no idea and no faith, and even less do we have a political conception to help us bring things back under human control. We look on helplessly as that coldly functioning machine we have created inevitably engulfs us, tearing us away from our natural affiliations (for instance from our habitat in the widest sense of that word, including our habitat in the biosphere) just as it removes us from the experience of 'being' and casts us into the world of 'existences'. This situation has already been described from many different angles and many individuals and social groups have sought, often painfully, to find ways out of it (for instance through oriental thought or by forming communes). The only social, or rather political, attempt to do something about it that contains the necessary element of universality (responsibility to and for the whole) is the desperate and, given the turmoil the world is in, fading voice of the ecological movement, and even there the attempt is limited to a particular notion of how to use technology to oppose the dictatorship of technology.

'Only a God can save us now', Heidegger says, and he emphasizes the necessity of 'a different way of thinking', that is, of a departure from what philosophy has been for centuries, and a radical change in the way in which humanity understands itself, the world and its position in it. He knows no way out and all he can recommend is 'preparing expectations'.

Various thinkers and movements feel that this as yet unknown way out might be most generally characterized as a broad 'existential revolution'. I share this view, and I also share the opinion that a solution cannot be sought in some technological sleight of hand, that is, in some external proposal for change, or in a revolution that is merely philosophical, merely social, merely technological or even merely political. These are all areas where the consequences of an 'existential revolution' can and must be felt; but their most intrinsic *locus* can only be human existence in the profoundest sense of the word. It is only from that basis that it can become a generally ethical – and, of course, ultimately a political – reconstitution of society.

What we call the consumer and industrial (or post-industrial) society, and Ortega y Gasset once understood as 'the revolt of the masses', as well as the intellectual, moral, political and social misery in the world today: all of this is perhaps merely an aspect of the deep crisis in which humanity, dragged helplessly along by the automatism of global technological civilization, finds itself.

The post-totalitarian system is only one aspect – a particularly drastic aspect and thus all the more revealing of its real origins – of this general inability of modern humanity to be the master of its own situation. The automatism of the post-totalitarian system is merely an extreme version of the global automatism of technological civilization. The human failure that it mirrors is only one variant of the general failure of modern humanity.

This planetary challenge to the position of human beings in the world is, of course, also taking place in the Western world, the only difference being the social and political forms it takes. Heidegger refers expressly to a crisis of democracy. There is no real evidence that Western democracy, that is, democracy of the traditional parliamentary type, can offer solutions that are any more profound. It may even be said that the more room there is in the Western democracies (compared to our world) for the genuine aims of life, the better the crisis is hidden from people and the more deeply do they become immersed in it.

It would appear that the traditional parliamentary democracies can offer no fundamental opposition to the automatism of technological civilization and the industrial–consumer society, for they, too, are being dragged helplessly along by it. People are manipulated in ways that are infinitely more subtle and refined than the brutal methods used in the post-totalitarian societies. But this static complex of rigid, conceptually sloppy and politically pragmatic mass political parties run by professional apparatuses and releasing the citizen from all forms of concrete and personal responsibility; and those complex focuses of capital accumulation engaged in secret manipulations and expansion; the omnipresent dictatorship of consumption, production, advertising, commerce, consumer culture, and all that flood of information: all of it, so often analysed and described, can only with great difficulty be imagined as the source of humanity's rediscovery of itself. In his June 1978 Harvard lecture, Solzhenitsyn describes the illusory nature of freedoms not based on personal responsibility and the chronic inability of the traditional democracies, as a result, to oppose violence and totalitarianism. In a democracy, human beings may enjoy many personal freedoms and securities that are unknown to us, but in the end they do them no good, for they too are ultimately victims of the same automatism, and are incapable of defending their concerns about their own identity or preventing their superficialization or transcending concerns about their own personal survival to become proud and responsible members of the *polis*, making a genuine contribution to the creation of its destiny.

Because all our prospects for a significant change for the better are very long range indeed, we are obliged to take note of this deep crisis of traditional democracy. Certainly, if conditions were to be created for democracy in some countries in the Soviet bloc (although this is becoming

increasingly improbable), it might be an appropriate transitio-
nal solution that would help to restore the devastated sense
of civic awareness, to renew democratic discussion, to allow
for the crystallization of an elementary political plurality, an
essential expression of the aims of life. But to cling to the
notion of traditional parliamentary democracy as one's
political ideal and to succumb to the illusion that only this
'tried and true' form is capable of guaranteeing human beings
enduring dignity and an independent role in society would,
in my opinion, be at the very least shortsighted.

I see a renewed focus of politics on real people as
something far more profound than merely returning to the
everyday mechanisms of Western (or if you like bourgeois)
democracy. In 1968 I felt that our problem could be solved by
forming an opposition party that would compete publicly for
power with the Communist Party. I have long since come to
realize, however, that it is just not that simple and that no
opposition party in and of itself, just as no new electoral laws
in and of themselves, could make society proof against some
new form of violence. No 'dry' organizational measures in
themselves can provide that guarantee, and we would be
hard pressed to find in them that God who alone can save us.

XXI

And now I may properly be asked the question: What then is
to be done?

My scepticism towards alternative political models and the
ability of systemic reforms or changes to redeem us does not,
of course, mean that I am sceptical of political thought
altogether. Nor does my emphasis on the importance of
focusing concern on real human beings disqualify me from
considering the possible structural consequences flowing
from it. On the contrary, if A was said, then B should be said
as well. Nevertheless, I will offer only a few very general
remarks.

Above all, any existential revolution should provide hope
of a moral reconstitution of society, which means a radical

renewal of the relationship of human beings to what I have called the 'human order', which no political order can replace. A new experience of being, a renewed rootedness in the universe, a newly grasped sense of 'higher responsibility', a new-found inner relationship to other people and to the human community – these factors clearly indicate the direction in which we must go.

And the political consequences? Most probably they could be reflected in the constitution of structures that will derive from this 'new spirit', from human factors rather than from a particular formalization of political relationships and guarantees. In other words, the issue is the rehabilitation of values like trust, openness, responsibility, solidarity, love. I believe in structures that are not aimed at the 'technical' aspect of the execution of power, but at the significance of that execution in structures held together more by a commonly shared feeling of the importance of certain communities than by commonly shared expansionist ambitions directed 'outward'. There can and must be structures that are open, dynamic and small; beyond a certain point, human ties like personal trust and personal responsibility cannot work. There must be structures that in principle place no limits on the genesis of different structures. Any accumulation of power whatsoever (one of the characteristics of automatism) should be profoundly alien to it. They would be structures not in the sense of organizations or institutions, but like a community. Their authority certainly cannot be based on long-empty traditions, like the tradition of mass political parties, but rather on how, in concrete terms, they enter into a given situation. Rather than a strategic agglomeration of formalized organizations, it is better to have organizations springing up *ad hoc*, infused with enthusiasm for a particular purpose and disappearing when that purpose has been achieved. The leaders' authority ought to derive from their personalities and be personally tested in their particular surroundings, and not from their position in any *nomenklatura*. They should enjoy great personal confidence and even great lawmaking powers based on that confidence. This would appear to be the only way out of the classic impotence of traditional democratic organizations, which frequently seem founded more on mistrust than mutual confidence, and more on collective irresponsibility than on responsibility. It is only with the full existential backing of every member of the community that a permanent bulwark against 'creeping totalitarianism' can be established. These structures should naturally arise from *below* as a consequence of authentic social 'self-organization'; they should derive vital energy from a living dialogue with the genuine needs from which they arise, and when these needs are gone, the structures should also disappear. The principles of their internal organization should be very diverse, with a minimum of external regulation. The decisive criterion of this 'self-constitution' should be the structure's actual significance, and not just a mere abstract norm.

Both political and economic life ought to be founded on the varied and versatile co-operation of such dynamically appearing and disappearing organizations. As far as the economic life of society goes, I believe in the principle of self-management, which is probably the only way of achieving what all the theorists of socialism have dreamed about, that is, the genuine (i.e. informal) participation of workers in economic decision-making, leading to a feeling of genuine responsibility for their collective work. The principles of control and discipline ought to be abandoned in favour of self-control and self-discipline.

As is perhaps clear from even so general an outline, the systemic consequences of an 'existential revolution' of this type go significantly beyond the framework of classical parliamentary democracy. Having introduced the term 'post-totalitarian' for the purposes of this discussion, perhaps I should refer to the notion I have just outlined – purely for the moment – as the prospects for a 'post-democratic' system.

Undoubtedly this notion could be developed further, but I think it would be a foolish undertaking, to say the least, because slowly but surely the whole idea would become alienated, separated from itself. After all, the essence of such a 'post-democracy' is also that it can only develop *via facti*, as a process deriving directly *from life*, from a new atmosphere and a new 'spirit' (political thought, of course, would play a role here, though not as a director, merely as a guide). It would be presumptuous, however, to try to foresee the structural expressions of this 'new spirit' without that spirit actually being present and without knowing its concrete physiognomy.

XXII

I would probably have omitted the entire preceding section as a more suitable subject for private meditation were it not for a certain recurring sensation. It may seem rather presumptuous, and therefore I will present it as a question: Does not this vision of 'post-democratic' structures in some ways remind one of the 'dissident' groups or some of the independent citizens' initiatives as we already know them from our own surroundings? Do not these small communities, bound together by thousands of shared tribulations, give rise to some of those special 'humanly meaningful' political relationships and ties that we have been talking about? Are not these communities (and they *are* communities more than organizations) – motivated mainly by a common belief in the profound significance of what they are doing since they have no chance of direct, external success – joined together by precisely the kind of atmosphere in which the formalized and ritualized ties common in the official structures are supplanted by a living sense of solidarity and fraternity? Do not these 'post-democratic' relationships of immediate personal trust and the informal rights of individuals based on them come out of the background of all those commonly shared difficulties? Do not these groups emerge, live and disappear under pressure from concrete and authentic needs, unburdened by the ballast of hollow traditions? Is not their attempt to create an articulate form of 'living within the truth' and to renew the feeling of higher responsibility in an apathetic society really a sign of some kind of rudimentary moral reconstitution?

In other words, are not these informed, non-bureaucratic, dynamic and open communities that comprise the 'parallel *polis*' a kind of rudimentary prefiguration, a symbolic model of those more meaningful 'post-democratic' political structures that might become the foundation of a better society?

I know from thousands of personal experiences how the mere circumstance of having signed Charter 77 has immediately created a deeper and more open relationship and evoked sudden and powerful feelings of genuine community among people who were all but strangers before. This kind of thing happens only rarely, if at all, even among people who have worked together for long periods in some apathetic official structure. It is as though the mere awareness and acceptance of a common task and a shared experience were enough to transform people and the climate of their lives, as though it gave their public work a more human dimension that is seldom found elsewhere.

Perhaps all this is only the consequence of a common threat. Perhaps the moment the threat ends or eases, the mood it helped create will begin to dissipate as well. (The aim of those who threaten us, however, is precisely the opposite. Again and again, one is shocked by the energy they devote to contaminating, in various despicable ways, all the human relationships inside the threatened community.)

Yet even if that were so, it would change nothing in the question I have posed.

We do not know the way out of the marasmus of the world, and it would be an expression of unforgivable pride were we to see the little we do as a fundamental solution, or were we to present ourselves, our community and our solutions to vital problems as the only thing worth doing.

Even so, I think that given all these preceding thoughts on post-totalitarian conditions, and given the circumstances and the inner constitution of the developing efforts to defend human beings and their identity in such conditions, the questions I have posed are appropriate. If nothing else, they are an invitation to reflect concretely on our own experience and to give some thought to whether certain elements of that experience do not – without our really being aware of it – point somewhere further, beyond their apparent limits, and whether right here, in our everyday lives, certain challenges are not already encoded, quietly waiting for the moment when they will be read and grasped.

For the real question is whether the 'brighter future' is really always so distant. What if, on the contrary, it has been here for a long time already, and only our own blindness and weakness has prevented us from seeing it around us and within us, and kept us from developing it?

Hrádeček
October 1978

3

Six asides about culture

I

While I consider it highly unlikely, I cannot exclude the theoretical possibility that tomorrow I shall have some fabulous idea and that, within the week, I shall have written my best play yet. It is equally possible that I shall never write anything again.

When even a single author – who is not exactly a beginner and so might be expected to have at least a rough idea of his abilities and limits – cannot foresee his literary future, how can anyone foresee what the overall development of culture will be?

If there is a sphere whose very nature precludes all prognostication, it is that of culture, and especially of the arts and humanities. (In the natural sciences we can, perhaps, make at least general predictions.)

There is a countless number of possibilities for culture in our country: perhaps the police pressure will intensify, perhaps many more artists and scholars will go into exile, many others will lose all desire to do anything and the last remnants of imagination with it, and the entire so-called 'second culture' will gradually die out while the 'first culture' will become entirely sterile. Or again, perhaps that second culture will suddenly, unexpectedly blossom to an unprecedent extent and form, to the amazement of the world and the astonishment of the government. Or again, perhaps the first culture will massively awaken, perhaps wholly improbable 'new waves' will arise within it and the second culture will quietly, inconspicuously and gladly merge into its shadow.

Perhaps wholly original creative talents and spiritual initiatives will suddenly emerge on the horizon, expanding somewhere in a wholly new space between the two present cultures so that both will only stare in amazement. Or again, perhaps nothing new will come up at all, perhaps everything will remain as it is: Dietl will go on writing his TV serials and Vaculík his feuilletons. I could continue listing such possibilities as long as I please without the least reason to consider one of them distinctly more probable than any other.

The secrets of culture's future are a reflection of the very secrets of the human spirit. That is why, having been asked to reflect on the prospects for Czechoslovak culture, I shall not write about those prospects, but will rather limit myself to a few, more or less polemical and marginal comments on its present. If anyone chooses to derive something from them for the future, that will be his business and on his head be it.

II

At one time, the state of culture in Czechoslovakia was described, rather poignantly, as a 'Biafra of the spirit'. Many authors, myself included, turned, when considering just what happened in Czechoslovak culture after 1968, to the metaphor of the graveyard. I must admit that recently, as I came across some such metaphor, something within me rebelled. We should, after all these years, at least specify the field to which the metaphor is supposed to apply.

It is certainly entirely valid with respect to the comportment of the regime in the area of culture with so-called 'cultural policy'. Something is always banned, now as then; virtually nothing is permitted, suppressed journals remain suppressed, manipulated institutions continue to be manipulated, and so on. The regime genuinely behaves like a gravedigger, while virtually all that is lively and yet has to be permitted lives almost by accident, almost by mistake, almost only on a word of honour, though with endless complications and no assurance about tomorrow.

What is true about the will of the regime, however, is not

necessarily true of the real spiritual potential of our community. However suppressed beneath the public surface, however silenced and even however frustrated, in some way that potential is still here. Somewhere, somehow it remains alive. And it certainly does not deserve to be pronounced dead. I simply do not believe that we have all lain down and died. I see far more than graves and tombstones around me.

I see evidence of this in far more than the hundreds of *samizdat* volumes, tens of typewritten magazines, private or semi-official exhibitions, seminars, concerts and other events: besides, there are theatres crammed full of people grateful for every nuance of meaning, frantically applauding every knowing smile from the stage (had we played to such houses in the early sixties in the theatre where I then worked, I can't imagine how we would have managed to complete any play!); all-night queues at some theatres when the month's tickets were about to go on sale; queues at book stores when one of Hrabal's books, emasculated though it may be, was about to appear; expensive books on astronomy printed in a hundred thousand copies (they would hardly find that many readers in the USA); young people travelling half way across the country to attend a concert that may not take place at all. Is all that – and more – really a graveyard? Is that really a 'Biafra of the spirit'?

I do not know what will happen in the culture of the years to come. I do know, though, that it will depend, if not entirely then to a great extent, on future developments in the confrontation between the graveyard intentions of the powers that be and this irrepressible cultural hunger of the community's living organism, or perhaps of that part of it which has not surrendered to total apathy. Nor would I dare predict what might come to life, given this or that change in our circumstances, and what would happen in that part which today appears to have given up.

III

I have read somewhere that martyrdom does better in a totalitarian system than thought.

I am a realist and as such far from the patriotic illusion that the world, due to its hopeless ignorance, remains deprived of some fabulous intellectual achievement waiting here on every corner. And yet something in me rebels as well against the claim that history has condemned us to the unenviable role of mere unthinking experts in suffering, poor relations of those in the 'free world' who do not have to suffer and have time to think.

First of all, it does not seem to me that many people here suffer from some kind of masochistic delight, or for want of better ways to kill time. Besides, what tends to be called 'martyrdom' – with a slightly contemptuous undertone, let's admit – in our country appears to me neither a particularly common pastime nor for the most part just a blind rush into an abyss. We live in a land of notorious realism, far removed from, say, the Polish courage for sacrifice. I would therefore be very hesitant about denying the capacity for thought to those who might be suspected of martyrdom among us. On the contrary, it seems to me that thought has been a prominent component of the Czech type of 'martyrdom'. Think of Jan Patočka: is it not symptomatic that the best-known victim of 'the struggle for human rights' in our country was our most important philosopher? And again, as I follow from a distance various individual actions and social upheavals in the 'free world', I am not at all sure that they are inevitably characterized by penetrating thought. I fear that far too often the idea comes limping behind the enthusiasm. And might that just not be because for the most part no great price need be paid for that enthusiasm? Are thought and sacrifice really so mutually exclusive? Might not sacrifice, under some circumstances, be simply the consequence of a thought, its proof or, conversely, its moving force?

In short, I simply would not dare claim that we think less in our country because we also suffer. On the contrary, I believe that with a bit of good will, a great deal that is generally relevant could be derived from our thought, perhaps precisely because it was bought at a price and because it grew out of something difficult. Admittedly, that thought is often tangled, hesitant and intermittent. Our texts do not display the easy virtuosity of global best-sellers. English elegance or French charm, alas, are really far more traditional to England and France and are not native to our somewhat heavy-handed central Europe, though I would avoid drawing any far-reaching conclusions from that: it is simply the way it is.

I do not know to what extent the fact that we do (occasionally) think will affect our prospects for the better, but it will surely not harm them. Neither will it harm them if, here and there, someone ignores the danger of being labelled a martyr for his stubbornness.

IV

What exactly is a 'parallel culture'? Nothing more and nothing less than a culture which for various reasons will not, cannot or may not reach out to the public through the media which fall under state control. In a totalitarian state, this includes all publishing houses, presses, exhibition halls, theatres and concert halls, scholarly institutes and so on. Such a culture, therefore, can make use only of what is left – typewriters, private studios, apartments, barns, etc. Evidently the 'parallel' nature of this culture is defined wholly externally and implies nothing directly about its quality, aesthetics or eventual ideology.

I think it important to stress this rather trivial fact if only because, in recent times, particularly in the exile press, various critiques of the 'parallel culture' as a whole have appeared, and they were possible only because their authors were not aware of this trivial definition of what it means to be 'parallel'.

To simplify it a little, such authors followed this common reasoning: the official culture is subservient to some official ideology, naturally bad. The 'parallel culture' is, or should be, a better alternative. To what better ideology is *it* subservient? Does it have any ideology at all? Any programme? Any conception? Or any orientation, any philosophy? They reached the disappointing conclusion that it does not.

They could have saved themselves disappointment if they had noted at the very start that, by its very nature, the 'parallel culture' can display none of those features. All those hundreds, perhaps thousands of people of all sorts and conditions – young, old, gifted, untalented, believers, unbelievers – gathered under the umbrella of 'parallel culture', were led to it exclusively by the incredible narrow-mindedness of a regime which tolerates practically nothing. They can never agree on a common programme because the only real thing they have in common (which is why they found themselves under the common umbrella in the first place) is their diversity and their insistence on being just what they are. And if, in spite of everything, they were to agree a common programme, it would be the saddest outcome of all: one uniform confronting another. If there is no great surplus of master works in the 'parallel culture' today, there would be nothing in it at all, were that to come to pass. If there is anything essentially foreign to culture, it is the uniform. The 'parallel culture' was born precisely because the official uniform was too constricting for the spiritual potential of our community, because it would not fit inside it and so spilled over beyond the limits within which a uniform is obligatory. It would be a suicide if, having done that, that potential voluntarily sought to fit into another uniform, no matter how much prettier than the one it had escaped.

I recall how, in my youth, I found it amusing that the lead paper at various writers' conferences and congresses would invariably be entitled: 'The tasks of literature in such and such a period' or '. . . after such and such a Party congress', or '. . . in a given five-year plan' – and that, in spite of all the tasks that were constantly assigned to it, literature would keep on doing only what it wanted. And if by chance it did not make an effort to carry out its assigned tasks, it was invariably the worse for it. Its only hope, no less so under the conditions of 'parallelism' (and especially then – that is why it chose them!) is to ignore the tasks anyone would assign to it, no matter how good his intentions, and go on doing only what it wants to do.

There are no more gifted writers, painters or musicians in Czechoslovakia today than there were at any time in the past. The disappointment that the 'parallel culture' is no better than it is, to be sure, is quite understandable. The more one is repelled by the official culture, the more one expects from the other, and the more one turns towards it. Still, such disappointment is not objectively relevant. By what odd whim of history would there be more of everything, and better, today in our stifled conditions, than ever before?

A great many people can peck at a typewriter and, fortunately, no one can stop them. But for that reason, even in *samizdat*, there will always be countless bad books or poems for every important book. If anything, there will be more bad ones than in the days of printing because, even in the most liberated times, printing is still a more complicated process than typing. But even if, objectively, there were some possibility of selection, who could claim the right to exercise it? Who among us would dare to say that he can unerringly distinguish something of value – even though it may still be nascent, unfamiliar, as yet only potential – from its counterfeit? Who among us can know whether what may seem today to be marginal graphomania might not one day appear to our descendants as the most substantial thing written in our time? Who among us has the right to deprive them of that pleasure, no matter how incomprehensible it may seem to us? Was not the basic presupposition of editorial selection in freer times that a rejected author could turn to a competitor or publish his manuscript at his own cost? Would any of our great editors and publishers – Firt, Škeřík, Vilímek, Otto, Laichter and all the others – ever have dared to make up their minds about anything, had it not been for that possibility?

Petlice Editions is by no means the only *samizdat* series; still, for those who measure parallel literature according to *Petlice* and the misery and hopes of the nation according to parallel literature, we should note that *Petlice* is something of an author-run service in which everyone is responsible for himself alone. Should anyone not like something that appears in *Petlice*, let him sing his disappointment to the author and not blame anyone else. Fortunately, there is no editor-in-chief of *Petlice*, or director-in-chief of *Samizda* *and Co.* responsible for what had been allowed to be typed.

All this, I know, is obvious. Still it seems that even such obvious matters need to be aired from time to time, especially for our exiles whose perspective, often influenced by the random selection of domestic texts that they happen to come across, might at times be distorted.

V

In an essay, 'Prague 1984' (written for *Art Forum*, Czech version in *samizdat* journal, *Kritický sborník*, 1984, No. 2) Jindřich Chalupecký writes that the artist 'either submits to the state power, produces works that propagate socialism and is respected and rewarded, or he protests in the name of freedom and leads the romantic life of a rebellious bohemian. If such official art arouses little interest, we can hardly expect much from the anti-official art. Both are equally conditioned by political perspectives and though certain political goals might be most noble and relevant, it turns out again and again that the world of modern art is not the world of modern politics. Neither politics nor art can profit from such efforts.' It is not quite clear whether Chalupecký is speaking for himself here, or whether he is paraphrasing the perspective of Hans-Heinz Holze whose views he outlines in his preceding paragraph. He is, however, clearly speaking for himself when he writes, later on, in reference to several recent exhibits of Czechoslovak artists in the West: 'It was not "socialist realism". Neither was it "anti-official art". The political context was missing, and there was no way of supplying it.'

Such formulations, along with other passages in Chalupecký's essay, might give the impression that there are, in Czechoslovakia, actually three cultures, or rather three kinds of art: official art, adapted to the ruling ideology; 'anti-official art, evidently of the 'dissident' variety, produced by the people with a peculiar penchant for the 'romantic life of rebellious bohemian', a culture as feebleminded as the official one and differing from it only in the political ideas it serves; and finally true, modern art which alone is good because it stands aside from politics and all ideologies.

Chalupecký's text, for the most part informative, does not make it entirely clear whether the author really sees those three divisions in the panorama of contemporary Czech art, and so I do not wish to argue with Chalupecký, but solely with that odd 'trinitarian' vision.

If we start with the presupposition that art constitutes a distinctive way of seeking truth – truth in the broadest sense of the word, that is, chiefly the truth of the artist's inner experience – then there is only one art, whose sole criterion is the power, the authenticity, the revelatory insight, the courage and suggestiveness with which it seeks its truth, or perhaps the urgency and profundity of this truth. Thus, from the standpoint of the work and its worth it is irrelevant to which political ideas the artist as a citizen claims allegiance, which ideas he would like to serve with his work or whether he holds any such ideas at all. And just as the attractiveness or repulsiveness of political ideas guarantees nothing about a work of art and likewise does not disqualify it in advance, so, too, whether or not an artist is interested in politics neither authorizes nor disqualifies him at the start. If so much of the art shown in official exhibits is indeed below average, and better art can be found only on the periphery of public art (in marginal or semi-official exhibition halls) or entirely beyond public view (in studios), then this is so not because the creators of the former involve themselves in politics while those of the latter do not, but simply because the prospect of public recognition and lucrative commissions in our country, today more than at other times and in other places, is incompatible with that stubborn, uncompromising effort to reach out for some personal truth without which, it seems, there can be no real art. The more an artist compromises to oblige power and gain advantages, the less good art can we expect from him; the more freely and independently, by contrast, he does his own thing – whether with the expression of a 'rebellious bohemian' or without it – the better his chances of creating something good – though it remains only a chance: what is uncompromising need not automatically be good.

Thus, it does not seem to me particularly meaningful to divide art between the official and anti-official on the one hand and the independent (that is, politically neutral) on the other. Surely the measure of artistic power is something other than whether or not the art displays a political concern. If we do speak of 'two cultures', one official and one 'parallel', it does not mean – at least as I understand it – that the one serves one set of political ideas and the second another set (which would force us to assume, in addition, a 'third' culture, subservient to no politics), but refers solely to the external framework of culture. The 'first' culture resides in the vaguely defined area of what is permitted, subsidized or at least tolerated, an area that naturally tends to attract more of those who, for reasons of advantage, are willing to compromise their truth, while the 'second' refers to culture in an area constituted through self-help, which is the refuge, voluntary or enforced, of those who refuse all compromise (regardless of how overtly 'political' or 'non-political' their work is).

Any *a priori* division of art into the 'anti-official' (necessarily inferior) and the 'apolitical' (necessarily better) seems to me rather dangerous. Unwittingly, it applies to art a notorious extra-artistic standard, albeit this time turned inside out: the value of art is no longer judged in terms of its overtly political nature but, conversely in terms of its overtly non-political nature. Surely, if Magda Jetelová constructs somewhere her evocative staircases and Ludvík Vaculík writes a novel about cops and dissidents, the artistic power of each has nothing to do with the fact that a staircase (albeit only on a primitive, thematic basis) is considered non political while the confrontation of cops and dissidents is eminently political. The 'non-political' stairness of staircases and the 'political' copness of the cops *of themselves* neither guarantee nor preclude anything. The only thing that matters is the urgency of artistic truth which both artists pursue (and I believe that is indubitable in both cases). The degree to which politics is present or absent has no connection with the power of artistic truth. If anything matters, it is, quite logically, only the degree to which an artist is willing, for external reasons, to compromise the truth.

In any case, it seems that our regime can sniff out far better than many an art theoretician what it should consider really dangerous to itself. Hundreds of examples testify that the regime prosecutes most vigorously not what threatens it overtly but has little artistic power, but whatever is artistically most penetrating, even though it does not seem all that overtly 'political'. The essence of the conflict, that is, is not a confrontation between two ideologies (for instance a socialist with a liberal one) but a clash between an anonymous, soulless, immobile and paralysing ('entropic') power, and life, humanity, being and its mystery. The counterpart of power in this conflict is not an alternative political idea but the autonomous, free humanity of man and with it necessarily also art – precisely as art! – as one of the most important expressions of this autonomous humanity.

VI

At times we do encounter something we might call a sectarian view of parallel culture, that is, the view that whatever does not circulate only in typescript or whatever was not recorded only privately is necessarily bad and that not being printed, publicly performed or exhibited is in itself an achievement or an honour while the reverse is always and automatically a mark of moral and spiritual decay, if not of outright treason.

I could name quite a few very worthwhile and important achievements of the most varied kinds which I have encountered in the sphere of the 'first' culture and which deny the legitimacy of such a view. I refrain from naming them solely because it might complicate the lives of the authors or call them to the attention of those thanks to whose inattention they were able to do what they did. I never take any pleasure in seeing someone from the 'first' culture fall into the 'second'; rather, I am always happy whenever I encounter anything in the 'first' culture that I would have tended to expect in the 'second'.

Even though the 'second' or 'parallel' culture represents an important fertile ground, a catalytic agent, and often even the sole bearer of the spiritual continuity of our cultural life, like it or not, it is the 'first' culture that remains the decisive sphere. Only once the suppressed spiritual potential of our community begins more distinctly to win back this culture (and, to be sure, without its 'interim' existence in the 'parallel' culture it would really have no base of operation) will things begin visibly to improve, not only in culture itself but in a broader and related social sense as well. It will be in the 'first' culture that the decision will be made about the future climate of our lives; through it our citizens will have the first genuine wide-scale chance to stand up straight and liberate themselves. The 'second' culture's relation to it will be analogous to that of a match to a glowing stove; without it, the fire might not have started at all, yet by itself it cannot heat the room.

Perhaps such a notion might be suspected of treating culture instrumentally – as if I wished artists to have public opportunity because it increases hope of some overall improvement of our conditions. So let me make it a bit more precise: every meaningful cultural act – wherever it takes place – is unquestionably good in and of itself, simply because it exists and because it offers something to someone. Yet can this value 'in itself' really be separated from 'the common good'? Is one not an integral part of the other from the start? Does not the bare fact that a work of art has meant something to someone – even if only for a moment, perhaps to a single person – already somehow change, however minutely, the overall condition for the better? Is it not itself an inseparable component of that condition, transforming it by its very nature? And does not a change in conditions mediated by a cultural achievement open the door to further cultural achievements? Is not culture itself something that is a common good? Is not some 'improvement in conditions' – in the most general, the deepest and, I would say, the existential sense of the word – precisely what makes culture culture? Being happy if five thousand rather than five people can read a good text or see a good painting is, I think, a wholly legitimate understanding of the meaning of culture – even when that joy comes from our perception that 'things are beginning to move'. Or is not precisely some 'impulse to move' – again in that deeper, existential sense – the primordial intent of everything that really belongs to culture? After all, that is precisely the mark of every good work of culture: it sets our drowsy souls and our lazy hearts 'moving'! And can we separate the awakening human soul from what it always, already is – an awakening human community?

Hrádeček
11 August 1984

4

Politics and conscience

I

As a boy, I lived for some time in the country and I clearly remember an experience from those days: I used to walk to school in a nearby village along a cart track through the fields and, on the way, see on the horizon a huge smokestack of some hurriedly built factory, in all likelihood in the service of war. It spewed dense brown smoke and scattered it across the sky. Each time I saw it, I had an intense sense of something profoundly wrong, of humans soiling the heavens. I have no idea whether there was something like a science of ecology in those days; if there was, I certainly knew nothing of it. Still that 'soiling the heavens' offended me spontaneously. It seemed to me that, in it, humans are guilty of something, that they destroy something important, arbitrarily disrupting the natural order of things, and that such things cannot go unpunished. To be sure, my revulsion was largely aesthetic; I knew nothing then of the noxious emissions which would one day devastate our forests, exterminate game and endanger the health of people.

If a medieval man were to see something like that suddenly on the horizon – say, while out hunting – he would probably think it the work of the Devil and would fall on his knees and pray that he and his kin be saved.

What is it, actually, that the world of the medieval peasant and that of a small boy have in common? Something substantive, I think. Both the boy and the peasant are far more intensely rooted in what some philosophers call 'the natural world', or *Lebenswelt*, than most modern adults. They

136

have not yet grown alienated from the world of their actual personal experience, the world which has its morning and its evening, its *down* (the earth) and its *up* (the heavens), where the sun rises daily in the east, traverses the sky and sets in the west, and where concepts like 'at home' and 'in foreign parts', good and evil, beauty and ugliness, near and far, duty and work, still mean something living and definite. They are still rooted in a world which knows the dividing line between all that is intimately familiar and appropriately a subject of our concern, and that which lies beyond its horizon, that before which we should bow down humbly because of the mystery about it. Our 'I' primordially attests to that world and personally certifies it; that is the world of our lived experience, a world not yet indifferent since we are personally bound to it in our love, hatred, respect, contempt, tradition, in our interests and in that pre-reflective meaningfulness from which culture is born. That is the realm of our induplicable, inalienable and non-transferable joy and pain, a world in which, through which and for which we are somehow answerable, a world of personal responsibility. In this world, categories like justice, honour, treason, friendship, infidelity, courage or empathy have a wholly tangible content, relating to actual persons and important for actual life. At the basis of this world are values which are simply there, perennially, before we ever speak of them, before we reflect upon them and inquire about them. It owes its internal coherence to something like a 'pre-speculative' assumption that the world functions and is generally possible at all only because there is something beyond its horizon, something beyond or above it that might escape our understanding and our grasp but, for just that reason, firmly grounds this world, bestows upon it its order and measure, and is the hidden source of all the rules, customs, commandments, prohibitions and norms that hold within it. The natural world, in virtue of its very being, bears within it the presupposition of the absolute which grounds, delimits, animates and directs it, without which it would be unthinkable, absurd and superfluous, and which we can only quietly respect. Any attempt to spurn it, master it or replace it with something else appears, within the framework of the natural world, as an expression of *hubris* for which humans must pay a heavy price, as did Don Juan and Faust.

To me, personally, the smokestack soiling the heavens is not just a regrettable lapse of a technology that failed to include 'the ecological factor' in its calculation, one which can be easily corrected with the appropriate filter. To me it is more, the symbol of an age which seeks to transcend the boundaries of the natural world and its norms and to make it into a merely private concern, a matter of subjective prefer ence and private feeling, of the illusions, prejudices and whims of a 'mere' individual. It is a symbol of an epoch which denies the binding importance of personal experience - including the experience of mystery and of the absolute – and displaces the personally experienced absolute as the measure of the world with a new, man-made absolute, devoid of mystery, free of the 'whims' of subjectivity and, as such, impersonal and inhuman. It is the absolute of so-called objectivity: the objective, rational cognition of the scientific model of the world.

Modern science, constructing its universally valid image of the world, thus crashes through the bounds of the natural world which it can understand only as a prison of prejudices from which we must break out into the light of objectively verified truth. The natural world appears to it as no more than an unfortunate left-over from our backward ancestors, a fantasy of their childish immaturity. With that, of course, it abolishes as mere fiction even the innermost foundation of our natural world; it kills God and takes his place on the vacant throne so that henceforth it would be science which would hold the order of being in its hand as its sole legitimate guardian and be the sole legitimate arbiter of all relevant truth. For after all, it is only science that rises above all individual subjective truths and replaces them with a super ior, trans-subjective, trans-personal truth which is truly objective and universal.

Modern rationalism and modern science, though the work

of man that, as all human works, developed within our natural world, now systematically leave it behind, deny it, degrade and defame it – and, of course, at the same time colonize it. A modern man, whose natural world has been properly conquered by science and technology, objects to the smoke from the smokestack only if the stench penetrates his apartment. In no case, though, does he take offence at it *metaphysically* since he knows that the factory to which the smokestack belongs manufactures things that he needs. As a man of the technological era, he can conceive of a remedy only within the limits of technology – say, a catalytic scrubber fitted to the chimney.

Lest you misunderstand: I am not proposing that humans abolish smokestacks or prohibit science or generally return to the Middle Ages. Besides, it is not by accident that some of the most profound discoveries of modern science render the myth of objectivity surprisingly problematic and, via a remarkable detour, return us to the human subject and his world. I wish no more than to consider, in a most general and admittedly schematic outline, the spiritual framework of modern civilization and the source of its present crisis. And though the primary focus of these reflections will be the political rather than ecological aspect of this crisis, I might, perhaps, clarify my starting point with one more ecological example. For centuries, the basic component of European agriculture had been the family farm. In Czech, the older term for it was *grunt* – which itself is not without its etymological interest. The word, taken from the German *Grund*, actually means ground or foundation and, in Czech, acquired a peculiar semantic colouring. As the colloquial synonym for 'foundation', it points out the 'groundedness' of the ground, its indubitable, traditional and pre-speculatively given authenticity and veridicality. Certainly, the family farm was a source of endless and intensifying social conflict of all kinds. Still, we cannot deny it one thing: it was rooted in the nature of its place, appropriate, harmonious, personally tested by generations of farmers and certified by the results of their husbandry. It also displayed a kind of optimal mutual proportionality in extent and kind of all that belonged to it; fields, meadows, boundaries, woods, cattle, domestic animals, water, toads and so on. For centuries no farmer made it the topic of a scientific study. Nevertheless, it constituted a generally satisfactory economic and ecological system, within which everything was bound together by a thousand threads of mutual and meaningful connection, guaranteeing its stability as well as the stability of the product of the farmer's husbandry. Unlike present-day 'agrobusiness', the traditional family farm was energetically self-sufficient. Though it was subject to common calamities, it was not guilty of them – unfavourable weather, cattle disease, wars and other catastrophes lay outside the farmer's province.

Certainly, modern agricultural and social science could also improve agriculture in a thousand ways, increasing its productivity, reducing the amount of sheer drudgery, and eliminating the worst social inequities. But this is possible only on the assumption that modernization, too, will be guided by a certain humility and respect for the mysterious order of nature and for the appropriateness which derives from it and which is intrinsic to the natural world of personal experience and responsibility. Modernization must not be simply an arrogant, megalomaniac and brutal invasion by an impersonally objective science, represented by a newly graduated agronomist or a bureaucrat in the service of the 'scientific world view'.

That is just what happened to our country: our word for it was 'collectivization'. Like a tornado, it raged through the Czechoslovak countryside thirty years ago, leaving not a stone in place. Among its consequences were, on the one hand, tens of thousands of lives devastated by prison, sacrificed on the altar of a scientific Utopia about brighter tomorrows. On the other hand, the level of social conflict and the amount of drudgery in the countryside did in truth decrease while agricultural productivity rose quantitatively. That, though, is not why I mention it. My reason is something else: thirty years after the tornado swept the traditional family farm off the face of the earth, scientists are amazed to discover what even a semi-literate farmer previously knew – that human beings must pay a heavy price for every attempt to abolish, radically, once for all and without trace, that humbly respected boundary of the natural world, with its tradition of scrupulous personal acknowledgement. They must pay for the attempt to seize nature, to leave not a remnant of it in human hands, to ridicule its mystery; they must pay for the attempt to abolish God and to play at being God. The price, in fact, fell due. With hedges ploughed under and woods cut down, wild birds have died out and, with them, a natural, unpaid protector of the crops against harmful insects. Huge unified fields have led to the inevitable annual loss of millions of cubic yards of topsoil that have taken centuries to accumulate; chemical fertilizers and pesticides have catastrophically poisoned all vegetable products, the earth and the waters. Heavy machinery systematically presses down the soil, making it impenetrable to air and thus infertile; cows in gigantic dairy farms suffer neuroses and lose their milk while agriculture siphons off ever more energy from industry – manufacture of machines, artificial fertilizers, rising transportation costs in an age of growing local specialization, and so on. In short, the prognoses are terrifying and no one knows what surprises coming years and decades may bring.

It is paradoxical: people in the age of science and technology live in the conviction that they can improve their lives because they are able to grasp and exploit the complexity of nature and the general laws of its functioning. Yet it is precisely these laws which, in the end, tragically catch up on them and get the better of them. People thought they could explain and conquer nature – yet the outcome is that they destroyed it and disinherited themselves from it. But what are the prospects for man 'outside nature'? It is, after all, precisely the sciences that are most recently discovering that the human body is actually only a particularly busy intersection of billions of organic microbodies, of their complex mutual contacts and influences, together forming that incredible megaorganism we call the 'biosphere' in which our planet is blanketed.

The fault is not one of science as such but of the arrogance of man in the age of science. Man simply is not God, and playing God has cruel consequences. Man has abolished the absolute horizon of his relations, denied his personal 'pre-objective' experience of the lived world, while relegating personal conscience and consciousness to the bathroom, as something so private that it is no one's business. Man rejected his responsibility as a 'subjective illusion' – and in place of it installed what is now proving to be the most dangerous illusion of all: the fiction of objectivity stripped of all that is concretely human, of a rational understanding of the cosmos, and of an abstract schema of a putative 'historical necessity'. As the apex of it all, man has constructed a vision of a purely scientifically calculable and technologically achievable 'universal welfare', demanding no more than that experimental institutes invent it while industrial and bureaucratic factories turn it into reality. That millions of people will be sacrificed to this illusion in scientifically directed concentration camps is not something that concerns our 'modern man' unless by chance he himself lands behind barbed wire and is thrown drastically back upon his natural world. The phenomenon of empathy, after all, belongs with that abolished realm of personal prejudice which had to yield to science, objectivity, historical necessity, technology, system and the *'apparat'* – and those, being impersonal, cannot worry. They are abstract and anonymous, ever utilitarian and thus also ever a priori innocent.

And as for the future? Who, personally, would care about it or even personally worry about it when the perspective of eternity is one of the things locked away in the bathroom, if not expelled outright into the realm of fairy tales? If a contemporary scientist thinks at all of what will be in two hundred years, he does so solely as a personally disinterested observer who, basically, could not care less whether he is doing research on the metabolism of the flea, on the radio signals of pulsars or on the global reserves of natural gas.

And a modern politician? He has absolutely no reason to care, especially if it might interfere with his chances in an election, as long as he lives in a country where there are elections . . .

II

A Czech philosopher, Václav Bělohradský, suggestively unfolded the thought that the rationalistic spirit of modern science, founded on abstract reason and on the presumption of impersonal objectivity, has, beside its father in the natural sciences, Galileo, also a father in politics – Machiavelli, who first formulated, albeit with an undertone of malicious irony, a theory of politics as a rational technology of power. We could say that, for all the complex historical detours, the origin of the modern state and of modern political power may be sought precisely here, that is, once again in a moment when human reason begins to 'free' itself from the human being as such, from his personal experience, personal conscience and personal responsibility and so also from that to which, within the framework of the natural world, all responsibility is uniquely related, his absolute horizon. Just as the modern scientists set apart the actual human being as the subject of the lived experience of the world, so, ever more evidently, do both the modern state and modern politics.

To be sure, this process of anonymization and depersonalization of power and its reduction to a mere technology of rule and manipulation, has a thousand masks, variants and expressions. In one case it is covert and inconspicuous, while in another case it is just the contrary, entirely overt; in one case it sneaks up on us along subtle and devious paths, in another case it is brutally direct. Essentially, though, it is the same universal trend. It is the essential trait of all modern civilization, growing directly from its spiritual structure, rooted in it by a thousand tangled tendrils and inseparable even in thought from its technological nature, its mass characteristics and its consumer orientation.

The rulers and leaders were once personalities in their own

right, with concrete human faces, still in some sense personally responsible for their deeds, good and ill, whether they had been installed by dynastic tradition, by the will of the people, by a victorious battle or by intrigue. But they have been replaced in modern times by the manager, the bureaucrat, the *apparatchik* – a professional ruler, manipulator and expert in the techniques of management, manipulation and obfuscation, filling a depersonalized intersection of functional relations, a cog in the machinery of state caught up in a predetermined role. This professional ruler is an 'innocent' tool of an 'innocent' anonymous power, legitimized by science, cybernetics, ideology, law, abstraction and objectivity – that is, by everything except personal responsibility to human beings as persons and neighbours. A modern politician is transparent: behind his judicious mask and affected diction there is not a trace of a human being rooted by his loves, passions, interests, personal opinions, hatred, courage or cruelty in the order of the natural world. All that he, too, locks away in his private bathroom. If we glimpse anything at all behind the mask, it will be only a more or less competent power technician. System, ideology and *apparat* have deprived humans – rulers as well as the ruled – of their conscience, of their common sense and natural speech and thereby, of their actual humanity. States grow ever more machine-like, men are transformed into statistical choruses of voters, producers, consumers, patients, tourists or soldiers. In politics, good and evil, categories of the natural world and therefore obsolete remnants of the past, lose all absolute meaning; the sole method of politics is quantifiable success. Power is a priori innocent because it does not grow from a world in which words like guilt and innocence retain their meaning.

This impersonal power has achieved what is its most complete expression so far in the totalitarian systems. As Bělohradský points out, the depersonalization of power and its conquest of human conscience and human speech have been successfully linked to an extra-European tradition of a 'cosmological' conception of the empire (identifying the empire, as the sole true centre of the world, with the world as such, and considering the human as its exclusive property). But, as the totalitarian systems clearly illustrate, this does not mean that the modern impersonal power is itself an extra-European affair. The truth is the very opposite: it was precisely Europe, and the European West, that provided and frequently forced on the world all that today has become the basis of such power: natural science, rationalism, scientism, the industrial revolution, and also revolution as such, as a fanatical abstraction, through the displacement of the natural world to the bathroom down to the cult of consumption, the atomic bomb and Marxism. And it is Europe – democratic western Europe – which today stands bewildered in the face of this ambiguous export. The contemporary dilemma, whether to resist this reverse expansionism of its erstwhile export or to yield to it, attests to this. Should rockets, now aimed at Europe thanks to its export of spiritual and technological potential, be countered by similar and better rockets, thereby demonstrating a determination to defend such values as Europe has left, at the cost of entering into an utterly immoral game being forced upon it? Or should Europe retreat, hoping that the responsibility for the fate of the planet demonstrated thereby will infect, by its miraculous power, the rest of the world?

I think that, with respect to the relation of western Europe to the totalitarian systems, no error could be greater than the one looming largest: that of a failure to understand the totalitarian systems for what they ultimately are – a convex mirror of all modern civilization and a harsh, perhaps final call for a global recasting of that civilization's self-understanding. If we ignore that, then it does not make any essential difference which form Europe's efforts will take. It might be the form of taking the totalitarian systems, in the spirit of Europe's own rationalistic tradition, as some locally idiosyncratic attempt at achieving 'general welfare', to which only men of ill-will attribute expansionist tendencies. Or, in the spirit of the same rationalistic tradition, though this time in the Machiavellian conception of politics as the technology of power, one might perceive the totalitarian regimes as a purely external threat by expansionist neighbours who can be driven back within acceptable bounds by an appropriate demonstration of power, without having to be considered more deeply. The first alternative is that of the person who reconciles himself to the chimney belching smoke, even though that smoke is ugly and smelly, because in the end it serves a good purpose, the production of commonly needed goods. The second alternative is that of the man who thinks that it is simply a matter of a technological flaw, which can be eliminated by technological means, such as a filter or a scrubber.

The reality, I believe, is unfortunately more serious. The chimney 'soiling the heavens' is not just a technologically corrigible flaw of design, or a tax paid for a better consumerist tomorrow, but a symbol of a civilization which has renounced the absolute, which ignores the natural world and disdains its imperatives. So, too, the totalitarian systems warn of something far more serious than Western rationalism is willing to admit. They are, most of all, a convex mirror of the inevitable consequences of rationalism, a grotesquely magnified image of its own deep tendencies, an extremist offshoot of its own development and an ominous product of its own expansion. They are a deeply informative reflection of its own crisis. Those regimes are not merely dangerous neighbours and even less some kind of an avant-garde of world progress. Alas, just the opposite: they are the avant-garde of a global crisis of this civilization, first European, then Euro-American, and ultimately global. They are one of the possible futurological studies of the Western world, not in the sense that one day they will attack and conquer it, but in a far deeper sense – that they illustrate graphically to what the 'eschatology of the impersonal', as Bělohradský calls it, can lead.

It is the total rule of a bloated, anonymously bureaucratic power, not yet irresponsible but already operating outside all conscience, a power grounded in an omnipresent ideological fiction which can rationalize anything without ever having to brush against the truth. Power as the omnipresent monopoly of control, repression and fear; power which makes thought, morality and privacy a state monopoly and so dehumanizes them; power which long since has ceased to be the matter of a group of arbitrary rulers but which, rather, occupies and swallows up everyone so that all should become integrated within it, at least through their silence. No one actually possesses such power, since it is the power itself which possesses everyone; it is a monstrosity which is not guided by humans but which, on the contrary, drags all persons along with its 'objective' self-momentum – objective in the sense of being cut off from all human standards, including human reason and hence entirely irrational – to a terrifying, unknown future.

Let me repeat: it is a great reminder to contemporary civilization. Perhaps somewhere there may be some generals who think it would be best to dispatch such systems from the face of the earth and then all would be well. But that is no different from an ugly woman trying to get rid of her ugliness by smashing the mirror which reminds her of it. Such a 'final solution' is one of the typical dreams of impersonal reason – capable, as the term 'final solution' graphically reminds us, of transforming its dreams into reality and thereby reality into a nightmare. It would not only fail to resolve the crisis of the present world but, assuming anyone survived at all, would only aggravate it. By burdening the already heavy account of this civilization with further millions of dead, it would not block its essential trend to totalitarianism but would rather accelerate it. It would be a Pyrrhic victory, because the victors would emerge from a conflict inevitably resembling their defeated opponents far more than anyone today is willing to admit or able to imagine. Just as a minor example: imagine what a huge Gulag Archipelago would have to be built in the West, in the name of country, democracy, progress and war discipline, to contain all who refuse to take part in the effort, whether from naivety, principle, fear or ill-will!

No evil has ever been eliminated by suppressing its symptoms. We need to address the cause itself.

III

From time to time I have a chance to speak with various
Western intellectuals who visit our country and decide to
include a visit to a dissident in their itinerary – some out of
genuine interest, or a willingness to understand and to
express solidarity, others simply out of curiosity. Beside the
Gothic and Baroque monuments, dissidents are apparently
the only thing of interest to a tourist in this uniformly dreary
environment. Those conversations are usually instructive: I
learn much and realize much. The questions most frequently
asked are these: Do you think you can really change anything
when you are so few and have no influence at all? Are you
opposed to socialism or do you merely wish to improve it? Do
you condemn or condone the deployment of the Pershing II
and the Cruise missiles in western Europe? What can we do
for you? What drives you to do what you are doing when all it
brings you is persecution, prison – and no visible results?
Would you want to see capitalism restored in your country?

Those questions are well intended, growing out of a desire
to understand and showing that those who ask do care about
the world, what it is and what it will be.

Still, precisely these and similar questions reveal to me ever
anew how deeply many Western intellectuals do not understand – and in some respects, cannot understand – just what
is taking place here, what it is that we, the so-called
'dissidents', are striving for and, most of all, what is the
overall meaning of it. Take, for instance, the question, 'What
can we do for you?' A great deal, to be sure. The more
support, interest and solidarity of free-thinking people in the
world we enjoy, the less the danger of being arrested, and the
greater the hope that ours will not be a voice crying in the
wilderness. And yet, somewhere deep within the question
there is a built-in misunderstanding. After all, in the last
instance the point is not to help us, a handful of 'dissidents',
to keep out of jail a bit more of the time. It is not even a
question of helping these nations, Czechs and Slovaks, to live
a bit better, a bit more freely. They need first and foremost to

help themselves. They have waited for the help of others far too often, depended on it far too much, and far too many times came to grief: either the promised help was withdrawn at the last moment or it turned into the very opposite of their expectations. In the deepest sense, something else is at stake – the salvation of us all, of myself and my interlocutor equally. Or is it not something that concerns us all equally? Are not my dim prospects or, conversely, my hopes *his* dim prospects and hopes as well? Was not my arrest an attack on him and the deceptions to which he is subjected an attack on me as well? Is not the destruction of humans in Prague a destruction of all humans? Is not indifference to what is happening here or even illusions about it a preparation for the kind of misery elsewhere? Is not their misery the presupposition of ours? The point is not that some Czech dissident, as a person in distress, needs help. I could best help myself out of distress simply by ceasing to be a 'dissident'. The point is what that dissident's flawed efforts and his fate tell us and mean, what they attest about the condition, the destiny, the opportunities and the problems of the world, the respects in which they are or could be food for thought for others as well, for the way they see their, and so our, shared destiny, in what ways they are a warning, a challenge, a danger or a lesson for those who visit us.

Or the question about socialism and capitalism! I admit that it gives me a sense of emerging from the depths of the last century. It seems to me that these thoroughly ideological and often semantically confused categories have long since been beside the point. The question is wholly other, deeper and equally relevant to all; whether we shall, by whatever means, succeed in reconstituting the natural world as the true terrain of politics, rehabilitating the personal experience of human beings as the initial measure of things, placing morality above politics and responsibility above our desires, in making human community meaningful, in returning content to human speaking, in reconstituting, as the focus of all social action, the autonomous, integral and dignified human I, responsible for ourself because we are bound to something higher, and capable of sacrificing something, in extreme cases even everything, of his banal, prosperous private life – that 'rule of everydayness' as Jan Patočka used to say – for the sake of that which gives life meaning. It really is not all that important whether, by accident of domicile, we confront a Western manager or an Eastern bureaucrat in this very modest and yet globally crucial struggle against the momentum of impersonal power. If we can defend our humanity, then, perhaps, there is a hope of sorts – though even then it is by no means automatic – that we shall also find some more meaningful ways of balancing our natural claims to shared economic control and to dignified social status, with the tried driving force of all work: human enterprise realized in genuine market relations. As long, however, as our humanity remains defenceless, we will not be saved by any technical or organizational trick designed to produce better economic functioning, just as no filter on a factory smokestack will prevent a general dehumanization. To what purpose a system functions is, after all, more important than how it does so. Might it not function quite smoothly, after all, in the service of total destruction?

I speak of this because, looking at the world from the perspective which fate allotted me, I cannot avoid the impression that many people in the West still understand little of what is actually at stake in our time.

If, for instance, we take a second look at the two basic political alternatives between which Western intellectuals oscillate today, it becomes apparent that they are no more than two different ways of playing the same game, proffered by the anonymity of power and as such, no more than two diverse ways of moving toward the same global totalitarianism. One way of playing the game of anonymous reason is to keep on toying with the mystery of matter – 'playing God' – inventing and ever deploying further weapons of mass destruction, all, of course, intended 'for the defence of democracy' but in effect further degrading democracy to the 'uninhabitable fiction' which socialism has long since become on our side of Europe. The other form of the game is the tempting vortex that draws so many good and sincere people into itself, the so-called 'struggle for peace'. Certainly it need not always be so. Still, often I do have the impression that this vortex has been designed and deployed by that same treacherous, all-pervasive impersonal power as a more poetic means of colonizing human consciousness. Please note, I have in mind impersonal power as a principle, globally, in all its instances, not only Moscow – which, if the truth be told, lacks the capability of organizing something as widespread as the contemporary peace movement. Still, could there be a better way of rendering an honest, free-thinking man, the chief threat to all anonymous power, ineffectual in the world of rationalism and ideology than by offering him the simplest thesis possible, with all the apparent characteristics of a noble goal? Could you imagine something that would more effectively fire a just mind – preoccupying it, then occupying it and ultimately rendering it intellectually harmless – than the possibility of 'a fight against war'? Is there a more clever means of deceiving men than with the illusion that they can prevent war if they interfere with the deployment of weapons (which will be deployed in any case)? It is hard to imagine an easier way to a totalitarianism of the human spirit. The more obvious it becomes that the weapons will indeed be deployed, the more rapidly does the mind of a person who has totally identified with the goal of preventing such deployment become radicalized, fanaticized and, in the end, alienated from itself. So a man sent off on his way by the noblest of intentions finds himself, at the journey's end, precisely where anonymous power needs to see him: in the rut of totalitarian thought, where he is not his own and where he surrenders his own reason and conscience for the sake of another 'uninhabitable fiction'! As long as that goal is served, it is not important whether we call that fiction 'human well-being', 'socialism' or 'peace'. Certainly, from the standpoint of the defence and the interests of the Western world, it is not very good when someone says 'better Red than dead'. Still, from the viewpoint of the global, impersonal power, transcending power blocs and truly devilish in its omnipresence, there could be nothing better. That slogan is an infallible sign that the speaker has given up his humanity. For he has given up the ability personally to guarantee something that transcends him and so to sacrifice, *in extremis*, even life itself to that which makes life meaningful. Patočka once wrote that a life not willing to sacrifice itself to what makes it meaningful is not worth living. It is just in the world of such lives and of such a 'peace' – that is, under the 'rule of everydayness' – that wars happen most easily. In such a world, there is no moral barrier against them, no barrier guaranteed by the courage of supreme sacrifice. The door stands wide open for the irrational 'securing of our interests'. The absence of heroes who know what they are dying for is the first step on the way to the mounds of corpses of those who are slaughtered like cattle. The slogan 'better Red than dead' does not irritate me as an expression of surrender to the Soviet Union, but it terrifies me as an expression of the renunciation by Western people of any claim to a meaningful life and of their acceptance of impersonal power as such. For what the slogan really says is that nothing is worth giving one's life for. However, without the horizon of the highest sacrifice, all sacrifice becomes senseless. Then nothing is worth anything. Nothing means anything. The result is a philosophy of sheer negation of our humanity. In the case of Soviet totalitarianism, such a philosophy does no more than offer a little political assistance. With respect to Western totalitarianism, it is what constitutes it, directly and primordially.

In short, I cannot overcome the impression that Western culture is threatened far more by itself than by SS–20 rockets. When a French leftist student told me with a sincere glow in his eyes that the Gulag was a tax paid for the ideals of socialism and that Solzhenitsyn is just a personally embittered man, he cast me into a deep gloom. Is Europe really incapable of learning from its own history? Can't that dear lad ever understand that even the most promising project of 'general well-being' convicts itself of inhumanity the moment it demands a single involuntary death – that is, one which is not a conscious sacrifice of a life to its meaning? Is he really incapable of comprehending that until he finds himself incarcerated in some Soviet-style jail near Toulouse? Did the newspeak of our world so penetrate natural human speech that two people can no longer communicate even such a basic experience?

IV

I presume that after all these stringent criticisms, I am expected to tell just what I consider to be a meaningful alternative for Western humanity today in face of political dilemmas of the contemporary world.

As all I have said suggests, it seems to me that all of us, East and West, face one fundamental task from which all else should follow. That task is one of resisting vigilantly, thoughtfully and attentively, but at the same time with total dedication, at every step and everywhere, the irrational momentum of anonymous, impersonal and inhuman power – the power of ideologies, systems, *apparat*, bureaucracy, artificial languages and political slogans. We must resist their complex and wholly alienating pressure, whether it takes the form of consumption, advertising, repression, technology, or cliché – all of which are the blood brothers of fanaticism and the wellspring of totalitarian thought. We must draw our standards from our natural world, heedless of ridicule, and reaffirm its denied validity. We must honour with the humility of the wise the bounds of that natural world and the mystery which lies beyond them, admitting that there is something in the order of being which evidently exceeds all our competence; relating ever again to the absolute horizon of our existence which, if we but will, we shall constantly rediscover and experience; making values and imperatives into the starting point of all our acts, of all our personally attested, openly contemplated and ideologically uncensored lived experience. We must trust the voice of our conscience more than that of all abstract speculations and not invent other responsibilities than the one to which the voice calls us. We must not be ashamed that we are capable of love, friendship, solidarity, sympathy and tolerance, but just the opposite: we must set these fundamental dimensions of our humanity free from their 'private' exile and accept them as the only genuine starting point of meaningful human community. We must be guided by our own reason and serve the truth under all circumstances as our own essential experience.

I know all that sounds very general, very indefinite and very unrealistic, but I assure you that these apparently naive words stem from a very concrete and not always easy experience with the world and, if I may say so, I know what I am talking about.

The vanguard of impersonal power, which drags the world along its irrational path, lined with devastated nature and launching pads, is composed of the totalitarian regimes of our time. It is not possible to ignore them, to make excuses for them, to yield to them or to accept their way of playing the game, thereby becoming like them. I am convinced that we can face them best by studying them without prejudice, learning from them and resisting them by being radically different, with a difference born of a continuous struggle against the evil which they may embody most clearly, but which dwells everywhere and so even within each of us. What is most dangerous to that evil are not the rockets aimed at this or that state but the fundamental negation of this evil in the very structure of contemporary humanity: a return of humans to themselves and to their responsibility for the world; a new understanding of human rights and their persistent reaffirmation, resistance against every manifestation of impersonal power that claims to be beyond good and evil, anywhere and everywhere, no matter how it disguises its tricks and machinations, even if it does so in the name of defence against totalitarian systems.

The best resistance to totalitarianism is simply to drive it out of our own souls, our own circumstances, our own land, to drive it out of contemporary humankind. The best help to all who suffer under totalitarian regimes is to confront the evil which a totalitarian system constitutes, from which it draws its strength and on which its 'vanguard' is nourished. If there is no such vanguard, no extremist sprout from which it can grow, the system will lose ground. A reaffirmed human responsibility is the most natural barrier to all irresponsibility. If, for instance, the spiritual and technological potential of the advanced world is spread truly responsibly, not solely under the pressure of a selfish interest in profits, we can prevent its irresponsible transformation into weapons of destruction. It surely makes much more sense to operate in the sphere of causes than simply to respond to their effects. By then, as a rule, the only possible response is by equally immoral means. To follow that path means to continue spreading the evil of irresponsibility in the world, and so to produce precisely the poison on which totalitarianism feeds.

I favour 'anti-political politics', that is, politics not as the technology of power and manipulation, of cybernetic rule over humans or as the art of the useful, but politics as one of the ways of seeking and achieving meaningful lives, of protecting them and serving them. I favour politics as practical morality, as service to the truth, as essentially human and humanly measured care for our fellow humans. It is, I presume, an approach which, in this world, is extremely impractical and difficult to apply in daily life. Still, I know no better alternative.

V

When I was tried and then serving my sentence I experienced directly the importance and beneficial force of international solidarity. I shall never cease to be grateful for all its expressions. Still, I do not think that we who seek to proclaim the truth under our conditions find ourselves in an asymmetrical position, or that it should be we alone who ask for help and expect it, without being able to offer help in the direction from which it also comes.

I am convinced that what is called 'dissent' in the Soviet bloc is a specific modern experience, the experience of life at the very ramparts of dehumanized power. As such, that 'dissent' has the opportunity and even the duty to reflect on this experience, to testify to it and to pass it on to those fortunate enough not to have to undergo it. Thus we too have a certain opportunity to help in some ways those who help us, to help them in our deeply shared interest, in the interest of mankind.

One such fundamental experience, that which I called 'anti-political politics', *is* possible and can be effective, even though by its very nature it cannot calculate its effect beforehand. That effect, to be sure, is of a wholly different nature from what the West considers political success. It is hidden, indirect, long term and hard to measure; often it exists only in the invisible realm of social consciousness, conscience and subconsciousness and it can be almost impossible to determine what value it assumed therein and to what extent, if any, it contributes to shaping social development. It is, however, becoming evident – and I think that is an experience of an essential and universal importance – that a single, seemingly powerless person who dares to cry out the word of truth and to stand behind it with all his person and all his life, ready to pay a high price, has, surprisingly, greater power, though formally disfranchised, than do thousands of anonymous voters. It is becoming evident that even in today's world, and especially on this exposed rampart where the wind blows most sharply, it is possible to oppose personal experience and the natural world to the 'innocent' power and to unmask its guilt, as the author of *The Gulag Archipelago* has done. It is becoming evident that truth and morality can provide a new starting point for politics and can, even today, have an undeniable political power. The warning voice of a single brave scientist, besieged somewhere in the provinces and terrorized by a goaded community, can be heard over continents and addresses the conscience of the mighty of this world more clearly than entire brigades of hired propagandists can, though speaking to themselves. It is becoming evident that wholly personal categories like good and evil still have their unambiguous content and, under certain circumstances, are capable of shaking the seemingly unshakeable power with all its army of soldiers, policemen and bureaucrats. It is becoming evident that politics by no means need remain the affair of professionals and that one simple electrician with his heart in the right place, honouring something that transcends him and free of fear, can influence the history of his nation.

Yes, 'anti-political politics' is possible. Politics 'from below'. Politics of man, not of the apparatus. Politics growing from the heart, not from a thesis. It is not an accident that this hopeful experience has to be lived just here, on this grim battlement. Under the 'rule of everydayness' we have to descend to the very bottom of a well before we can see the stars.

When Jan Patočka wrote about Charter 77, he used the term 'solidarity of the shaken'. He was thinking of those who dared resist impersonal power and to confront it with the only thing at their disposal, their own humanity. Does not the perspective of a better future depend on something like an international community of the shaken which, ignoring state boundaries, political systems, and power blocs, standing outside the high game of traditional politics, aspiring to no titles and appointments, will seek to make a real political force out of a phenomenon so ridiculed by the technicians of power – the phenomenon of human conscience?

Prague
February 1984

This presentation is intended for the University of Toulouse where I would have presented it while receiving an honorary doctorate, had I been able to be present.

5

Thriller

Before me lies the famous *Occult Philosophy* of Heinrich Cornelius Agrippa von Nettesheim, where I read that the ingestion of the living (and if possible still beating) heart of a hoopoe, a swallow, a weasel, or a mole will bestow upon one the gift of prophecy. It is nine o'clock in the evening and I turn on the radio. The announcer. a woman, is reading the news in a dry, matter-of-fact voice: Mrs Indira Gandhi has been shot by two Sikhs in her personal bodyguard. The corpse of Father Popieluszko, kidnapped by officers of the Polish police, has been fished out of the Vistula river. International aid is being organized for Ethiopia where a famine is threatening the lives of millions, while the Ethiopian regime is spending almost a quarter of a billion dollars to celebrate its tenth anniversary. American scientists have developed plans for a permanent observatory on the Moon and for a manned expedition to Mars. In California, a little girl has received a heart transplanted from a baboon; various animal welfare societies have protested.

Ancient myths are certainly not just a manifestation of archetypal images from man's collective unconsciousness. But they are undoubtedly that as well. Much of the mystery of being and of man, many of his dark visions, obsessions, longings, forebodings, much of his murky 'pre-scientific' knowledge and many important metaphysical certainties are obviously encoded in old myths. Such myths, of course, transcend their creators: something higher spoke through them, something beyond their creators, something that not even they were fully able to understand and give a name to. The authority invested in old myths by people of ancient cultures indicates that this higher power, whatever it is, was once generally felt and acknowledged. If we go no further than Jung's interpretation of myths, it is obvious that they introduced a partial or temporary 'order' into the complex world of those unconscious forebodings, unprovable certainties, hidden instincts, passions, and longings that are an intrinsic part of the human spirit. And they obviously exercised something like a 'check' or 'supervisory power' over those forces of the human unconscious.

The civilization of the new age has robbed old myths of their authority. It has put its full weight behind cold, descriptive Cartesian reason and recognizes only thinking in concepts.

I am unwilling to believe that this whole civilization is no more than a blind alley of history and a fatal error of the human spirit. More probably it represents a necessary phase that man and humanity must go through, one that man – if he survives – will ultimately, and on some higher level (unthinkable, of course, without the present phase), transcend.

Whatever the case may be, it is certain that the whole rationalistic bent of the new age, having given up on the authority of myths, has succumbed to a large and dangerous illusion: it believes that no higher and darker powers – which these myths in some ways touched, bore witness to, and whose relative 'control' they guaranteed – ever existed, either in the human unconscious or in the mysterious universe. Today, the opinion prevails that everything can be 'rationally explained', as they say, by alert reason. Nothing is obscure – and if it is, then we need only cast a ray of scientific light on it and it will cease to be so.

This, of course, is only a grand self-delusion of the modern spirit. For though it make that claim a thousand times, though it deny a thousand times the 'averted face' of the world and the human spirit, it can never eliminate that face, but merely push it further into the shadows. At the most, it will drive this entire complex world of hidden things to find surrogate, counterfeit, and increasingly confusing manifestations; it will compel the 'order' that myth once brought into this world to vanish along with the myth, and the 'forces of the night' to go on acting, chaotically and uncontrollably, shocking man again and again by their, for him, inexplicable presence, which glimmers through the modern shroud that conceals them. But more than that: the good powers – because they were considered irrational as well – were buried along with the dark powers. Olympus was completely abolished, leaving no one to punish evil and drive the evil spirits away. Goodness, being well mannered, has a tendency to treat these grand obsequies seriously and withdraw; evil, on the contrary, senses that its time has come, for people have stopped believing in it altogether.

To this day, we cannot understand how a great, civilized nation – or at least a considerable part of it – could, in the twentieth century, succumb to its fascination for a single, ridiculous, complex-ridden, *petit bourgeois*, could fall for his pseudo-scientific theories and in their name exterminate nations, conquer continents, and commit unbelievable cruelties. Positivistic science, Marxism included, offers a variety of scientific explanations for this mysterious phenomenon, but instead of eliminating the mystery, they tend rather to deepen it. For the cold, 'objective' reason that speaks to us from these explanations in fact only underlines the disproportion between itself – a power that claims to be the decisive one in this civilization – and the mass insanity that has nothing in common with any form of rationality.

Yes, when traditional myth was laid to rest, a kind of 'order' in the dark region of our being was buried along with it. And what modern reason has attempted to substitute for this order, has consistently proved erroneous, false, and disastrous, because it is always in some way deceitful, artificial, rootless, lacking in both ontology and morality. It may even border on the ludicrous, like the cult of the 'Supreme Being' during the French Revolution, the collectivist folklore of totalitarian systems, or their 'realist', self-celebrating art. It seems to me that with the burial of myth, the barn in which the mysterious animals of the human unconscious were housed over thousand of years has been abandoned and the animals turned loose – on the tragically mistaken assumption that they were phantoms – and that now they are devastating the countryside. They devastate it, and at the same time they make themselves at home where we least expect them to – in the secretariats of modern political parties, for example. These sanctuaries of modern reason lend them their tools and their authority so that ultimately the plunder is sanctioned by the most scientific of world views.

Generally, people do not begin to grasp the horror of their situation until too late: that is, until they realize that thousands of their fellow humans have been murdered for reasons that are utterly irrational. Irrationality, hiding behind sober reason and a belief that the inexorable march of history demands the sacrifice of millions to assure a happy future for billions, seems essentially more irrational and dangerous than the kind of irrationality that, in and through myth, admits to its own existence, comes to terms with the 'positive powers' and, at most, sacrifices animals. The demons simply do what they want while the gods take diffident refuge in the final asylum to which they have been driven, called 'human conscience'. And so at last bloodlust, disguised as the most scientific of the world's views (which teaches, by the way, that conscience must submit to historical necessity) throws a twentieth-century John of Nepomuk into the Vistula. And the nation immediately canonizes its martyr in spirit.

In the events which chance tossed together in a single newcast, and juxtaposed with Agrippa's *Occult Philosophy*, I begin to see a sophisticated collage that takes on the dimensions of a symbol, an emblem, a code. I do not know what message is hidden in that unintentional artefact, which might be called 'Thriller', after Michael Jackson's famous song. I only feel that chance – that great poet – is stammering an indistinct message about the desperate state of the modern world.

First, Marxist demonologists in the Polish papers label Popieluszko a practitioner of black magic who, with the assistance of the Devil, serves the black mass of anti-communism in the church of St Stanislav Kostka; then, other scientific Marxists waylay him at night, beat him to death and throw him into the Vistula; and finally, still other 'scientists' on one-sixth of the earth's surface claim that the Devil in disguise – the CIA, in other words – is behind it. It is all pure medieval history. Except that the actors are scientists, people shielded by science, possessing an allegedly scientific world view. Of course that makes the whole thing so much more powerful. The demons have been turned loose and go about, grotesquely pretending to be honourable twentieth-century men who do not believe in evil spirits. The Sikhs do not even need to masquerade as men of science. Confronting this modern world with modern machine guns in their hands, they believe themselves to be instruments of providence: after all, they are merely meting out punishment in accordance with the ancient prophecy about the desecrator of their Golden Temple. The Hindus then turn around and murder Sikhs, burning them alive, as though all Sikhs, to the last man, had taken part in Mrs Gandhi's murder. How can this happen in the century of science and reason? How can science and reason explain it? How does it relate to colonizing the Moon and making ready an expedition to Mars? How does it relate to an age capable of transplanting the heart of a baboon into a person? Could we be getting ready to go to Mars in the secret hope of leaving our demons behind on the earth and so disposing of them? And who, in fact, has a baboon heart: that little girl in California – or the Marxist government of Ethiopia, building its mausoleums in a time of famine; or the Polish police; or the Sikhs in the personal bodyguard of the Indian prime minister who died – thanks to their belief in ancient prophecies – like an antique emperor at the hands of his own servants?

It seems to me that man has what we call a human heart, but that he also has something of the baboon within him. The modern age treats the heart as a pump and denies the presence of the baboon within us. And so again and again, this officially non-existent baboon, unobserved, goes on the rampage, either as the personal bodyguard of a politician, or wearing the uniform of the most scientific police force in the world.

Modern man, that methodical civil servant in the great bureaucracy of the world, mildly frustrated by the collapse of his 'scientific' world view, finally switches on his video recorder to watch Michael Jackson playing a vampire in 'Thriller', the best-selling video cassette in the history of the world, then goes into the kitchen to remove from a thermos flask – behind the backs of all animal welfare societies – the still warm heart of a hoopoe. And he swallows it, hoping to have the gift of prophecy conferred upon him.

6

An anatomy of reticence

I

Western peace groups, it seems, are turning in ever greater numbers not to the official, state-sponsored Peace Committees in the eastern part of central Europe but to those ordinary citizens who concern themselves with global issues independently of their governments, that is, they are turning to the so-called 'dissidents'. We are being invited to peace congresses – the fact that we are unable to attend them is another matter. We are receiving visitors representing various peace groups; we are being called upon for dialogue and co-operation. All this, to be sure, does not mean that this is a spontaneous and universal attitude within the Western peace movement. The opposite appears closer to the truth. When it comes to the 'dissidents' in east-central Europe, the prevailing mood seems to be one of reticence, of caution, if not of outright distrust and uneasiness. The reasons for this reticence are not hard to imagine. Our governments resent anyone contacting us. And, after all, it is not we but our governments that can most affect the fortunes of the world, and so they need the primary contacts. Besides, to the Western peace fighters the 'dissidents' in the eastern half of central Europe must seem to be people strangely absorbed in their provincial concerns, exaggerating human rights (as if human survival were not more important!), suspiciously prejudiced against the realities of socialism, if not against socialist ideals themselves, people not sufficiently critical of Western democracy and perhaps even sympathizing, albeit secretly, with those detested Western armaments. In short, for them the 'dissidents' tend to appear as a fifth column of Western establishments east of the Yalta line.

The reticence, to be sure, is mutual. It is not less noticeable in the attitude of east-central European dissidents toward the Western peace movement. When we read Western texts dealing with the issues of peace, we usually find in them shadows and reasons for reticence, as well.

I do not know whether I shall succeed in contributing to better mutual understanding – I tend to be sceptical in that respect. Still, I want to try to describe some of the reasons for one of those two cases of reticence, the one on our side.

Seen from the outside, the 'dissidents' present the appearance of a minuscule and rather singular enclave – singularly radical, that is – within a monolithic society which speaks with an entirely different voice. In a sense, they really are such an enclave: there is but a handful of them and the state does everything in its power to create a chasm between them and society at large. They are in fact different from the majority in one respect: they speak their mind openly, heedless of the consequences. That difference, however, is hardly significant. What matters is whether the views they express differ significantly from those of the majority of their fellow citizens. I do not think they do. Quite the contrary, almost every day I come across some piece of heartening evidence that the dissidents are really saying nothing other than what the vast majority of their fellow citizens think privately. Actually, if we were to compare what the dissidents write in their texts with what we can hear their fellow citizens saying – albeit privately or, at most, over beer – we would reach the paradoxical conclusion that the dissidents constitute the less radical, more loyal, and more peaceful segment of the population. I say this because, if we want to consider the particular reticence among the dissidents when it comes to issues of peace, we need first to consider the social context of their actions, that is, the common experiences, perspectives and feelings they echo, express politically, or follow through in their own distinctive way.

II

Perhaps the first thing to understand is that, in our part of the world, the word 'peace' has been drained of all content. For thirty-seven years every possible and impossible open space in Czechoslovakia has been decorated with slogans such as 'Building up our homeland strengthens peace', 'The Soviet Union, guarantor of world peace', 'For the even greater flowering of the peaceful labour of our people!' and so on and so forth. For thirty-seven years our newspapers and the other media have been saturated with the same weary clichés about peace. For thirty-seven years our citizens have been required to carry the same old peace placards in the mandatory parades. For thirty-seven years a few individuals clever enough to establish themselves as our professional 'peace fighters', being particularly adept at repeating the official pronouncements, have engaged in extensive peace-congress tourism at state expense. That is, for thirty-seven years 'the struggle for peace' has been part and parcel of the ideological façade of the system within which we live. Yet every citizen knows from a thousand daily, intensely personal experiences that this official façade conceals an utterly different reality that grows ever more disheartening: the wasteland of life in a totalitarian state, with its all-powerful centre and all-powerless inhabitants. The word 'peace' – much like the words 'socialism', 'homeland', and 'the people' – has been reduced to serving both as one rung on the ladder up which clever individuals clamber and as a stick for beating those who stand aloof. The word has become one of the official incantations which our government keeps muttering while doing whatever it wants (or perhaps whatever it has been ordered) to do, and which its subjects must mutter along with it to purchase at least a modicum of peace.

Can you wonder, under these circumstances, that this word awakens distrust, scepticism, ridicule and revulsion among our people? This is not distaste for peace as such: it is distaste for the pyramid of lies into which the word has been traditionally integrated.

The extent of that distaste – and so its seriousness as a social phenomenon – can be illustrated by the fact that when our 'dissidents' occasionally attempt to express their views on peace issues publicly, no matter how much they differ from the views of the government, they become mildly suspect to the public simply because they express serious interest in the issues of peace at all. While people listen with interest to other Charter 77 documents in foreign broadcasts, seek them out, and copy them, Charter 77's documents dealing with 'peace' are guaranteed universal lack of interest in advance. A citizen of our country simply starts to yawn whenever he hears the word 'peace'.

The complete devaluation and trivialization of this word by official propaganda is, to be sure, only one reason – and a rather superficial one at that – for the reserve which people here display (including to some extent the dissidents themselves, since they live in a climate not unlike that of others) when they regard the 'struggle for peace' and the peace movement.

III

Against whom exactly is this officially sponsored 'struggle for peace' in our country directed? Naturally, against Western imperialists and their armaments. Thus the word 'peace' in our country means nothing more than unswerving concurrence with the policies of the Soviet bloc with its uniformly negative attitude toward the West. That is, in our newspeak, the phrase 'Western imperialists' does not refer to certain individuals obsessed by a vision of world domination, but rather the more or less democratically elected Western governments and the more or less democratic Western political system.

Add to this one more circumstance: our media, in reporting world news, have systematically sought for decades to create the impression that virtually the only thing which ever happens in the West is the 'peace struggle' – naturally in the sense that word has here. That is to say, the peace movement

is used as evidence of the eagerness with which the people o
the West await Soviet-style communism.

In such circumstances, what do you expect the averag
citizen thinks? Simply that those Western peace fighter
should get their wish – let them be punished for their naivet
and their inability to learn!

Try to imagine what would happen if a young, enthusia
tic, and sincere Western peace fighter were to approach not
prominent dissident but an ordinary Czechoslovak citize
and and were to ask him to sign, say, a petition against th
completion of NATO's armament plans. In principle I ca
imagine two possibilities. One is that this ordinary citize
would politely show his visitor the door. The other (probabl
more likely) possibility is that he would take him for an agen
of the secret police and would promptly sign the proffere
paper just as he signs scores of similar papers presented fo
his signature at work – without studying it, simply and solel
to stay out of trouble. (A more alert citizen, regardless of hi
attitude to armament plans, might try to squeeze an invita
tion to the West out of the whole thing. Ultimately he i
accustomed to looking out for 'number one': there might b
time to visit Paris for the first time in his life before Europ
perishes in an atomic conflagration.)

Let me make it even more emphatic. Imagine that throug
some unfortunate coincidence our Western visitor happene
to hit upon an older citizen who has lived all his life on Letn
in Prague – and who, together with hundreds of others, i
soon to be forcibly moved to some housing development o
the outskirts of Prague, losing his lifelong home and bein
forced to pay perhaps double the rent (out of what??), simpl
because Soviet officers have selected Letná for their settle
ment. Soviet officers – the most militant peace fighters of all
Would the Western enthusiast be justified in his surprise ove
the cold reception he would receive in this household?

I know that some people in the West believe the entir
Western peace movement is a Soviet plot. Others perceive i
as a collection of naive dreamers whose great enthusiasm an
minimal knowledge are cleverly utilized by the Soviets.

I do not share these views. Still, I have the impression that if one could determine what the people of east-central Europe really think, it would turn out that these views have more supporters there than in the West itself.

I think that a mutual exchange of such hard truths, with no punches pulled, is the first precondition for any meaningful European *rapprochement*.

IV

The more enlightened among the Western peace fighters demand not only the disarmament of their own countries but the simultaneous disarmament of everyone. For that reason they expect the people of east-central Europe to struggle against the various Soviet rockets rather than against the Pershings. This surely makes sense: let everyone first put his own house in order.

Since my topic today is the 'peace reticence' in our part of Europe, I need to call attention to something that tends to be overlooked: that any, even the most diffident, expression of disagreement with government policy in an area as sensitive as defence is infinitely more dangerous in our countries than in the West. After all, whereas the Western press publishes maps showing projected or completed rocket bases, the location of any weapons whatever is considered a state secret in our countries. Simply revealing the location of a base would undoubtedly lead to a prison term of many years. And when I try to imagine someone daring to come near a rocket base with an anti-war placard or – perish the thought! – trying to interfere with its construction, I break out in a cold sweat. It would mean not fourteen days in jail, with visits and packages, as in England, but fourteen cruel years in Valdice, our Czech Sing-Sing. When I once mentioned this to one of my interrogators during a police interrogation occasioned by an encounter of mine with some Western peace activists, he floored me with his answer. 'Different countries, different customs', he said.

Yes, different country, different customs. To my countrymen I have always stressed that we should not lie our way out of our responsibility and blame everything on overall conditions, on the superpowers and on the bad, bad world at large. To readers abroad, though, I would like to point out that we live in a country where the 'customs' are different. To speak out against the rockets here means, in effect, to become a 'dissident'. Concretely, it means the complete transformation of one's life. It means the acceptance of a prison term as one of life's natural possibilities. It means giving up at a stroke many of the few openings available to a citizen in our country. It means finding oneself, day after day, in a neurotic world of constant fear of the doorbell. It means becoming a member of that microscopic 'suicide-pact' enclave surrounded, to be sure, by the unspoken good wishes of the public but at the same time by unspoken amazement over the fact that anyone would choose to risk so much for something as hopeless as seeking to change what cannot be changed.

The peace movement in the West has a real impact on the dealings of parliaments and governments, without risking jail. Here the risk of prison is real and, at least at this point, the impact on the government's decision-making is zero.

I do not claim that all action here is pointless. I only want to explain why so few people choose to act. I do not believe that, as a nation, we are significantly more cowardly. If the same conditions obtained in the West, I doubt that significantly more people there would choose to act than among us.

All this, I hope, is obvious. Still it is important to repeat it over and over again – among other reasons, to prevent the gradual growth in European minds of the wholly erroneous impression that only those weapons are dangerous which are surrounded by encampments of demonstrators.

V

I would not presume to speak about conditions in the entire Soviet bloc. I believe, however, that I can say at least of the Czechoslovak citizen that his world is characterized by a perennial tension between 'their' omnipotence and his impotence.

That is to say, this citizen knows 'they' can do anything they want – take away his passport, have him fired from his job, order him to move, send him to collect signatures against the Pershings, bar him from higher education, take away his driver's licence, build a factory producing mostly acid fumes right under his windows, pollute his milk with chemicals to a degree beyond belief, arrest him simply because he attended a rock concert, raise prices arbitrarily, any time and for any reason, turn down all his humble petitions without cause, prescribe what he must read before all else, what he must demonstrate for, what he must sign, how many square feet his apartment may have, whom he may meet and whom he must avoid. The citizen picks his way through life in constant fear of 'them', knowing full well that even an opportunity to work for the public good is a privilege 'they' have bestowed upon him, conditionally. (One of my friends, an expert in a certain area of medicine, had her request to attend a scholarly congress in her speciality in the neighbouring German Democratic Republic – to which she had been invited and to which her own scholarly society wanted to send her – turned down by her all-powerful superior, a representative, of course, of the bureaucracy rather than of medicine, simply because – as he made clear – learning about the methods of scientists in other countries is not, in this country, a question of natural interest in scientific development and in patient-care, but a favour bestowed upon doctors by their bureaucratic superiors.) The average citizen living in this stifling atmosphere of universal irritability, servility, perpetual defensiveness, backbiting, nervousness, and an ever smouldering compensatory contentiousness, knows perfectly well, without having to read any 'dissident' literature, that 'they' can do anything and he can do nothing. (That there is no clear division between those 'down under' and those 'up above', that no one really knows who 'they' are and that all of us, drawn into the same plot, are in part 'they', while 'they' are at the same time partly 'we', 'they' are subordinate citizens dependent on some other 'they' – this is a different matter outside the present context.)

And now try to imagine, my dear Western peace activist, that you confront this half-exhausted citizen with the question of what he is willing to do for world peace. Are you surprised to find him staring at you uncomprehendingly, wondering to himself what kind of trap has been laid for him this time?

You see, for him matters far simpler than questions of peace and war are – or, under our present conditions, appear to him to be – utterly beyond the reach of his competence. Since he can have absolutely nothing to say about the possible conversion of a large part of his homeland into a desert for the sake of a bit of inferior coal that God knows what industry needs for God knows what purpose, since he cannot protect even his children's teeth from deteriorating due to environmental pollution, since he cannot even obtain a permit to move for the sake of his children's teeth and souls from northern to southern Bohemia, how could he influence something of the order of some sort of 'star wars' between two superpowers? All that appears to him to be so terribly distant, as far beyond his influence as the stars above, that it really can exercise only people free of all his 'ordinary' concerns and restless from sheer boredom.

Mrs Thatcher was enchanted with the charm of Mr Gorbachev. In a completely rationalized world of computers, even capable, I have heard, of launching a nuclear war, the entire civilized world is irrationally fascinated by the fact that Mr G drinks whisky and can play golf – thanks to which, we are told, humankind is not utterly bereft of all hope of survival. But how does this appear to our weary little Czech? As yet another proof of what he has known all along: that war and peace are the business of Messrs G and R. What could he add to it? How can he enter into their thoughts? Can he join them for a glass of whisky and a few holes of golf? He cannot even enter into the thoughts of some petty bureaucrat at the passport office who will decide, with no appeal possible, whether to permit him to have the two-week vacation in

Yugoslavia for which he had been saving all year long. Is it surprising that he does not consider some mysterious star pact between Messrs R and G as an 'important step toward peace' but simply as yet another plot against him?

I am trying to show that the general reserve in questions of war and peace is not – at least in my country – the result of some genetically determined indifference to global problems but rather a completely understandable consequence of the social atmosphere in which it is our lot to live.

I repeat, I do not claim that there is nothing we can do. I am trying to say only that I can understand why so many people around me think they can do nothing. I would beg our friends – the peace fighters in the West – to try to empathize with the situation of these people. Please try, in our common interest!

VI

From time to time there appear in this world people who can no longer bear the spectacle of life's outrageous chaos and mysterious fertility. They are the people tragically oppressed by the terror of nothingness and fear of their own being, who need to gain inner peace by imposing order ('peace') upon a restless world, placing in a sense their whole unstable existence into that order, ridding themselves of their obsessions once and for all. The desperate impatience of such people drives them compulsively to construct and impose various projects directed toward a rationally ordered common good, their purpose is to make sure that, at long last, things will be clear and comprehensible, that the world will stride onward toward a goal, finally putting an end to all the infuriating contingency of history. No sooner do they set out to achieve this – if the world has had the misfortune to give them the opportunity – than they encounter difficulties. A great many of their fellow humans would prefer to go on living as they like. Their proposal, for all its perfection, does not attract those people. They treat it spitefully, putting obstacles in its path, whether intentionally or simply by their very nature. The fanatic of the abstract project, that practising Utopian, is quite naturally incapable of tolerating that sort of thing, not only because it destabilizes his own centre of gravity, but because he has long since lost all sensitivity to the integrity of all that is, and can see only his own dream of what should be and of the goal it should pursue. So he decides to impose his project upon the world – for its own good, to be sure. That is the beginning. Then that strange 'calculus of the common good' comes into play, demonstrating that it is right and proper to sacrifice a few thousand recalcitrants for the contentment of millions, or perhaps to sacrifice a few millions for the contentment of billions. How it must end is evident – in universal misery.

It is the tragic story of a 'mental short circuit': Why bother with never ending, genuinely hopeless search for truth when a truth can be had so readily, all at once, in the form of an ideology or a doctrine? Suddenly it is all so simple. Think of all the difficult questions which are answered in advance! Think of all the laborious existential tasks from which our minds are freed once and for all! The essence of this short-circuit is a fatal mistake: the tacit assumption that some ingenious, universally applicable artefact – and is a doctrine or an ideology ever anything more than a human artefact? – can lift from our shoulders the burden of the incessant, always unique, and essentially inalienable question and utterly transform man from a questioning being into an existing answer. This is the illusion that the demanding, unending, and unpredictable dialogue with conscience or with God can be replaced by the clarity of a pamphlet, that some artefact, like a set of pulleys freeing us from physical effort, can liberate us from the weight of personal responsibility and timeless sorrow.

Various extreme examples of this mental short circuit, some quite sad, some rather tragic, and some nothing short of monstrous, are familiar from history – Marat, Robespierre, Lenin, Baader, Pol Pot. (I would not include Hitler and Stalin in this category; if I did, it would have to include every criminal.) However, I am less concerned with these well-

known luminaries of fanaticism than I am with the inconspicuous temptation containing the germ of Utopianism (and
with it of totalitarianism) present in perhaps every man who
is not wholly indifferent to everything. Visions of a better
world and dreams about it are surely a fundamental aspect of
authentic humanity; without them and without that transcendence of the given which they represent, human life loses
all meaning, dignity, its very humanness. Is it any wonder
then that the devilish temptation is no less omnipresent? An
atom of it is hidden in every beautiful dream!

So it is only a matter of a 'detail': to recognize in time that
fateful first moment of deterioration, when an idea ceases to
express the transcendent dimension of being human and
degenerates into a substitute for it, the moment when the
artefact, the project for a better world, ceases to be an
expression of man's responsible identity and begins, on the
contrary, to expropriate his responsibility and identity, when
the abstraction ceases to belong to him and he instead begins
to belong to it.

I believe that a distinctive central European scepticism is
inescapably a part of the spiritual, cultural, and intellectual
phenomenon that is central Europe as it has been formed and
is being formed by certain specific historical experiences,
including those which today seem to lie dormant in our
collective unconscious. That scepticism has little in common
with, say, English scepticism. It is generally rather stranger, a
bit mysterious, a bit nostalgic, often tragic, and at times even
heroic, occasionally somewhat incomprehensible in its
heavy-handed way, in its caressing cruelty and its ability to
turn a provincial phenomenon into a global anticipation of
things to come. At times it gives the impression that people
here are endowed with some inner radar capable of recogniz-
ing an approaching danger long before it becomes visible and
recognizable as a danger.

Among the dangers for which our mind has such an
exceptionally keen sense is the one of which I have been
speaking, Utopianism. Or, more precisely, we are keenly
sensitive to the danger that a living idea, at once the product

and the emblem of meaningful humanity, will petrify into a Utopia, into technical instructions for doing violence to life and intensifying its pain. (This scepticism may also be reinforced by the fact that, in our area, it must coexist permanently with a great deal that is not far from the Utopian mentality. I am thinking for instance of our provincial enthusiasm, our periodic inclination to illusions, our tendency to trust, at times to the point of servility, everything that comes to us from elsewhere, the grand words and short breath of our courage, an inclination to sudden euphoria which, predictably, turns to frustration, resignation, and apathy at the first setback, and so on and so forth.)

Once and only once in this country did a number of Czechs and Slovaks fall prey to unambiguous Utopianism (and for historically intelligible reasons at that – it was in the atmosphere of the moral collapse of the older orders). That was when they came to believe that the merciless introduction of Leninist-Stalinist socialism (with the help, of course, of its global centre) would secure those 'glowing tomorrows' for us – and when, heedless of the will of the rest of the inhabitants, they proceeded to carry out that intent. (After many tragic experiences and after what was for some a long process of self-liberation and for others an awakening, we did attempt something like a revision of the misfortune, a 'socialism with a human face'. Also, even that was coloured by the Utopianism preserved in many of us as a fundamental habit, more persistent than the individual illusions on which it had focused. The Utopian aspect of that effort was not so much the faith that democratic institutions could be erected under Moscow's rule as the faith that we might secure approval from above – that the Kremlin, if only we could explain it all properly, must understand and approve. As it turned out, this faith proved a rather insecure foundation for such an undertaking. The answer to the plea for understanding came in the form of armoured divisions.) Our country has paid a cruel price for its postwar lapse into Utopianism. It helped cast us into a subjugation – and for God knows how long – in which we need not have found ourselves at all.

The result of this story is obvious – a new, far-reaching reinforcement of our central European scepticism about Utopianism of all colours and shadings, about the slightest suggestion of Utopianism. Today there is actually more of this scepticism than is good for us – extending from Utopianism to the will to resist evil as such. In the end, even a very timid, hesitant, tactful attempt to appeal to justice – and officially proclaimed justice at that – even though it calls for nothing, has been tested by both individual reflection and conscience, and is anti-Utopian in its entire moral essence, will be suspected of Utopianism (which is something the dissidents in particular know well.)

I have spoken about all this at length because I suspect that the reserve of our people with respect to the Western peace movement is rooted not merely in the banal suspicion that it is all a communist plot but much more in our region's fundamental scepticism about any Utopianism. Rightly or wrongly – but not surprisingly – our people ask themselves whether the Western peace fighters aren't just more Utopians. Bogged down in his wearying, exhausting everyday existence, crushed in the name of his putative wellbeing by bureaucratic might, the Czechoslovak citizen tends to ask who is this proposing still more 'glowing tomorrows' for us this time? Who is disturbing us again with some Utopia? And what new catastrophes are being prepared for us – with the best of intentions? Why should I get burned in some attempt to save the world when who knows what baleful news, without appeal, my boss will break to me tomorrow, naturally in the name of a better world? As if I didn't have enough problems already! Should I create more problems with pipe-dreams about a peaceful, disarmed, democratic Europe of free nations when merely a whisper about such a dream can bring me troubles for the rest of my life – while Mr G will still go on playing golf just as he pleases? Isn't it better to attempt, quite modestly, to live with dignity even in this morass, so I will not have to be ashamed in front of my children, than to get mixed up in some platonic construction of the Europe of the future? Western peace fighters will get me into trouble without giving it a second thought, they'll be off to a demonstration somewhere in Hanover or God knows where, while I'll be left here at the mercy of the nearest secret police office which, in exchange for my concern about the future of the world, will take away the work I like – and in addition my children will have to pay with their very real futures! (For the sake of accuracy, let us note that this distrust applies to every Utopianism, not to the leftist variety only: militant anti-communism, in which reason is crowded out by obsession and reality by a dream, evokes, I think, the same reactions, at least among more sensible people.)

Hand in hand with scepticism about all Utopias goes, quite understandably, scepticism about the various types and manifestations of the ideological mentality. In the course of my life I have sat through enough political debate to be used to quite a bit, at least in this respect. In spite of that, I must admit that even I am taken aback by the extent to which so many Westerners are addicted to ideology, much more than we who live in a system which is ideological through and through. Those perennial reflections about whom this or that view serves or abets, what political tendency it reinforces or weakens! What idea can or cannot be misused by someone . . . That perennial, exhausting examination of this or that attitude, opinion, or person, whether they are rightist or leftist, left or right of the centre, right of the left or left of the right! As if the proper pigeon-hole were more important than the substance of an opinion! I can understand that in a world where political forces interact freely this might be to some extent unavoidable. Still, I wish it could be understood why for us, against the background of our experiences, under conditions in which ideology has utterly terrorized the truth, this all seems petty, erroneous, and far removed from what is actually at stake.

Perhaps my description is overstated and oversimplified. Still, it appears to me that anyone who is seriously concerned about the future of Europe would do well to familiarize himself in as much detail as possible, for his own good as well as for their general educational value, with the various aspects of the scepticism which people here in the heart of Europe feel with respect to all visions of 'glowing tomorrows'. Few people would be happier than a Pole, a Czechoslovak, or a Hungarian were Europe soon to turn into a free community of independent countries in which no great power would have its armies and its rockets. And at the same time, I am sure that no one would be more sceptical about any hope that this can be accomplished by appeals to anyone's good will, even assuming someone might get around to making such appeals. Let us not forget that few people have had such a good opportunity to learn about the purpose of the superpower military and rocket presence in certain European countries. Their purpose is not so much defence against a putative enemy as it is supervision of conquered territories.

VII

Some time ago, two appealing young Italian women arrived in Prague with a women's proclamation calling for all things good: respect for human rights, disarmament, demilitarization of children's education, respect for all human beings. They were collecting signatures from both parts of our divided Europe. I found them touching: they could easily have been cruising the Mediterranean on the yachts of wealthy husbands (they would surely have found some) – and here they were, rattling around Europe, trying to make the world better. I felt all the more sorry for them because virtually none of the better-known Prague women dissidents wanted to sign (the petitioners understandably did not even try to approach non-dissidents). The reason was not that Prague women dissidents could not agree with the content of the declaration. Without conferring in any way about it, they all, individually, agreed on a different reason: it seemed to them ridiculous that they should sign something 'as women'. Men, who had nothing to sign, treated this feminine action with gallant attentiveness and a quiet smile, while among the ladies the prevalent mood was one of vigorous distaste for the whole matter, a distaste all the more vigorous for the fact that they were not absolved from deciding whether to sign or not; they experienced no need to be gallant. (Incidentally, in the end about five of them did sign.)

I wondered whence came this sudden, spontaneous distaste for associating on the basis of gender among my women friends. It surprised me.

Only some time later did I come up with an explanation. One of the traditions of the central European climate of which I have been speaking is, after all, a deepened sense of irony and self-irony, together with humour and black humour, and perhaps most important in this context, an intense fear of exaggerating our own dignity unintenionally to a comic degree, a fear of pathos and sentimentality, of overstatement and of what Kundera calls the lyric relation to the world. Yes, my women friends were suddenly seized with the fear that, as participants in an international women's venture, they would make themselves ridiculous. It was the fear that they would become 'dada', to borrow a term from the Czech theoretician of art, Karel Teige – that, unwittingly, they would become laughable in the earnestness with which they sought to reinforce their civic opinion by stressing their helpless femininity. Apparently they were seized by a sudden remembrance of how repulsive it was when in their televised talks, the vice-president of Czechoslovak Television, Mrs Baláš, larded the official 'peace' theses with constant references, full of fake sentimentality, to women and children. My women friends among the dissidents undoubtedly know a great deal about the sad position of women in our country. Despite this they found even the vague suggestion of feminism which could be read into the fact that the declaration in question was to be strictly a women's affair somehow internally objectionable. I do not wish to ridicule feminism; I know little about it and am prepared to believe that it is far from being the invention of a few hysterics, bored housewives, or rejected mistresses. Still, I have to note that in our country, even though the position of women is incomparably worse than in the West, feminism seems simply 'dada'.

Feminism, to be sure, is not at issue here. I want only to illustrate that strange, almost mysterious horror of everything overstated, enthusiastic, lyrical, pathetic, or overly serious that is inseparable from our spiritual climate. It is of the same kind, and stems from analogous roots, as our scepticism about Utopianism, with which it is often coextensive: emotional enthusiasm and rationalistic Utopianism are often no more than two sides of the same coin.

I can cite another example. It would be obviously inappropriate for Charter 77 to make jokes in its documents. Recently, however, it occurred to me in a particular context that some people might be getting bored with Charter 77 because it may seem to them to be taking itself much too seriously. Knowing only its documents and not its authors, they might easily gain the impression that Charter 77, forced for years to repeat the same theme over and over, has become stuck in the rut of its own seriousness, its martyrdom, its fame, that it lacks the ability to rise above itself, to look at itself from a distance, the ability to make light of itself – and for that very reason its rigidly serious expression might end up by making it unintentionally ridiculous. I do not know whether such an impression really exists, and if it exists, how widespread it may be; even less can I judge whether, if such an impression exists, to what degree it is justified or unfair to us. In any case, this speculative idea is something to think about.

It seems that in our central European context what is most earnest has a way of blending in a particularly tense manner with what is most comic. It seems that it is precisely the dimension of distance, of rising above oneself and making light of oneself, which lends to our concerns and actions precisely the right amount of shattering seriousness. Is not Franz Kafka, one of the most serious and tragic authors of this century, at the same time a humorist? I think that whoever does not laugh when reading his novels (as Kafka himself is supposed to have laughed when he read them out loud to his friends) does not understand them. Is not a Czech Hašek or an Austrian Musil a master of tragic irony or of ironic tragedy? Is not Vaculík's *Czech Dreambook* (to cite a contemporary dissident writer) a book oppressive in its humour and merry in its hopelessness?

The life of a dissident in Czechoslovakia is really not particularly jolly, and spending time in Czechoslovak jails is even less so. Our frequent jesting about these matters is not in conflict with their seriousness; rather, it is their inevitable consequence. Perhaps we simply would not be able to bear it if we were not at once aware of how absurd and so how comic it all is. Many of those who sympathize with us abroad would not understand our joking or would take it for cynicism. (More than once I have noted that, when meeting with foreigners, I do not translate much of what we say, just to be sure.) And when a dissident friend of mine, tasting various exotic (for us) delights at the American embassy, hailed them with Patočka's famous remark, 'There are things worth suffering for', we all laughed; it never occurred to any of us to consider this unworthy of the dignity of Patočka's heritage, of his tragic death, and of the moral foundations of the dissident stance in general.

In short, perhaps it is part of the plebeian tradition of Czech culture, but here we tend to be more acutely aware of the fact that anyone who takes himself too seriously soon becomes ridiculous, while anyone who always manages to laugh at himself cannot be truly ridiculous.

People in the West are, for various reasons, more afraid of war than we are. They are also significantly more free, they live more freely, and their opposition to armaments has no unacceptably serious consequences for them. Perhaps all of this makes the peace fighters on the other side seem, at least from here, a bit too earnest, perhaps even somewhat pathetic. (There is something else here as well, something which we are probably insufficiently aware of – that for them the fight for peace is probably more than a simple matter of particular demands for disarmament, it is an opportunity to erect unconforming, uncorrupted social structures, an opportunity for life in a humanly richer community, for self-realization outside the stereotypes of a consumer society and for expressing their resistance to those stereotypes.)

Our distrust of all overstatement and of any cause incapable of seeing itself in perspective may also affect that reticence which I have sought to analyse here. Since we pay a somewhat harsher price for our interest in the destiny of the world, we may also have a stronger need to make light of ourselves, to desecrate the altar, as so aptly described by Bakhtin. For this reason alone we have to be a bit more reserved than we might wish in our reaction to the various overly earnest exaggerations (which, at the same time, and not accidentally, are not purchased at a high price) with which some Western peace fighters come to us. It would be absurd to force on them our black humour and our invincible scepticism or even to demand of them that they undergo our serious tribulations and learn to see them in an ironic perspective. It would, however, be equally absurd if they expected from us their own brand of overstatement. To understand each other does not mean to become like each other, only to understand each other's identity.

VIII

There are, to be sure, still other reasons for the reticence with which I am concerned here. For instance: Czechoslovaks learned only too well, from their own fate, where a policy of appeasement can lead – they still have not quite got over it. For many years to come, historians are likely to conjecture whether the world could have avoided the Second World War with its millions of corpses if the Western democracies had been able to resist Hitler forcefully and in time. Is it any wonder that in this country, whose present decline began at Munich, people are especially sensitive to anything even remotely reminiscent of the pre-war capitulation to evil? I do not know how much genuine courage there would be in this country in any extreme situation. I do know, however, that one idea is firmly rooted in our common awareness: that the inability to risk, *in extremis*, even life itself to save what gives it meaning and a human dimension leads not only to the loss of meaning but finally and inevitably to the loss of life as well

– and not one life only but thousands and millions of lives. Certainly in a world of nuclear arms capable of exterminating all of humankind, many things have changed. Still, experience's fundamental lesson, that one must not tolerate violence in silence in the hope that it will simply run its course, retains its validity. (To believe the opposite would mean, among other things, to surrender to the inhumanity of technology once and for all.) Should such an attitude by some miracle avert rather than accelerate the coming of war, I cannot imagine to what kind of world, to what kind of humanity, to what kind of life and to what kind of 'peace' it would open the door. To be sure, a universal moral imperative and concrete political techniques for implementing it are two different things. I believe there are more effective and more meaningful ways of resisting violence or the threat of violence than its blind imitation (that is, promptly matching each of your opponent's actions with one of our own). That question, however, would take me too far afield from today's topic.

So let me cite just one example to complete the sketch. How much trust or even admiration for the Western peace movement can we expect from a simple yet sensitive citizen of east-central Europe when he has noticed that this movement has never, at any of its congresses or at demonstrations involving hundreds of thousands of participants, got around to protest the fact that one important European country attacked a small neutral neighbour five years ago, and since that time has been conducting on its territory a war of extermination which has already claimed a million dead and three million refugees? Seriously, what are we to think of a peace movement, a European peace movement, which is virtually unaware of the only war being conducted today by a European state? As for the argument that the victims of aggression and their defenders enjoy the sympathies of Western establishments and so are not worthy of support from the left, its incredible ideological opportunism can provoke only one reaction – total disgust and a sense of limitless hopelessness.

IX

It should be evident that the reticence of the inhabitants of the Soviet bloc with respect to peace issues has various causes; some are probably found in all its countries, some are primary in one land, others in another.

Understandably, these various elements enter to a greater or lesser degree into the reflections of east European dissidents as well. If we also take into account the fact that the specific social situation differs somewhat in each of the Soviet bloc countries, that each nation has its own historical, social, and cultural traditions, experiences, and models of behaviour, and finally, when we consider that the dissidents, though not numerous, are still a highly variegated company (in a certain sense the dissent in each of these nations mirrors the whole spectrum of political attitudes as would become evident if it were ever allowed to emerge), it becomes quite clear that the Western peace movement is unlikely ever to receive a unified and specific peace programme from our side.

And yet there is, it seems to me, something like a 'common denominator' even here, some basic thoughts upon which we could in all likelihood all agree if we ever had the opportunity to do so. At least that is my impression from the texts I have seen: certain motifs recur in them with a surprising regularity. That cannot be a coincidence. Evidently analogous experiences lead to analogous considerations, perspectives, and convictions. And if they indeed represent something like a common denominator of the east-central European experience and thought, it is surely worth noting.

It is not the aim of this essay to formulate this 'common denominator'. I shall only try to sum up some of the points that appear to be common to all independent east-central European thinking about peace and the peace movement and are characteristic of it.

1 Most important, despite the general reticence, there appears to be a certain basic sympathy for the moral ethos of

those who, living in a mature consumer society, place their concern for the destiny of the world ahead of a mere concern for personal well-being. Are we not doing something similar here, albeit in different ways and under different conditions? This 'pre-rational' consideration guarantees of itself a certain basic weakness for the Western peace movement among our dissidents.

2 Close second, however, may be a clearly polemical conviction: the cause of the danger of war is not weapons as such but political realities (including the policies of political establishments) in a divided Europe and a divided world, realities which make possible or simply require the production and installation of these weapons and which in the end could lead to their utilization as well. No lasting, genuine peace can be achieved simply by opposing this or that weapons system, because such opposition deals only with consequences, not with causes. Opposition to weapons – assuming, of course, that it is an opposition to all weapons and not only to those suitable for protest encampments – can at best induce governments to accelerate various disarmament negotiations, that being probably the most we can expect.

3 Nor can disarmament negotiations alone resolve the present crisis, even if they are successful (which in the light of our experience thus far seems unlikely). After all, to date everything an agreement had slowed down soon accelerated again, without any agreement, a short time later. At best, successful negotiations might create a more favourable atmosphere for a real resolution of the crisis. Atmospherics, however, are one thing, the will to resolve the crisis something else again. Basically, they can achieve nothing more than the perpetuation of an explosive status quo – but with a smaller amount of explosive technology.

4 Thus the sole meaningful way to genuine European peace – and not simply to some armistice or 'non-war' – is the path of a fundamental restructuring of the political realities that are at the roots of the current crisis. This would require both sides to abandon in a radical manner their defensive

policy of maintaining the status quo (that is, the division of Europe into blocs) as well as their policy of power or superpower 'interests', subordinating all their efforts to something quite different – to the ideal of a democratic Europe as a friendly community of free and independent nations. What threatens peace in Europe is not the prospect of change but the existing situation.

5 Without free, self-respecting, and autonomous citizens there can be no free and independent nations. Without internal peace, that is, peace among citizens and between the citizens and the state, there can be no guarantee of external peace: a state that ignores the will and the rights of its citizens can offer no guarantee that it will respect the will and the rights of other peoples, nations, and states. A state that refuses its citizens their right to public supervision of the exercise of power will not be susceptible to international supervision. A state that denies its citizens their basic rights becomes a danger to its neighbours as well: internal arbitrary rule will be reflected in arbitrary external relations. The suppression of public opinion, the abolition of public competition for power and its public exercise opens the way for the state power to arm itself in any way it sees fit. A manipulated population can be misused in serving any military adventure whatever. Unreliability in some areas arouses justifiable fear of unreliability in everything. A state that does not hesitate to lie to its own people will not hesitate to lie to other states. All of this leads to the conclusion that respect for human rights is the fundamental condition and the sole, genuine guarantee of true peace. Suppressing the natural rights of citizens and peoples does not secure peace – quite the contrary, it endangers it. A lasting peace and disarmament can only be the work of free people.

Both the posture and perspective I have tried to sketch here have been presented in detail and with supporting arguments in innumerable, highly diverse works devoted to this topic by independent writers in our part of Europe. To quote them at length or to repeat what has already been written about it would be superfluous. This is roughly the attitude of various independent civic initiatives and groupings in the countries of the Soviet bloc.

It has become evident that reflection on the bitter daily experiences of the citizen in a totalitarian state always leads quite logically to the same point – a new appreciation of the importance of human rights, human dignity, and civic freedom. This is the focus of my remarks, and the focus, with good reason, of all reflections about peace as well. It may be that this understanding of the fundamental preconditions of peace, purchased at a high price and marked by a new vehemence, is the most important contribution that independently thinking people in our part of the world can make to our common awareness today.

For us it is simply no longer comprehensible how anyone can still believe in the possibility of any disarmament which would bypass human beings or be purchased at the cost of their enslavement. This appears to us to be the most foolish of all Utopias, comparable perhaps only to a hope that all the weapons in the world will, on their own, turn themselves in for scrap metal or turn into musical instruments.

The intensity and the approach to emphasizing the continuity between peace and human freedom tend naturally to vary at different times and in different places in our part of the world, and they depend, in various ways, on the specific situation and context. Still, when we are confronted with the view that our insistent introduction of human rights into every discussion about peace complicates the situation and interferes with agreement, we all, for evident reasons, fall prey to the hopeless feeling that those who will not hear are beyond help.

X

Since the matters which I have just discussed have appeared to us to be almost banally obvious, it strikes us as awkward to be forced to explain them again and again. It seems, however, that they are anything but obvious to many adherents of the peace movement and that we have no option other than to go on explaining. More than once in conversations with peace activists or while signing shared points of view, I myself have encountered the notion that our ideas may be remarkable, perhaps even surprising (!), but they are also too abstract, too 'philosophical', not sufficiently political, clearly comprehensible, and hard-hitting, and thus difficult to implement. I had the impression that my interlocutors are far more accustomed to the kind of slogans, proclamations, and clear, unambiguous demands that are fit for placards and T-shirts than they are to any global considerations. What can we do – they come to us from the world of practical, real politics!

Still, our position remains simple enough as long as we are asked for nothing other, and for no more, than clarification of our fundamental perspective on the topic of peace. More serious complications arise when, for whatever reason, we are asked to explain how we imagine projecting our global or 'philosophical' conception into the reality of political action: what should we actually be demanding, and what political measures, and in what order, would we expect Europe to take in the light of our perspective?

An initial difficulty here is that even when east European dissidents have more difinite views on this matter, those views differ widely.

There are some, for instance in Poland and Hungary, who believe that the first and perhaps the most important step toward transforming the status quo in Europe and thus toward genuine peace should be the creation of a belt of neutral states in central Europe in place of the present abrupt frontier between the two blocs. The objection of many to this suggestion is that this is the least realistic of all possible demands – surely the Soviet Union will not be willing to give up several of its European client states and to guarantee their neutrality to boot! Besides, it is said, this would be immoral because it would in fact mean a solution at the cost of others – as long as we are free, let the rest of Europe manage as best it can! According to the critics of such a solution, that immorality is linked with its hopelessness: a 'no-man's-land' between the blocs into which Europe is divided will not bring peace. The danger of conflict would continue, and were it to come, the central European states would be the first to be blown sky high (was it ever otherwise in our remembered history?) while the neutrality, behind which, Swiss style, they sought to hide from the world's turmoils, would become a scrap of paper overnight.

Others would suggest a straightforward dissolution of the two military blocs and withdrawal of American and Soviet armies from the territories of their European allies (which would naturally lead to the liquidation of all nuclear weapons stationed in or aimed at Europe). Speaking personally, this seems simply lovely . . . although it is not quite clear to me who or what could induce the Soviet Union to dissolve the entire phalanx of its European satellites – especially since it is evident that, with its armies gone from their territories, it would sooner or later have to abandon its political domination over them as well.

Another voice, incidentally a particularly authoritative one, seeks to show that Europe will remain divided as long as Germany remains divided. For that reason (and not simply because of the German right to unification) we should first of all demand a German peace treaty which would confirm the present European frontiers but would at the same time offer the two German states the prospect of gradual confederation. With the German problem resolved, a dissolution of the two pacts might be far more realistic. This perspective is rather persuasive: would a Europe without pacts and without the protection – actually 'protection' – of the superpowers be imaginable if Berlin were to remain cut in two by a wall and the German problem left unresolved?

This proposal also evokes a series of objections: it is said to be provocative, stirring up all kinds of ghosts and emotions on every side; many judicious people fear the reconstitution of a great Germany, with its danger of automatic German predominance in Europe, and so on.

Finally, still others believe there is no point in raising any of these bold proposals since no one is prepared to act on them in any case, and the mighty find them needlessly irritating. It makes more sense, they would say, to take the various treaties already on the books at face value (for example, the Concluding Act of the Helsinki Agreement) and to demand that they be observed. Or perhaps it might be better to support without bombastic gestures a variety of small steps which would gradually lead to a healthier climate throughout Europe, to cooler heads and so to a gradual limitation of armaments, and to a relaxation of tensions.

In all likelihood, numerous other proposals and perspectives exist. (For completeness' sake, although this is not directly related to the various perspectives on the restructuring of Europe, I would like to mention one other point that divides the dissidents rather significantly – their attitude toward the US. On one side of the spectrum, anti-Americanism is nearly as strong as it is among Western leftists; on the other, the viewpoint tends to be Reaganite: the Soviet Union is the evil empire, the US the land of the good. As for myself – should anyone care – I have no great illusions about America, about the American establishment, and about American foreign policy. Still, the degree of internal freedom and consequently of international political credibility characteristic of the two superpowers appears to me so profoundly different that to consider the current situation simply symmetrical, in the sense that both colossi are equally dangerous, appears to me a monstrous oversimplification. Yes, both are dangerous, each in a different way, they definitely are not dangerous in the same way.)

Another difficulty involved in considerations of this kind in our part of Europe is more serious than that deriving from the difference of opinion we have just described. It is rooted in a rather vague, difficult to explain, and yet immensely powerful sense of the futility and senselessness of all such considerations. It may seem strange, however, as I shall try to explain, that ultimately it is quite reasonable that this feeling came over us when we confined ourselves to 'philosophizing' generally about peace, but only at the point when our reflections had to touch upon concrete politics.

A central European mind – a sceptical, sober, anti-Utopian, understated mind, crushed by daily confrontation with unprincipled power – when suddenly cast in the role of arbiter of Europe's future, cannot avoid the feeling that this is 'dada'. It is no great problem for one of our dissidents to concoct this or that vision of European development and of Europe's future. The problem is how to shake off the feeling of the utter hopelessness and pointlessness of such work, how to rid himself of the fear that any concrete, so to speak technical, conception of the longed-for transformation of Europe into a continent of peace is nowadays every bit as ludicrous as any other Utopian construct, how to rid himself both of the fear that he will become a target for his sober neighbours' ridicule, and of the feeling that, for the first time, he is actually drifting away from real life and up into the stratospheric realm of fairy tales.

A trace of the heroic dreamer, something mad and unrealistic, is hidden in the very genesis of the dissident perspective. In the very nature of things, the dissident is something of a Don Quixote. He writes his critical analyses and demands freedoms and rights all alone, merely with a pen in his hand, face to face with the gargantuan might of the state and its police. He writes, cries out, screams, requests, appeals to the law – and all the time he knows that, sooner or later, they will lock him up for it. Why, then, such scruples? Amid clouds of folly should he not feel like a fish in water? I will attempt to explain the difference between the 'naturally foolish' world of the dissident and the type of folly that terrifies him when he is asked to sign some programme for the peaceful reordering of Europe.

As I have written more than once, I believe the phenomenon of dissidence grows out of an essentially different conception of the meaning of politics than that prevailing in the world today. That is, the dissident does not operate in the realm of genuine power at all. He is not seeking power. He has no desire for office and does not gather votes. He does not attempt to charm the public, he offers nothing and promises nothing. He can offer, if anything, only his own skin – and he offers it solely because he has no other way of affirming the truth he stands for. His actions simply articulate his dignity as a citizen, regardless of the cost. The innermost foundation of his 'political' undertaking is moral and existential. All he does, he does first of all for himself: something within has simply revolted and left him incapable of continuing to 'live a lie'. Only after and dependent on that thoroughly existential motivation does there follow (and can there possibly follow) a 'political' motive: the hope – vague, indefinite, and difficult to justify – that this course of action is also good for something in general. It is the hope that 'politics outside politics', that 'politics outside the sphere of power', does make some sense, that by whatever hidden and complex ways it leads to something, summons something, produces some effect. That even something as seemingly ephemeral as the truth spoken aloud, as an openly expressed concern for the humanity of humans, bears within itself a certain power and that even a word is capable of a certain radiation, of leaving a mark on the 'hidden consciousness' of a community. (It is an intrinsic aspect of a perspective with this foundation that the dissident is more likely to describe and analyse the present than to project a future. He is far more the one who criticizes what is wrong here and now than the one who plans something better which is to be. He sees his mission more in defending man against the pressures of the system than in imagining better systems. As for the future, he is more concerned with the moral and political values on which it should rest than with utterly premature speculations about how and by whom these values will be secured for humankind. He knows, after all, that the nature of this future does not depend on his present wishes but on the difficult-to-predict course of things to come.)

This, then, is the 'naturally mad' world of dissent. It is meaningful because, within its limits, it is consistent. It is tactical because it does not let itself be guided by tactical considerations. It is political because it does not play politics.

It is concrete, real, effective – not in spite of its madness but because of it. To be sure, it is also this because there is something honest about its 'madness', it is faithful to itself, it is whole and undivided. This may be a world of dreams and of the ideal, but it is not the world of Utopia.

Why deny it, this world of truth, however uncomfortable to live in, offers at the same time definite advantages: finding himself outside the universe of real power and traditional practical politics, that is, outside the matrix of utility, tactics, success, compromise, and the inevitable manipulations of half-truths and deceptions, the dissident can be significantly himself and can even make fun of himself without danger of becoming ridiculous to everyone.

A dissident runs the risk of becoming ridiculous only when he transgresses the limits of his natural existence and enters into the hypothetical realm of real power, that is, in effect, into the realm of sheer speculation. For only then can he become a Utopian. Here he accepts the perspective of real power without having any genuine power whatever; he enters the world of tactics incapable of tactical manoeuvre and without being either justified or compelled to do so by real power; he leaves the world of service to truth and attempts to smuggle his truth into the world of service to power without being able or even willing to serve it himself. He attempts to go on speaking the truth outside the world of truth; standing outside the world of power, he attempts to speculate about power or to organize it. He is trading the respectable role of a champion for the somewhat grotesque role of a self-appointed adviser to the mighty. He was not ludicrous formerly in the role of a dreamer, just as a tactician is not ludicrous in a tactician's role. He became ludicrous only when he became a dreamer playing at tactics. A dreamer playing at tactics is a minister without a ministry, a general without an army, a president without a republic. Alienated from his role as a witness of history, yet unwelcome in the role of its organizer, he finds himself in a strange vacuum – outside the credibility of power and outside the credibility of truth.

In all of this I do not wish to suggest that Soviet bloc dissidents should not comment on the political realities and political possibilities existing in the part of the world where they live, that they should not examine the various limits on their effectiveness and seek to expand them, that they should not reflect on how and where they can or cannot project their truth. (Besides, history is unpredictable, and we need to be prepared for a whole range of eventualities: recall, for instance, how the dissidents of the Polish Workers' Defence Committee (KOR) had to become practical politicians overnight.)

I have sought only to explain why I believe that east European dissidents are, and in the future in all likelihood will remain, cautious in their own distinctive manner whenever they are called upon to take part in peace activities.

Prague
April 1985

PART TWO

SIXTEEN TEXTS FOR VÁCLAV HAVEL

1

Samuel Beckett: Catastrophe

For Václav Havel

Director (D).

His female assistant (A).

Protagonist (P).

Luke, in charge of the lighting, offstage (L).

Rehearsal. Final touches to the last scene. Bare stage. A and L have just set the lighting. D has just arrived.

D in an armchair downstairs audience left. Fur coat. Fur toque to match. Age and physique unimportant.

A standing beside him. White overall. Bare head. Pencil on ear. Age and physique unimportant.

P midstage standing on a black block 18 inches high. Black wide-rimmed hat. Black dressing-gown to ankles. Barefoot. Head bowed. Hands in pockets. Age and physique unimportant.

D and A contemplate P. Long pause.

D: [*Finally.*] Like the look of him?

A: So so. [*Pause.*] Why the plinth?

D: To let the stalls see the feet.

  [*Pause.*]

A: Why the hat?

D: To help hide the face.

  [*Pause.*]

A: Why the gown?

D: To have him all black.

  [*Pause.*]

A: What has he on underneath? [A *moves towards* P.] Say it. [A *halts.*]

A: His night attire.

D: Colour?

A: Ash

    [D *takes out a cigar.*]

D: Light. [A *returns, lights the cigar, stands still.* D *smokes.*]
    How's the skull?

A: You've seen it.

D: I forget. [A *moves towards* P.] Say it.
    [A *halts.*]

A: Moulting. A few tufts.

D: Colour?

A: Ash.

    [*Pause.*]

D: Why hands in pockets?

A: To help have him all black.

D: They mustn't.

A: I make a note. [*She takes out a pad, takes pencil, notes.*] Hands
    exposed.
    [*She puts back pad and pencil.*]

D: How are they? [A *at a loss. Irritably.*] The hands, how are the
    hands?

A: You've seen them.

D: I forget.

A: Crippled. Fibrous degeneration.

D: Clawlike?

A: If you like.

D: Two claws?

A: Unless he clench his fists.

D: He mustn't.

A: I make a note. [*She takes out pad, takes pencil, notes.*] Hands limp
    [*She puts back pad and pencil.*]

D: Light. [A *returns, relights the cigar. stands still.* D *smokes.*] Good
    Now let's have a look. [A *at a loss. Irritably.*] Get going. Los
    that gown. [*He consults his chronometer.*] Step on it, I have a
    caucus.

    [A *goes to* P, *takes off the gown.* P *submits, inert.* A *steps back, the
    gown over her arm.* P *in old grey pyjamas, head bowed, fists
    clenched. Pause.*]

A: Like him better without? [*Pause.*] He's shivering.

D: Not all that. Hat.

[A *advances, takes off hat, steps back, hat in hand. Pause.*]

A: Like that cranium?

D: Needs whitening.

A: I make a note. [*She takes out pad, takes pencil, notes.*] Whiten cranium.

[*She puts back pad and pencil.*]

D: The hands. [A *at a loss. Irritably.*] The fists. Get going. [A *advances, unclenches fists, steps back.*] And whiten.

A: I make a note. [*She takes out pad, takes pencil, notes.*] Whiten hands.

[*She puts back pad and pencil. They contemplate* P.]

D: [*Finally.*] Something wrong. [*Distraught.*] What is it?

A: [*Timidly.*] What if we were . . . were to . . . join them?

D: No harm trying. [A *advances, joins the hands, steps back.*] Higher. [A *advances, raises waist high the joined hands, steps back.*] A touch more. [A *advances, raises breast-high the joined hands.*] Stop! [A *steps back.*] Better. It's coming. Light.

[A *returns, relights cigar, stands still.* D *smokes.*]

A: He's shivering.

D: Bless his heart.

[*Pause.*]

A: [*Timidly.*] What about a little . . . a little . . . gag?

D: For God's sake! This craze for explicitation! Every i dotted to death! Little gag! For God's sake!

A: Sure he won't utter?

D: Not a squeak. [*He consults his chronometer.*] Just time. I'll go and see how it looks from the house.

[*Exit* D, *not to appear again.* A *subsides in the armchair, springs to her feet no sooner seated, takes out a rag, wipes vigorously back and seat of chair, discards rag, sits again. Pause.*]

D: [*Off, plaintive.*] I can't see the toes. [*Irritably.*] I'm sitting in the front row of the stalls and can't see the toes.

A: [*Rising.*] I make a note. [*She takes out a pad, takes pencil, notes.*] Raise pedestal.

D: There's a trace of face.

A: I make a note.

[*She takes out pad, takes pencil, makes to note.*]

D: Down the head. [A *at a loss. Irritably.*] Get going. Down his head. [A *puts back pad and pencil, goes to* P, *bows his head further, steps back.*] A shade more. [A *advances, bows the head further.*] Stop! [A *steps back.*] Fine. It's coming. [*Pause.*] Could do with more nudity.

A: I make a note.

[*She takes out pad, makes to take her pencil.*]

D: Get going! Get going! [A *puts back the pad, goes to* P, *stands irresolute.*] Bare the neck. [A *undoes top buttons, parts the flaps, steps back.*] The legs. The shins. [A *advances, rolls up to below knee one trouser-leg, steps back.*] The other. [*Same for other leg, steps back.*] Higher. The knees. [A *advances, rolls up to above knees both trouser-legs, steps back.*] And whiten.

A: I make a note. [*She takes out pad, takes pencil, notes.*] Whiten all flesh.

D: It's coming. Is Luke around?

A: [*Calling.*] Luke! [*Pause. Louder.*] Luke!

L: [*Off, distant.*] I hear you. [*Pause. Nearer.*] What's the trouble now?

A: Luke's around.

D: Blackout stage.

L: What?

[A *transmits in technical terms. Fade-out of general light. Light on* P *alone.* A *in shadow.*]

D: Just the head.

L: What?

[A *transmits in technical terms. Fade-out of light on* P's *body. Light on head alone. Long pause.*]

D: Lovely.

[*Pause.*]

A: [*Timidly.*] What if he were to . . . were to raise his head . . . an instant . . . show his face . . . just an instant.

D: For God's sake! What next? Raise his head? Where do you think we are? In Patagonia? Raise his head? For God's

sake! [*Pause.*] Good. There's our catastrophe. In the bag.
Once more and I'm off.

A: [*To* L.] Once more and he's off.

[*Fade-up of light on* P's *body. Pause. Fade-up of general light.*]

D: Stop! [*Pause.*] Now . . . let 'em have it. [*Fade-out of general
light. Pause. Fade-out of light on body. Light on head alone.
Long pause.*] Terrific! He'll have them on their feet. I can
hear it from here.

[*Pause. Distant storm of applause.* P *raises his head, fixes the
audience. The applause falters, dies.
Long pause.
Fade-out of light on face.*]

*In a letter to Samuel Beckett written in April 1983, six weeks after
his release, the Czech dramatist Václav Havel described 'the shock I
experienced during my time in prison when, on the occasion of one of
her one-hour visits allowed four times a year, my wife told me in the
presence of an obtuse warder that at Avignon there had taken place a
night of solidarity with me, and that you had taken the opportunity
to write, and to make public for the first time, your play
Catastrophe. For a long time afterwards there accompanied me in
prison a great joy and emotion which helped me to live on amidst all
the dirt and baseness.'*

2

Heinrich Böll: Courtesy towards God

(On Václav Havel's *Letters to Olga*)

It is scarcely possible to do any justice at all to this publication; the 145 letters have been censored; no deletion was remedied, for obvious reasons, and Havel himself offered no explanation.

It would have been preferable to include the epilogue by Jiří Dienstbier, 'Writing letters (in prison)', as an introduction this sets the scene in a way which Havel himself is unable to describe in his letters. 'One is allowed to write', says Dienstbier, 'only about personal and family matters. Nothing can be written about the conditions in prison, for example The reason is that conditions in prison are the most persona of matters at this time.'

This ironical flashlight should serve as the reading lamp for the 300 pages in this book. It would also be useful to be aware in advance of what Dienstbier has written about Havel 'Václav Havel was a particular target for persecution.' His overall manner of courtesy, of having been 'well brought up', gave the impression that he was 'soft and easily broken'. It was seductive. 'Those around him reacted all the more excitedly to Havel's unyieldingness, to this "inaccessible systematist", who even tidied up his prison cell in so precise and presentable a fashion that it could have served as the model for the graduates of an officers' training school.' There was ambivalence towards this fellow prisoner: the 'ordinary criminals' slipped this political prisoner pastries, bacon and lard, and even clothes, and gave any informers a beating; but the fact that Havel was an internationally renowned author also aroused envy.

These could well be elements of a fantastic prison diary, which Havel did *not* write or add to his censored letters. The 'entertainment value' of these letters is thus small for anyone who seeks to 'amuse' himself with the author of spiritually absurd and 'humorous' dramas who here reveals the brooding seriousness on which his work is founded. Havel does not make his own ego the subject of his brooding, but rather portrays himself as an example of the human genus. His introspection is not an egomaniac preoccupation with pain, but – and one is justified in saying it here – is existential in its nature.

It would also have been a good idea to include a brief preliminary remark to the effect that letters 138 and 139 contain the crucial message, the motive for this 'trial' which drags on for three years. The accused in this trial is Havel himself, who says of himself that, 'my imprisonment is only a necessary period in my life which had to happen (the fact that it happened so late is, in itself, quite surprising).'

For years he was unable to forgive himself for the fact that, in 1977, when Charter 77 came into being, and at the time of his first arrest, he had given in for an instant in a moment of inattention rather than weakness – still being unfamiliar with the vicissitudes of the system – and had revealed a weak point by submitting to the public prosecutor an application for release which was subsequently published (!).

This weakness of the moment was then turned against him publicly to the extent that his credibility as spokesman for Charter 77 was called into question. 'There were weeks, months and even years of quiet despair, and years of shame, when I was eaten up by inner reproach.' Only in prison, brooding for years at a time, does he eventually find occasional 'peace of mind', when 'all the pain of existence ceases to be pain and becomes what Christians call mercy'. A person will then readily accept a punishment, even if it has been meted out by the wrong authorities for a given offence – making that person a penitent – but to what authority?

Again and yet again the values and authorities which are proposed and are considered are the very ones which are falling increasingly into discredit in the free and 'free' world: consciousness, conscience, order and responsibility. These are juxtaposed with surprising concepts such as 'recollection of being', 'spiritual order' and 'absolute horizon'.

Does this make the penitent who is searching for an authority a 'God-seeker'?

This could well be someone who shrinks from saying the word 'God'; what we are possibly dealing with here is the manifestation of a new form of religiousness, which out of *courtesy* no longer addresses God with the name which has been trampled underfoot by politicians.

Havel allows the word to slip out from time to time, albeit rather colloquially and in passing. He avoids its *intentional* use. When asked about it, he admits that, 'I am still not capable of speaking of God here'. At other times he stated, 'and yet I am aware of the paradox: should God not exist in that place which I am trying to define, then all this will appear to be nothing more than some form of abstract construction and subterfuge.'

Other comments on the same theme include: 'I have the feeling that there is something more than intellectualistic subterfuge that is preventing me from admitting my belief in a personal God. Something deeper is concealed behind these subterfuges: what I am lacking is that extremely important "last drop" in the form of the mystical experience of the enigmatic address and revelation. There is no doubt that I could substitute the word "God" for my "something" or for the "absolute horizon", and yet this does not seem to me to be a very serious approach.' And: 'I acknowledge this closeness to Christian feelings, and I am pleased whenever I sense that this closeness has been perceived by others, and yet one must be very careful in these matters and one must consider one's words well (it was the Archbishop of Prague himself who told me this in the course of a conversation).'

And is it really the case that a bishop in the free world could suggest to the politicians that they should be more 'careful' in their use of the word 'God', and even more careful in their use of the word 'Christian'? There, this is seen as the courteous use of the word 'God' by a brooding detainee – and yet here, there would be permanent repercussions of these words in the vocabulary of persons, probably not *all* of whom had undergone the 'mystical' experience which Havel was aware he lacked. What a mad world, where authors are here reproached (see Schelsky and the other persons, primarily Christians, who latched on to Schelsky, who was certainly not a Christian) for claiming to 'impart consciousness' – and where a person there makes consciousness, order, conscience and responsibility the subject of years of profound brooding.

We are familiar with order here only in the context of public order policy, and we are familiar with conscience perhaps only because it is a part of the language of irresponsibility. Metaphysics is a new fashion here, a breeze which one breathes in because it has now surprisingly become the 'in' thing to do, whereas over there a person adopts the metaphysical concept of 'recollection of being'; this person is 'gentle' and 'courteous' by nature, is given to agility of mind, enjoys his food and drink, likes to celebrate, and knows how to make the most of the material aspects of earthly life.

How can a 'master's son', who was spoilt as a child, develop this astonishing hardness towards the specimen of humanity which he himself represents? The 'spoilt child', the 'master's son', endured the privileges, found them to be inequitable, and yet at the same time was ridiculed as a 'fatty' precisely because of them. The question is whether the new masters' sons and daughters of the nomenclature (corresponding more or less to the 'golden gang' of the Ceausescus) will ever be capable of such sensitivity, or of applying the power embodied therein, which Havel had, as I see it, predestined precisely for what should in future be referred to with confidence as 'socialism with a human face'. From what other direction will the rebellion come, if not from within the ranks of the privileged 'masters' sons'? And in what other way could they be expected to do penance?

There is little of a biographical nature in the accepted sense to be found in these 145 letters, in the 300 and more pages of this book. There are just one or two droplets, which add some colour and are expanded upon in the epilogue by Dienstbier. There can scarcely be any objection, even piecemeal, if toothache, haemorrhoids and emergency operations are a little overdone, and if the ordeals of imprisonment predominate. This wide-ranging and persistent examination of the consciousness and the conscience is constantly concerned with the question of the reason for human existence. He exists in order to fulfil the need for 'higher responsibility'. Havel is not at all interested to know why man commits evil acts. 'Why does man do good deeds, in spite of the fact that he has nothing to gain from so doing (for example if no one at all is aware of it, and if no one will ever experience it)? And if he neglects to do it, then why does he apologize to himself?' 'It is for this reason, too, that responsibility provides the main key to human identity.'

Yet again, we see consciousness, conscience, responsibility and order represented as 'recollection of being'. Strange thoughts entered my head as I read through these letters: Is it not the case that Europe not only exists, as we sometimes condescendingly accept, but exists above all in the consciousness of the intellectuals in the socialist countries, whereas here in the West, which is suffering from its chronic security disease, Europe is in decline and is racked with problems of markets and arms, and with the absurdity of over-armament, over-production and growth?

The order which Havel is seeking is not the order which comes from the calmness imposed by social order policy, just as the God which he is seeking is not the God of peace through 'order'. God is not a secure possession which may even attract interest if at all possible; these are mere words relating to the pursuit of wealth which is no longer in control of its own absurdities and should perhaps be seen as representing 'spiritual order'.

Unrest, searching, the lack of security and risk are also to be found in art, of course. 'The artist makes use of something without being precisely aware of what so-called significance his creation will have. The work, it seems to me, should always be a little more clever than its author.' How clever, then, must those people be who are judged to be cleverer than the work and its author together: the critics? Is a 'spiritual order' available to them?

What interests Havel about the theatre is its 'social' and personal aspect, and not what is generally referred to as its surrounding field. He is interested in what is happening on the stage and in the audience. He is bored by the 'chaos and licence' which he has experienced so many times; he has a 'polite and cold' respect for Brecht, although he enjoys only his 'un-Brechtian' aspects, which I understand to mean Brecht when he is not being didactic. He loves plays and, of course, the enjoyment associated with them. And Beckett, who is far removed from 'chaos and licence', could naturally be neither imagined out nor wished out of the situation, being so irreplaceable – and yet he is not the very last word, either. Can any word at all occupy that position? After all these years of brooding, in which he longed to write, how will Havel the theatre author give expression to his play and to his enjoyment of the performance?

What would the censor have thought as he 'let through' all this? What were his thoughts when Havel identified himself with the weather girl who was so distressingly embarrassed as the result of a technical failure and was suffering in consequence? Time after time Havel has written pages and pages about this weather girl, although in the context of a state medium which cannot but appear hostile to him? Did the censor smile or laugh when he had to assess the humanity of this conscientious and highly courteous detainee? Could it possibly be that there is a play concealed behind all this?

Havel nevertheless managed, in spite of the censorship, to smuggle out a scale of his moods: melancholy, anxiety, hypersensitivity, apathy, indifference, resignation and total self-doubt to the point of feeling worthless; he devotes himself at great length to the 'dejectedness of Sunday', to what he calls this 'problem of civilization bearing the name Sunday'. These moods, in particular those on Sundays, are to him 'the typical cracks through which nothingness finds its way to man, this modern face of the Devil'. He does not shrink from calling it by name. As we are told by Dienstbier, Havel was forbidden from continuing with this scale of moods.

'The global wonder of existence', that peace of mind which 'Christians call mercy', was also allowed through. One would have had to be a censor in order to *review* these letters. Is not so much metaphysics more dangerous than many a direct message? The following resulted from a particularly beautiful moment in the prison yard: 'The more beautiful the moment, the more distinct is the growth of the eerie question: What else? What more? What now? What next? What am I to do, and what will I achieve? I would describe this as the feeling of having arrived at a kind of end to the finite.' Asians sometimes commit suicide after such moments, in order to ensure that they pass on into the expected infinity.

Bitterness is heard only rarely, if he has to wait too long for mail, if the recipient shows little interest in his preoccupations, or if he complains about the absence of the 'personal note', in spite of the fact that all these letters are notes addressed in person to Václav Havel.

It is surprising that the censor has allowed the comments relating to Klaus Juncker to pass unchallenged, who – defined by Havel as the ideal publisher – 'does not regard culture as a means to making profit, but regards profit as a means to disseminating culture'. He observes with interest the inflated linguistic style used in the language of the media: for example, the use of 'made of wooden material' instead of 'made of wood'.

As demonstrated in Dienstbier's description of the circumstances, the apparently monastic peace with which he writes from his cell is deceptive. This 'God-seeker' who admits his penitence does not complain about his circumstances. He feels *bound*; the Latin *'religari'* means restrained – one of the etymological definitions of religion. Havel's shyness, his courteousness, his timidity and his love of order, which has nothing to do with social order policy, all of whose victim he is, together leave no room for demonstrative declarations. His air of quiet restlessness is here scarcely noticeable in our plethora of information, which sometimes becomes information terrorism when 'surrounded' by music and enables us simply to perform reflex actions rather than to reflect.

Perhaps there are still some individuals sitting in their theologists' and philosphers' cells, without a 'Walkman' to their ears, who can hear these preoccupations and will not cease to resist and to reflect. I dare say that Christ is speaking in these letters, albeit a Christ who does not describe himself by that name and yet is still a Christ, and yet I must quickly erase this description again before those ever ready Christian drummer boys, representing their explosive form of Christianity, lay their hands on it. These first signs of a new Christian spirit can only be misused by the authorities here, where brotherhood and humanity are being tried before a church court. If an objection is raised against Havel to the effect that 'this' – resistance, endurance and hope – 'serves no purpose, then my reply will be quite simply that it does in fact have a purpose'.

The anti-communists and all those who seek to trap dissidents, but who do not usually read books and simply acquire blindly and clumsily everything which comes within their clutches, these killers of intellectuals should be warned, before laying their hands on Havel, by what he says in the following passage, which is repeated by Dienstbier in his epilogue:

The roots of my controversial attitude are not only based on the structure of the concrete 'nonego' into which I was thrown by fate, but are in fact also on a much deeper plane in my relationship with 'the world as a whole'. If I were a West German, for example, I would probably be involved at this time [February 1982] amongst many other things, in preventing the construction of the new runway at Frankfurt, in collecting signatures against the siting of Pershing II and Cruise missiles, and in voting for the 'Green Party'. I feel deep down inside that the long-haired young people who do this and whom I am able to see almost every day on television are my brothers and sisters, which is a new experience for me, moreover: during my visit to the USA in 1968, I rarely felt so much at ease as in the company of the revolutionary youth.

Beware, you who would take precipitate action, for here speaks a rebel, one of the quite dangerous kind, the gentle and courteous kind.

Review of Václav Havel's Letters to Olga *published in German* Briefe an Olga, Identität und Existenz, Betrachtungen aus dem Gefängnis; *translated by Joachim Bruss, Reinbek bei Hamburg: Rowohlt, 1984. First published in* Die Zeit, *No. 37 of 7 September 1984. Now in Heinrich Böll,* Die Fähigkeit zu trauern, Schriften und Reden 1983–1985, *Lamuv Verlag 1985.*

3

Timothy Garton Ash:
Prague – a poem, not disappearing

'Karel is out', she says. 'You know he works during the day. I mean', she blushes, 'of course he does his real work at night. Work – bricklaying. Real work – writing. You know, if you earn your living by writing, it's regarded as quite suspicious and, well, almost unworthy.'

Now here is a room full of writers, few of whom do anything so – unworthy. They sit around, feet in slippers, drinking wine and swapping jokes about Chernobyl. They have just produced the best journal of new writing in Czechoslovakia. It took about twenty minutes. This is how it's done. Once a month they meet for a small 'party' at somebody's flat. The invited guests bring, instead of (perhaps as well as) a bunch of flowers, twenty copies of their latest text. (Most are carbon copies. It is a recognized fact that twelve is the largest number of legible copies achievable at one typing. Twelve is therefore the *samizdat* unit of reckoning – the 'writer's dozen'. A few *samizdat* texts are photocopied, although all photocopiers are closely controlled by the state.) The editorial meeting then has only one task: to decide the order of texts and type the contents page, also in twenty copies. This done, the texts are arranged in order in twenty blank cardboard folders, with the contents page on top and – presto – you have the Czech *Granta*. For the purposes of literary criticism it is a journal called *Contents*. For those of police search or legal defence, it is a miscellaneous collection of typewritten papers in a blank folder. If students want to sit up half the night typing further copies, that is their own business. (They do.) If Czech exiles in the West want to reissue *Contents* in print (they do), how can the writers prevent them? And if people want to bring these printed copies back to Prague, what on earth can the poor writers do? Grin and bear it.

The old Jewish cemetery. The famous tomb of Rabbi Löw, its pale grey-pink coping decorated with beautiful Hebrew script. 'Rabbi Löw', says the guide to a party of German tourists, 'is reputed to be able to grant your wishes. Just write your wish on a piece of paper and tuck it into that corner of the tomb.' She points to a crack beneath the coping, already stuffed with wish-papers. The party looks blank-faced, bored, not even embarrassed. (Germans, Jewish cemetery . . .) 'Don't you have a wish?' says a fat-faced *Hausfrau* to a muscular young man with an artificial suntan. 'No,' says the young man sadly, 'he couldn't grant *my* great wish.' 'What's that?' 'To change places with my boss.'

The Olšany cemetery. Here, every year, in January, young Czechs light candles and lay wreaths with the simple message 'We remember' on one modest grave. The headstone declares this to be the grave of Marie Jedličková. Who was Marie Jedličková? I don't know. Her mourners don't know either. All they know is that seventeen years ago a young man was buried in this grave. His name was Jan Palach and he immolated himself to bear witness against the Soviet occupation. To extinguish his memory the Husák regime subsequently had his remains removed to a country churchyard, and put the unknown Marie J in his place. But Palach's mourners will not be cheated. So every year, on the anniversary of his self-immolation in January 1969, they light candles before the tombstone of an unknown stranger.

Remembering and forgetting.

Early evening. A cellar beneath a ponderous red-brick, nineteenth-century office building, now part of the Ministry of Culture. The cellar contains a grimy strip of carpet, two easy chairs (one with springs), an old office desk, a camp bed, a tin percolator, a typewritter, and a piano which looks as if it first saw service at the Café Europa in 1896. On the walls, a newspaper portrait of Stalin surrounded by his adoring subjects, *circa* 1951, and a black wire silhouette of a girl, *circa* 1963, with breasts that can only be described as proud. A dirty T-shirt hangs from one nipple. Through a small skylight I see the rain splashing off the cobbles on the street outside, but in here it is dry and very warm, thanks to the huge coal-fired boiler in the next room.

My host, courteously ushering me to the chair with springs, starts to discuss the philosophy of Hayek. At one point he says: 'You know – but this is a *private* conversation isn't it? You won't tell my friends?' 'No, of course not.' 'Well, you know I have to say that I myself don't entirely reject *all* elements of socialism.' When he left university he knew there was no chance of pursuing an academic career in his subject, and remaining honest. So he decided to become a stoker. It gives him time for his real work – philosophy. Income: small. Prospects: none. Spirit: unbroken.

'Now, would you like to hear my rags?' he asks, after two hours' quiet argument. He sits down at the old piano and starts to pound out 'the Sting'. Then 'Bohemia' – 'our national rag'. Against the white keys, I notice how his fingernails are broken and black from shovelling coal. He's not really a good player – he wouldn't pass muster in any jazz club in New York City – but endless practice has brought him up to an impressive tempo, and his playing, here, is somehow electrifying. It has a kind of defiant ferocity. I see him pounding out 'Bohemia'. I see the music leap out of the basement skylight, like an escaping genie, force its way up through the pouring rain, giving the two-fingers salute to the Ministry of Culture as it passes, and then up, up, high above the sodden city, above the smoke from his boiler's chimney, above the rain clouds, the two fingers turn the other way now, proclaiming V for victory.

When you've spent a few days in this world turned upside down, among the writers turned bricklayer or window cleaner, between the philosopher–stoker and the poet–dustman, you inevitably start playing the 'if' game. Philip Roth does it in his *Prague Orgy*: 'I imagine Styron washing glasses in a Penn Station bar-room, Susan Sontag wrapping buns at a Broadway bakery, Gore Vidal bicycling salamis to school luncheons in Queens – I look at the filthy floor and see myself sweeping it.' Anyone can play. Just insert your own favourite characters. End up with yourself. 'Me? Oh, me I'd be cleaning lavatories. Sure. I wouldn't last five minutes under a dictatorship. Fascist or communist – they'd never publish *me*.' But hold on: what makes you so sure? Maybe they would and maybe you (we, I) wouldn't. Maybe you (we, I) would still be – perish the thought – published writers. And then, what about all these official publishers and literary journals? Their former editors are all working as window cleaners, or in exile. But who edits them now? Somebody must. Window cleaners? It would be more fun if they did. But the answer is: writers, journalists, men of letters. Second or third rate, semi-literate and corrupt writers, to be sure, but are there none such in our own literary establishments?

Here's the other half of the 'if' game, the half we leave out because it's not so pretty. It would be invidious to name names. Come on, let's be invidious: 'I imagine—editing the *New York Review*,—taking over at the *TLS*,—getting a rave review from—, and—being published after making his self-criticism on television.' And why not: 'I look at this bookshop, and see my books adorning its front window'?

The Waldstein Inn. A stranger is placed at my table. About sixty. Stooping. Thick spectacles. Signet but no wedding ring. A mouthful of expensive gold fillings. He speaks an excellent, old fashioned German, which matches his fillings. He is a picture restorer, works near here, lives on his own. From a good family, I guess, perhaps even a noble one – the waiter treated him with a quite unusual deference. No, he says, there's no good picture restoration done in Czechoslo-vakia any more. No good painting either. No good professors at the art schools. There were some but they died. Now it's 'all stupidity', '*alles Eselei, Eselei*'. But aren't there still some good *writers*? '*Ach, wissen sie*, nothing they produce today can stand comparison with Shakespeare or Goethe. Though, of course', he adds cautiously, 'not everything Goethe wrote was up to scratch.' But is there really nothing more recent that is worth reading? '*Ach, wissen Sie*,' he sighs, 'a few things by Thomas Mann are just about possible (*einiges von Thomas Mann geht gerade*), but apart from that . . .'

What they all resent about Milan Kundera – and how! – is not, I think, his extraordinary success (perhaps that, a little, too), but his stylized nightmare vision of a Prague from which, by definition, no good thing can come. No, they say, the Prague in which we live and work is *not* a 'Biafra of the spirit'. One well-known writer (the gentlest of men) tells me Kundera has to justify to himself 'the fact that he ran away' (though he immediately adds: 'no, these are not the right words, "ran away", that's too strong'). And the self-justification, as for so many exiles, comes by depicting what you have left behind as hell – and, incidentally, painting how it was before as heaven. It wasn't heaven then. It isn't hell now.

I am determined to visit Václav Havel. It's not easy. He is staying at his remote farmhouse in northern Bohemia. It has no telephone. I am told the police will try to prevent such a visit. I set off early in the morning in a hired car. After two hours' driving, as I pass through a small town, there are suddenly three police cars in front of me, lights flashing. I am guided on to the verge. *Damn*! Three cars seem a little excessive. And how on earth did they *know*? Then I notice that other cars are being waved down too. This has nothing to do with me or Havel. We are all being stopped for a bicycle race. I watch as gaggles of prune-faced youngsters come whizzing by on their racing bikes. A *Tour de Bohème*. A banner in the window of the local toy shop says 'Socialism – is a child's smile'.

Off again, now winding up narrow lanes towards the Sudeten mountains, through the damp Bohemian pine woods; turn a corner, there is the house – and there are the police, a Lada estate parked right across the drive, two uniformed officers, one in plain clothes. Their eyes follow me as I drive past, inwardly cursing. Fortunately, however, I have about me my WITS, one of those marvels of Western science, which, like satellite television and the word processor, will confound the secret police and undermine the whole Soviet bloc. Activating my WITS, I become invisible, and only rematerialize inside the inner courtyard of the farmhouse.

Havel is a short, stocky man with curly blond hair; his moustache and lower face remind me of a friendly walrus. He is dressed entirely in shades of damask – slippers, cord trousers, and a T-shirt which declares 'Temptation is GREAT'. (His latest play is called *Temptation*.) He is warm, intense, a concentration of nervous energy. He tells me the police turned up yesterday evening and have been there ever since. 'When this happens it's usually because there is a Western visitor in Prague. Genscher or somebody.' He has been listening to Radio Free Europe and the BBC, trying to discover who it might be.

He talks about the nervous strain of writing under these conditions, when at any moment the police might walk in and confiscate a year's work. How he has crept out into the woods at night and buried parts of his typescript in the hole of a tree. How as a manuscript piles up he writes faster and faster: the fear of a house search concentrates the mind wonderfully. Far more effective than any publisher's deadline. Just yesterday he was writing about this nervous tension. Then his wife came in and said 'The police are outside again. I'm afraid they aren't our usual ones.' And so he got nervous about writing about the nervous strain of writing when . . .

This is nothing compared with the conditions under which he wrote in prison. There he was not allowed to write at all, except for one letter a week to his wife – maximum four sides, and only about 'personal matters', as the prison regulations specify. This was his only opportunity to express himself as a writer, over a period of almost four years. If any part of a letter was unacceptable, the whole letter would be confiscated. The commandant of the prison camp at Hermanice took a sadistic delight in enforcing these instructions. This commandant was an old man, nearing retirement. His great days had been the 1950s, when he had more than a thousand political prisoners – bishops, professors, former government ministers – on whom to exercise his will. Things had never been as good since. Worst of all in 1968. A little better since the invasion. But now, at last, he once again had some famous political prisoners, educated men, a writer, a journalist, a philosopher, to bully and abuse. His particular delight was censoring the writer's letters. Havel started writing a 'cycle' of letters about his philosophical views. He mentioned the 'order of being'. 'The only order you can write about', declared the commandant, 'is the prison order'. Then he decided Havel should not write about philosophy at all. 'Only about yourself.' So Havel designed another cycle of letters on the subject of his moods: sixteen of them, two to each letter, one good, one bad. And he numbered them. After eight, the commandant called him in: 'Stop numbering your moods!' 'No foreign words!' he ordered one week. 'No underlining!' the next. 'No exclamation marks!!'

The book written under these circumstances – for Havel conceived the series of letters to his wife as a book – is marvellous. Much of if consists of his philosophical reflections. In Havel's conception these were perhaps the most important part of the book. Yet for me, and I suspect for most of his readers, they are actually the least compelling passages: partly because, since he was not allowed to keep copies of his earlier letters, there is a great deal of repetition and recapitulation, partly because he had to write in a fearfully convoluted and elliptical way to smuggle his *pensées* past the commandant. Instead of writing 'the regime', for example, he had to write something like 'the social-collective manifestation of the not-I'. Havel laughingly tells me that when he rereads some of his deepest passages today, he hardly knows what he was talking about. (A warning to over-clever critics.) No, what makes this book so compelling is the incidental detail of prison life – the elaborate rituals that surround the drinking of tea, toasting the New Year in a foaming glass of soluble aspirin – and the intense personal detail of his relationship with his wife – as a present, he makes her a piece of jewellery out of dried bread . . . 'I have tried to give it a touch of *Jugendstil*'; above all it is the self-portrait of the writer, setting himself tasks for his four years in prison ('. . . 3 To write at least four plays. 4 To improve my English. 5 To learn German at least as well as I currently know English. 6 To study the whole Bible thoroughly.'), fretting about his health, fretting about old friends outside and, sounding through it all, again and again, his overwhelming determination to remain a *writer*, though he has only four pages a week and each word he chooses can endanger the whole work. ('Last week's letter did not come off' he writes – meaning, it was confiscated.) A portrait of the artist as prisoner.

Early in his imprisonment, in 1979, Havel writes several times about a 'Faust' play that he is mentally reworking. This is the piece which, seven years later, has its première in Vienna under the title *Temptation*. Like most of his plays, he has never seen it performed. He reads the reviews. Friends telephone from Vienna. And during rehearsals, the actors call him with questions which show that they have not *exactly* understood the piece. In this case, they ring up a few days before opening and ask 'Oh, by the way, is there really black magic in Czechoslovakia?' (Well, it *is* a communist country.) Yet this is what he regards as his real work. The rest, his political activity, his essays, his letters from prison, his role as a moral and political authority for thousands of Czechs and Slovaks (and by no means only those actively engaged in opposition), an authority which no writer in the west enjoys; all this is secondary. His real work is writing plays.

Since, unlike Havel, I can travel to Vienna, I go to see *Temptation*. His fears about the limited understanding of the Viennese company are justified. The director of the academic institute in which Havel's Dr Faustka works, a deeply corrupt party placeman, is played as if he was the manager of a

department store in the Kärntnerstrasse. And yet, and yet
. . . however heavily I discount for the Viennese factor, I still
cannot avoid a deeper disappointment. The play, even as
Havel has written it, is weak. And it is weak, it seems to me,
for reasons directly related to his situation. For a start, the
dramaturgy and the stage effects envisaged in his very
detailed stage directions are stilted, and if not stilted, then
dated – all stroboscopes and smoke, *circa* 1966. Not surprising, if you consider that he has been unable to work in a
theatre for eighteen years. The dénouement is desperately
predictable, and predictably political: the Mephisto figure
(called Fistula) turns out to be working for the secret police.
Despite some grimly amusing dialogue, which survives even
the Viennese production, most of the action is so carefully
plotted, and so obviously pointed, as to be quite schematic. It
feels like a plan for a play rather than the play itself. Not
surprising, when you consider that it was planned and
replanned through almost four years in prison. The thing is
overcooked.

So what of George Steiner's 'muse of censorship'? Here is a
rather clear case, it seems to me, of an artist's work being
deformed and diminished by censorship and persecution. If
he were a poet, it might be otherwise. But the playwright
needs his theatre as a musician needs his instrument. Not
merely the artist, the art has suffered. Yet at the same time,
through that persecution and that censorship, or rather,
through his defiance of it, he has produced a volume of
letters, and a body of essays, that will, I think, be read long
after *Temptation* is forgotten. And what will then be known as
his real work?

*This is part of a longer text which was originally published
in* Granta.

4

Jiří Gruša: Ex-prophets and storysellers

Whether he's the type of latter-day prophet found east of the
Prater, or the – shall we say – seller of tales found west of the
Prater, the man of letters likes to talk of his integrity. He
dreams of his integrity as though it were *Paradise Lost*. But
ever since he began seeking another paradise, this time on
earth, his dreams have been more or less in vain. It seems to
me there is a connecting link between the two.

The monk, or lord, of yesteryear, predecessors of today's
man of letters, were wont to write more naturally, the former
to the greater glory of God, the latter as time and inclination
took him. While we, the sons and daughters of a solid middle
class, write to fulfil ourselves.

We believe stubbornly that there must be something good
inside us that only needs to be brought out. It suffices, we
say, just to have the will. Nurtured on this belief, we have
lent ourselves to all the mechanisms of disintegration of the
last two centuries. There is no piece of tastelessness we have
not helped to cook up. Our inclination towards the prophetic
(again in that spirit of self-fulfilment) was a welcome
assistance to the work of renovation when the present was
used to destroy the past, when we set about laying down that
brave new world like a broad avenue stretching into the
future.

We were to be the prophets of a sanitized new megapolis in
which the people, free at last, would live each according to
his or her need. And, of course, this people would be
composed of children like ourselves, gifted minds who can
turn to writing interminable tales of self-fulfilment. With the

discovery that the megapolis was more like a megacamp and that our services were needed less and less the closer it came to being realized, sobriety caught up with us. Particularly in the land east of the Prater, where nowadays you find only ex-prophets.

West of that great Viennese pleasure park we still lack that sobriety, but we make up for it in domesticity. They've found a wonderful placebo: they want our words, but they want them merely as merchandise for the market. So we are ex-prophets too, unwitting, guileless ex-prophets. Getting to that stage was a hard slog. The yearned-for integrity somehow didn't measure up to the myth of self-fulfilment.

In the lands where tales are sold we yearn after those prophetic times like havens of integrity. We who must offer our words like wares cast envious glances in the direction of our brothers in the east. And this leads to misunderstanding. For those prophetic traits of our brothers in the east are paradoxically simple traits of a passionate anti-prophecy. Don't be deceived by their occasionally overdone gestures or baroque choice of phrase. Don't be deceived by their own life story, so full of dramatic narrative itself, so full in fact that both literary imagination and those twin false gods of the world of merchandise, originality and creativity, have nothing on offer to compete with it. Those in the east really only bear witness to the essential ambivalence of Western literary modes. They remind us of what we already know or can discover, if we take the trouble to explore all the sources of our writing, including the dark ones.

People like myself, who have known both worlds – the world of the ex-prophets and that of the word-vendors – are surprised at how little the West (which considers itself the best) takes account of this ambivalence. In the West, it's automatically assumed that writing has to do with decency – and integrity.

A man sobered out of his prophesying may well become a preacher of slowly dying passions. But he is never likely to become a scintillating super-commentator of the kind you come across in the West. The world of commentators is the kingdom of the safe insurance, a kingdom in which the strange incident, the sudden and the unexpected are regarded as mishaps. Therefore, where there is a dearth of good tales to tell you can well understand this desire to produce commentaries on anything and everything. And here we get back to our old *hubris*.

Even ex-prophets understandably try now and again to market a story, usually their own. And when they don't succeed because the story happens to be too true, they revile the corruption of the West (just as I'm doing now), often aiming at quite the wrong targets. They are arrogant and vain and they well know the dark side of writing. Nevertheless when we talk of the integrity of writing let us not forget their experience.

When we come to consider literature in exile let us not forget that it was Western (in the meaning of the culture common to us all, thus including the East) men of letters who were godfathers to the ideas which have driven people from their homelands. And when we talk of censorship let us never forget it was we who glorified the modern state, first as the embodiment of all that was godly, then as the ultimate source of all welfare. So we should not be surprised when it takes an interest in what we write even before we've lifted the pen. And when we consider the identity of literature let us not forget the myth about self-fulfilment which knows only one identity – the ego. Thus the principle of self-preservation and the extension of existence at all costs: no wonder our works are turning more and more into textbooks *à la* 'The joy of . . .' something or other. And when we come to dwell on the rights of minorities let us never forget our underlying contempt for all majorities, our provocations and our abuse of the public at large, our theories on whether a majority should be considered simply a numerical one or a real one. And finally, when we come to speak of the right to one's history, let us never lose sight of the fact that our patriotic odes are to be found in all the school-books of Europe, works which played such an important part in the catastrophe of this continent because they were the first to see history as the El Dorado of nationalism.

But I exaggerate. I know there were those who, in the struggle with the illusion of unlimited originality and creativity, fulfilled something more than just themselves.

But it is not they I'm talking about today. It has been my intention to invoke a certain scepticism, a necessary scepticism, which should be employed when we leaf through that favourite comic book of ours we call Progress. A message from the fields and glades where we prophets dwell. In acquiring such scepticism we might yet create the basic conditions for a world (and thank God we still live in a world in which a story can be enjoyed without the storyteller having to be offered up as a sacrifice to some bloody tribal idol) in which ex-prophets will not just be left to sink into the parochialism of their loneliness.

For Václav Havel, the great prophet of anti-prophecy, who couldn't himself come to Budapest where this speech was delivered.

5

Ladislav Hejdánek: From variations and reflections on topics in Václav Havel's prison letters

At the end of one of his letters, No. 62, Václav Havel wrote a warning valid not only for his wife, to whom the letter was addressed, but indeed to anyone who might read this particular message from prison, or any of the others. So I must immediately apologize for deciding to ignore that warning, and try to explain my reasons. What Václav Havel said was this:

> . . . you mustn't take these and similar meditations too literally; they are only attempts to capture something of the flow of my feelings and inner thoughts; sometimes I map them out with these formulations, at other times I may employ entirely different ones; I'm no philosopher and it is not my ambition to construct a conceptually fixed system; anyone who tries to understand it that way will soon discover that I am perpetually contradicting myself, that I leave many things unexplained, or I explain them differently each time, etc. etc.

If I have to agree – with every regret at such a waste of talent – that Václav Havel is no philosopher, he in turn must accept – with relief, no doubt – that I am no writer or poet. But for any thinking man his letters, or the reflections contained in them, are a challenge to meditation and self-questioning. Though they do not expound philosophy, they certainly raise exceptionally weighty philosophical issues. I hope neither Václav Havel nor anyone else will see in the pages that follow signs of professional arrogance. But the appropriate reaction, the 'answer' to Havel was, I thought, to put my cards on the table as openly as he had done. Unlike him (compare his letter No. 100) I am not troubled by a yearning for finality; I write best when not committed to a definitive statement, and make no such claims for these 'variations and reflections'.

It's a kind of paradox – I think I mentioned it during your last visit – that I, of all people, such a lover of harmony, who wants everyone to like each other and to be kind to each other – must live my entire life, in fact, in conflict, tension and nerve-racking situations. [Letter No. 40]

The real paradox lies deeper than the mere fact that people do not achieve their dreams. Human life remains formless if undirected toward any goal. The goal may, as Broch says, be either finite or infinite. A life directed toward a finite goal, or rather toward finite goals, has only a relative and partial form, possibly only a stunted and fragmented one. This is apparent when despite the achievement of finite ends a life is still unfulfilled, unsatisfied, 'unredeemed'. Orientation toward an infinite goal, by contrast, means by definition that it can never be attained, but such a life is endowed with the fulfilment that comes not from reaching its goal but, precisely, from falling ever short of it. The quality of this falling short is, of course, different in a life dedicated only to finite ends, and in one where every relationship to finite ends is controlled by, and subordinated to, the pursuit of infinite ones. One finite project will integrate one part of a man's life, another finite project will integrate another part, but none can effect the integration of a complete human existence, of a life as a single whole. An acute awareness of this leads some people into a special subterfuge by which they defraud and deceive others, incidentally, but primarily themselves. The trick consists in persuading themselves that some aptly chosen finite goal is in fact an infinite one. The aptly chosen finite goal may create the illusion of an infinite goal, and this illusion can in effect integrate their lives. But this kind of integrity, based on a false infinite goal, though real enough, is never genuine – it can only be a false integrity.

What kind of harmony can its devotees be seeking? If we were to accept without further thought the formulation about wanting everyone to 'be fond of each other and kind to each other', we would risk lapsing into the climate of religious revivalism or of escapist communities weary of life's conflicts. But these and suchlike remedies are only partial ones, since at best such communities can only bring about mutual fondness and kindness among a limited number of people, namely those who have withdrawn to their latter-day Kunvald* from the labyrinth of worldly strife. The infinite goal of the apostle of harmony, that *all* men should love one another, would thus have been replaced by the finite aim of 'universal' love between members of a new group that had turned its back on the world and its battles. But no real advocate of harmony amongst all men would or could accept such a substitution: his objective is truly universal concord, not concord within a restricted group that meet and join forces just to exercise reciprocal fondness and kindness among its members.

Again, to try and universalize the 'Kunvald' experiment and apply it to everyone would be an equally false solution. Either it would have only a superficial success, involving disgruntlement or even refusal to take life's problems seriously enough, or else it would amount to coercion, with everyone being persuaded or, if that failed, compelled to be kind and affectionate. The fanaticism of 'universal love' leads inevitably to two things directly contrary to love: hatred and – still worse perhaps – simulated love. For it is no more possible to force people into love than to force them into freedom. (Existentialist talk of being 'condemned to freedom' is either a recherché paradox or an intellectual contortion.) All we can do with love and freedom is offer them to others or rather, since neither is really ours to offer, point them out, inform others, that is, that love and liberty are available for

---

*a village in north-east Bohemia where the first community of Czech Brethren was founded in 1456.

them to choose, and therefore constitute a challenge. But harmony, a challenge? That would have to be an infinite goal!

Orientation of one's life toward an infinite goal can only be achieved – and then only in a given situation, always subject to renewal, never for good and all – in the context of a daily life committed necessarily to innumerable ends that are finite, and conditioned by other ends and so relative, but nevertheless binding for the moment. Which means that commitment to a finite aim must confront those other commitments, conflict with them repeatedly, and very often sustain defeats and setbacks – yet never, never go totally under. A life committed to an infinite end, however, is not even finally defeated in death. Not by any means, of course, that it can overcome death. Life is not capable of that, but it is capable of robbing death of its victory. Yet to snatch victory from the hands of death, or of chaos (as against harmony) or of hatred (as against love) and so on does not mean engaging in a struggle or battle or making mighty efforts and getting into all kinds of unpleasant conflicts, strains and nerve-racking situations. This is quite logical – neither contrary to logic nor even paradoxical. The paradox lies elsewhere.

Experience shows that harmony advocated and effected by human effort and organization either increases the sum of disharmony – paying for the achievement of harmony in one field, that is, by draining it off, or positively upsetting it, in others – or else simply collapses. And only then, from the wreckage, does a real harmony emerge, not for good and all but as a bonus, a gift, as the experience of something which it is in no man's power to bring about deliberately, yet which can never emerge without his labour, his efforts and commitment. Harmony as an infinite goal emerges on its own, here and now, not at the end of the course – but emerges only when people strive for it, yearn for it, love it and embark for its sake on undertakings where they willingly shoulder all the preliminaries, and fulfil the conditions, for its emergence. It is precisely here that the paradox arises. Genuine harmony never comes to those who seek it for themselves, and for their own group – which always comes to the same thing – but only to those who seek it for others, even at the cost of discord, conflicts, strains and nerve-racking situations for themselves, and their group.

Václav Havel finds it strange, indeed more than strange, that he, who is so fond of harmony, must live practically his entire life amid conflicts and stresses of one kind or another. Speaking purely for myself, let me say that it is just this deplorable circumstance that gives his love of harmony a convincing ring of truth for those who, like him, take harmony seriously enough to live their lives too amid conflicts and stresses. More than that, I feel empowered to tell Václav Havel that his sensitivity as an essayist and playwright gives him not only a heavier, but a more glorious cross to bear than any which we others carry. For it will sometimes result, not merely in things getting on his nerves, in his being intolerant, in his experiencing everything excessively and taking it to heart – it will enable him to savour more often and more intensely the real harmony which instead of trying to acquire for himself and his friends he has helped to prepare the way for, so that it should be granted to others, to the rest of us. Primarily, of course, to those who likewise live amidst stress and conflict. But in the last resort to everybody, as a hope and a promise.

Václav Havel's stresses and conflicts contribute, imponderably but genuinely, to the alleviation of our own difficulties and help us carry our own crosses. Indeed, is it not the case that Václav Havel – and others whom I must not forget at this point – have explicitly carried certain burdens on our behalf? And do they not continue to? Was he not chosen as a sacrificial representative, not so much to redeem the rest of us as to intimidate us? What has happened to the world-famous playwright could happen even more easily to people the world knows nothing about. It would have lent great point to the threat if Václav Havel had opted to go straight from prison into exile abroad. We are grateful that the point could not be made. We are grateful that Václav opted to remain with those strains and conflicts which he could never accommodate himself to, and never will. The situation

ontinues and cannot be otherwise, and will evidently remain
o. We are more than grateful, even if it all seems strange,
ery strange, to him.

But is it really?

*he above is a translation of the first of the author's five 'Variations
nd reflections on topics from Václav Havel's prison letters', together
vith part of his introduction.*

6

Harry Järv: Citizen *versus* state

For Václav Havel

Plato says that only Socrates possessed an 'inner voice' tha
warned him against carrying out unfitting actions.

If one reads the passages where the phenomenon i
described, one finds that it is not only a question of unethica
actions but also such as are harmful to him in a concrete
sense. Socrates himself used the word *daimonion*, deity, to
describe this 'inner voice'. There are many interpretations o
Socrates' *daimonion*, but I believe it is simply a question o
what we now call conscience.

Plato's remark that only Socrates had a *daimonion*, a
conscience, is puzzling only to those who think that consci
ence is something eternally and unchangeably the same in al
people, whether its source be biological or supernatural. I
this is not the case, and in my opinion it is not, then Plato
may to some extent be right: the Greek religion contained no
controversial elements of faith, neither did it constitute fertile
soil for emotionally tinged piety, which in turn leads to
conflicts of conscience and sectarian separations, of which
there are so many examples in the history of religion. As long
as the majority of citizens unreflectingly accept the prevalen
conceptions of faith, no problems will arise.

At the time of Socrates there was not yet a Greek word for
'conscience'; not until about a hundred years later was the
word *syneidesis* used by the Epicureans to denote this
phenomenon. It was later adopted by the evangelists in the
New Testament. But both the Sophists and Socrates began to
question old conceptions. The Sophists' doctrines were
highly individualistic and personal, going far beyond the

boundaries of egoism. Socrates attacked the Sophists, but he too was so individualistic that the contemporary comedy writer, Aristophanes, caricatured him as a hair-splitting and greedy Sophist. He was concerned with ethical problems and with individual free will, thus coming into conflict with the ethics of society that were based on conformism. Socrates himself said that his *daimonion* prevented him from participating in politics; he was obviously well aware of the lack of agreement between individual conscience and the demands of the state.

Yet he accepted his death sentence. He could have saved his life by demanding exile as an alternative punishment, but refused to take advantage of this possibility. He also refused to escape from prison, although his friends had prepared for this; he was guided by his *daimonion* and proved to Crito that it would be wrong to flee.

Although Socrates maintained the supremacy of the individual conscience, he accepted extreme measures on the part of the state authorities as a guarantee for social order. His disciple Plato, who has been mainly responsible for our picture of Socrates, says (also in *Crito*) that Socrates used to praise the constitutions of Sparta and Crete, which were both authoritarian (although he preferred to live in Athens), and Plato himself drew up the ideological model for a state that was first realized by Stalin and Hitler.

'Law and order' are not sufficient criteria for a good society. For this one must have *good* law and order. This allows for any amount of disputes on questions of values. Continual discussion is necessary. Laws can be unjust and harmful. There are at the present time thousands of millions of human beings, each with a historically developed private conscience. The possibilities of conflict are legion.

Plato's pronouncement that only Socrates had a private conscience is undermined by the fact that, in 442 BC, Socrates could have seen Sophocles' tragedy *Antigone* performed at the Dionysos theatre in Athens; he was at that time twenty-eight years old. In *Antigone* the dilemma of conflicting loyalties is shown vividly. In accordance with her religion

Antigone has a duty to bury her brother Polyneikes, whereas the state, represented by the Theban ruler Creon has decreed

> that no one in this town
> may give him burial or mourn for him.
> Leave him unburied, leave his corpse disgraced,
> a dinner for the birds and for the dogs.*

Antigone chooses to follow her private conscience and buries her brother. She refers to

> the gods' unwritten and unfailing laws.
> Not now, nor yesterday's, they always live.

In comparison to them, the commands of Creon, 'a mortal man', cannot weigh so heavily.

The drama has often been interpreted as an attempt by Sophocles to contrast a representative of Western humanity – 'I cannot share in hatred, but in love' – with a tyrant who is blindly guided by the interests of governmental power. Hegel saw the drama as a tragic conflict between the absolute right of the state and the equally absolute right of the family (though he thought that Antigone was to some extent in the wrong when she refused to obey the law); the two forces crush each other because they are incompatible. But this would not be a tragic conflict in the classical sense, which requires a conflict between justified but incompatible forces in the same person. However, this aesthetic requirement is met in the tragedy, and in both the main characters. Creon is not just the personification of blind, evil power; he has the legitimate role of ruler, but does not master it. His inadequacy is revealed when he is confronted with Antigone. Neither is she a perfect representative of the divine, infallible conscience, but is broken down by her arrogance, her *hubris* (a fundamental defect according to Greek ethics); this is demonstrated by her brusque treatment of her weaker sister

---

* The quoted passages from *Antigone* are from the translation by Elizabeth Wyckoff.

Ismene and her death-lament, in which she reveals the limitations of her humanity: she says that she would not have defied the state for the sake of a child or husband – these can be replaced – but only for her irreplaceable brother:

> Had I had children or their father dead,
> I'd let them moulder. I should not have chosen
> in such a case to cross the state's decree.

In an analysis from the 1920s (by John Dickinson) Antigone's attitude is judged primitive and that of Socrates mature, because he obeyed the law to his death. Even so, Socrates has put into words the essence of what nowadays is called 'civil disobedience'. Citizens must be prepared to sacrifice their lives for the state that has educated and nourished both them and their parents before them, they must accept any punishment that is given, both just and unjust. But in one domain they are immune from the demands of the state: their personal conscience. Socrates was prepared to *suffer* unjustly, but the Athenian state could not force him to *act* unjustly.

'An unjust law is no law', said Aristotle. Yet the consequence of this pronouncement was not drawn until the middle of the nineteenth century, when Henry David Thoreau created the concept of 'civil disobedience'.

On several occasions in 1848 Thoreau gave a speech on 'the individual's relationship to the state', which was published in 1849 under the title 'Resistance to Civil Government'. The better known title, 'Civil Disobedience', was not used for the text until 1866.

Thoreau had spent a night in jail in Concord, Massachusetts, for refusing to pay tax, his reasons being that the US was waging an imperialistic war against Mexico and that its attitude to the question of slavery was unacceptable. His basic proposition was that all governments – including those that are democratically elected – can become corrupted by abuse of power. The integrity of all governments depends on the individual citizen's feeling of responsibility. 'There will never be a really free and enlightened state until the state comes to recognize the individual as a higher and independent power, from which all its own power and authority are derived, and treats him accordingly.'

Thoreau sets the individual conscience against majority decisions, the individual's sense of justice against the law. When a government acts unjustly in the name of the state – as the US does when it wages an unjust war of conquest and keeps human beings in slavery – then every individual person with better judgement must offer moral resistance to the state. This is an extremely individualistic, anarchistic point of view. The motto for his speech was: 'That government is best which governs least.'

Goethe had formulated a similar but more exacting maxim: 'That government is best which teaches us to govern ourselves.'

'Civil Disobedience' did not excite interest when it was published, but it is the first text that theoretically propounds the individual's right against the state.

It is usual to point out a weakness in Thoreau's reasoning – and the criticism applies to all who criticize the state – namely that the boundary between an ordered society and anarchy is diffuse and easily crossed. In this context anarchy is used as a synonym for lack of order, chaos. But anarchy does not mean chaos but freedom from rulers. Anarchy in its true, etymological sense needs no motivation; it is self-evident. There is no reason of any weight that justifies that one person shall rule over another.

Thoreau's one-man struggle against the state cost him one night's freedom. He would have been spared even that if the jailer, Sam Staples, had not already taken off his boots when his daughter told him that someone had left an envelope containing the money for Thoreau's tax debt. Staples could not be bothered to put on his boots again; it would not harm the prisoner to spend the night in the cell, he thought. When Thoreau was let out the following morning he was furious because the shortness of his period in jail had ruined his civil-resistance profile. But that one night was enough to affect the course of history. It was Gandhi's inspiration for his campaign for passive resistance. The same principle was later applied by Martin Luther King. The person who paid Thoreau's tax was probably his aunt, Maria Thoreau. Incidentally, she went on paying it in advance for the rest of Thoreau's life. In 1849 it amounted to $1.50.

Antigone and Socrates paid with their lives.

Writing in 1939, one of Thoreau's biographers, Henry Seidel Canby, wonders how the author of 'Civil Disobedience' would react if he lived in a modern totalitarian state. In his opinion, Thoreau's reaction to totalitarian ideology would be that the great mass of people who support these states might for the moment be irresistible, like an avalanche that cannot be halted.

> The citizen will have to step back and, protecting integrity by any concessions possible to it, endeavor to make the nobler moral fervor prevail. But he would disobey rather than rebel, and wrestle with weakness in himself rather than use violence against the despot in the enemy. Gandhi took such a position. He struck at the pocket book of the state, not at its armies. He refused to conform, but did not attack his rulers.

The totalitarian states Canby alludes to are the Soviet Union and Germany. Since then the number of totalitarian regimes has increased considerably. Among those at the top of the list at the moment are South Africa and Chile.

The Soviet Union's relationship with its citizens is a directive for all states in the Eastern bloc and, therefore, of great importance to many millions of people who actually live beyond the Soviet Union's boundaries.

Freedom of expression, freedom of the press, freedom of assembly and freedom of demonstration are guaranteed to Soviet citizens according to article 50 of the Constitution (the fourth Soviet Constitution in power since 1977; the previous constitutions were also positive in this connection). But there is a reservation: the use of these freedoms must 'agree with the interests of the working class and aim at strengthening the socialist system'. Generally speaking, all rights are subject to the premise that nothing is allowed that may 'harm the interests of society or the state, or other citizens' rights'. In the new constitution there is for the first time a chapter on foreign policy: 'The Soviet Union continues to pursue Lenin's peace policy and aims to further the security of the peoples and to bring about extensive international co-operation.' (Section 1, article 28.)

The Helsinki Agreement, which was signed on 1 August 1975, aims at 'contributing to peace, security, justice and co-operation in Europe'. Host at the conference was Finland's president, Urho Kekkonen, but the initiative was taken by the Soviet Union, whose head of state, Leonid Brezhnev, also signed the document. The document has been signed by representatives of thirty-five states. It was agreed that the text should be published in all participating states, who would 'make it known as widely as possible'. The Soviet Union was the first to meet the last-mentioned stipulation: on 2 August, the day after the document was signed, the full text was published in the Soviet press.

The document raised hopes that the best and most humane of all worlds was to be realized. In the eastern states, however, the section on non-intervention in the internal affairs of other countries has come to be regarded as the principal point of the agreement. It has even been said that the Soviet Union pushed through the agreement in order to legitimate its hegemony of eastern Europe. In that case it can be considered a great success for the Soviet Union's foreign politics, even if it seems an unnecessary precaution. World peace was never in danger when the Soviet Union settled its internal affairs in Hungary in 1956 and in Czechoslovakia in 1968, neither is it threatened by the intervention in Afghanistan's internal affairs (Afghanistan is not, however, protected by the Helsinki Agreement); if it can ride out such crises, one can reasonably assume that its security does not depend on an agreement.

When, in April 1975, Olof Palme called Czechoslovakia's

present leaders 'creatures of dictatorship', the relationship between the two countries became strained, but only for a while. On 21 August 1976, the Swedish foreign minister, Sven Andersson, gave a reminder of what had happened in Czechoslovakia eight years earlier: 'This was a defeat for freedom and democracy. At the same time it showed up the inhumanity of communist society. The answer to citizens' demands for more participation in decision-making and freedom of choice was armed tanks and prison. And still at the present time the people are forced into silence.' This statement – which is still valid now, ten years later – also had the effect of cooling down relationships but did not lead to a serious crisis.

In the Soviet Union, *détente* does not mean a relaxation in ideology, as Brezhnev explained to the French president at that time, Giscard d'Estaing, when he visited Moscow in the autumn after the Helsinki conference. The same opinion was expressed by the member of the politburo, Alfred Pelshe, in a speech held on the anniversary of the October Revolution: 'While our party advocates peaceful coexistence between states, it knows no ideological reconciliation', he said, and pointed out that in the West there are still people who speculate on questions concerning human rights and in this connection shoot critical arrows at Soviet society. 'But they will not succeed in their attempts to find a weak spot here. In this country human rights are highly manifest and effective. They are guaranteed and protected by the socialist system, by a true democracy, more fully and effectively than in any capitalist country.'

All who read the newspapers know that, ever since the agreement was signed, the Soviet Union has reacted very sluggishly on questions of reunification and emigration. Jews in the Soviet Union who have referred to the Helsinki Agreement when they have applied for exit visas have been told by the authorities that 'it does not apply to Jews'. The agreement does not, however, contain one word regarding special negative treatment of Jews; on the contrary, it says that the participating states will respect human rights and fundamental freedoms, including the freedom of thought, conscience, religion or belief, 'for all without distinction as to race, sex, language or religion'.

In 1970, Andrei Sakharov and A. Tverdokhlebov founded the Committee for the Defence of Civil Rights, the first public dissident organization in the Soviet Union.

After the Helsinki conference 'Helsinki groups' were formed, first in Moscow, then in Ukraine, Lithuania, Georgia and Armenia, in order to monitor the Soviet Union's observance of human rights clauses in the agreement. Today they have all been crushed and the leaders are in prison. Punishment has recently hardened; ten to fifteen years in a labour camp and exile is now normal. Yuri Orlov, who founded the first Helsinki group, was interned in a labour camp in the Perm district, as was Ivan Kovalyev, the last effective leader of the group. The Solzhenitsyn Fund for support of the families of political prisoners – Solzhenitsyn's foreign royalties for the Gulag series – has been forced underground since the administrator of the fund in Moscow, Sergei Khodorovich, was arrested, as well as the local administrator in Leningrad, Valeri Repin.

When Yuri Andropov (later, during the last year of his life, leader of the Soviet Union) was head of the KGB he organized the campaign against the civil rights movement. The campaign began in the autumn of 1979 prior to the invasion of Afghanistan and the Olympic Games in Moscow. Since then at least 200 dissidents have been arrested each year; about 900 political prisoners known by name are now in labour camps, but the real figure is higher. According to the accusations, they are 'criminal renegades' and 'betrayers of the fatherland' in the pay of the CIA, who have tried to pull down the foundations of the Soviet Union. When Valeri Repin confessed on Leningrad's local TV in March 1983, and in court some months later, it was declarations of this kind he was made to utter: the activities of the Solzhenitsyn Fund were directed by the CIA, he himself had been an obedient tool of US imperialism, and he begged to be given a severe sentence. (He was, however, given only two years in a camp, followed by three years' exile.'

The civil rights movement has only demanded that the Soviet Union's laws shall be respected.

Gustáv Husák was arrested on 6 February 1951 and sentenced, on 24 April 1954, to life imprisonment and hard labour for high treason and sabotage. He was given amnesty and released on 10 May 1960. Six of those almost ten years had been spent in solitary confinement.

In his petition of 20 December 1962 for a new hearing, he describes the 'violations of the laws of the country' which were 'crowned by an illegal lawsuit and an illegal sentence'. He describes in detail the methods of interrogation, that 'transform many honourable citizens, who are loyal to the party, into spies, saboteurs, traitors, demoralized elements', how the leaders of the interrogations fabricated 'lies and deceptions' that were subsequently used as 'irrefutable evidence'. 'People's will to live was broken down, and the laws of the country were trampled underfoot. Honest people who served communism were driven . . . to the brink of madness and suicide.'

Husák was one of the approximately 18,000 people who applied for rehabilitation. He was rehabilitated in 1963 and regained his party membership, but was not to be allowed to carry out any political function. About 3,500 were in time to obtain full reparation before rehabilitation work ceased when the 'Prague Spring' came to an end. When Husák succeeded Alexander Dubček as Secretary General of the Communist Party on 17 April 1969, he had the following to say about political lawsuits: 'In Slovakia there is an old saying that anyone who wants to go into politics must spend some time in prison. I wish no one such a fate.'

And yet, since he came to power, people have been sent to prison in Czechoslovakia on grounds that he stigmatized in his own petition. The civil rights movement that began to take form in the middle of the seventies referred to the Helsinki Agreement, which was also signed by Husák. The fundamental Charter 77 manifesto of 1 January 1977 states that it does not form the basis for any oppositional political activity; it demands only respect for valid laws, for the Helsinki Agreement, for the UN's Declaration of Human Rights and other documents on freedoms and rights having legal force in Czechoslovakia and which the republic has pledged itself to follow.

The first three spokesmen for Charter 77, who would 'help to make it possible for all citizens in Czechoslovakia to live and work as free people', were Jan Patočka, Václav Havel and Jiří Hájek. These three and all who have signed the manifesto have been defamed and persecuted. 'A rabble of failures', they were called in an article in the Central Committee's official newspaper, *Rudé Právo*, of 12 January 1977: 'millionaire's son V. Havel', 'the failed politician J. Hájek, who under the cloak of neutrality tried to persuade us to leave the fellowship of the socialist camp' and 'the reactionary professor J. Patočka, who is in the service of anti-communism', etc. Charter 77 has been 'commissioned by the centres of anti-communism and Zionism and delivered to certain agents of the West by a small group of people from the ruined reactionary bourgeoisie of Czechoslovakia, but also some bankrupt organizers of the counter-revolution of 1968'.

It is symptomatic that the long article contains no defence against the accusations of violations of socialist laws set out in the Charter 77 manifesto.

Václav Havel was first arrested (together with two other Charter 77 men) when he was on his way to deliver the Charter 77 manifesto to the Czechoslovak government and parliament and to the news agency ČTK.

Havel gave his assurance in the spring of 1977 that he 'would no longer participate in activities that could be punishable' and that he would 'avoid public appearances of a political nature', but that he would not disclaim and would never disclaim his signature to Charter 77. 'Thus, I shall stand up for those who suffer injustice, and endeavour to take advantage of all possibilities that can be judged effective, constructive and in accordance with the Czechoslovak legal system.' Since then he has been arrested so many times that it must be difficult for him to keep count; altogether he has spent about five years in prison.

In the Charter 77 document No. 10 (29 April 1977) Jiří Hájek wrote:

> We are encouraged by the solidarity of communists, socialists and democrats all over the world, who believe in the same thing as Charter 77: respect for human rights and civic freedoms as a prerequisite for true peaceful coexistence and co-operation between different countries irrespective of social system or degree of economic development, as expressed in the Charter of the United Nations, the Universal Declaration of Human Rights and the Final Act of the Helsinki Conference.

Hájek spent the years 1939–45 in a German concentration camp. He was foreign minister in Dubček's government in 1968, but forced to resign after the occupation in August 1968. He was expelled from the Communist Party in 1970 and today he is isolated and under constant surveillance by the security police.

The Charter 77 document No. 10 was signed only by Hájek, since Havel was then in prison and Patočka had died the previous month. Patočka had been seized by the police and subjected to such long and exhausting interrogations that he had to be put in hospital, where he was also interrogated on 10 March 1977. The following day he had a stroke and died on 13 March. A few days earlier, on 8 March, he made a last statement on the citizen's relationship to unjust authorities:

> Accommodation has so far never led to an improvement in a situation, only to a deterioration.
> The greater the fear the servility have been, the greater has the lack of consideration been on the part of the authorities. There is no other way to make them lessen the pressure than to show them that injustice and arbitrariness are not ignored. People must always be dignified, refuse to let themselves be frightened and humiliated, say that which is true – behaviour that will make an impression just because it will be in such sharp contrast to the behaviour of the authorities.

Immanuel Kant showed in a penetrating essay that what is true in theory must also work in practice. It does not require much reflection to see that he was right. Yet a good law does not always work well in practice. How it fails is a complicated and difficult philosophical problem. We know, for instance, that the laws in the Soviet Union and Czechoslovakia are excellent. When Gustáv Husák was confronted with the legal machinery thirty-five years ago, he discovered that it worked scrupulously, pedantically and formalistically: no one was convicted without a signed confession that was properly recorded. He himself made three confessions (after torture) but retracted all three after he had been allowed to rest. He then made it clear to the leader of the interrogation that he would under no circumstances make another false confession. The interrogators then wrote out an eighty-page interrogation report, and asked a few unimportant questions, which Husák answered and signed. 'The three or four pages signed by me were then attached to the eighty pages they and their principal had fabricated. They explained that the whole was an interrogation report that I had signed with my name.' This was the document on which he was sentenced to life imprisonment.

Thus, the problem is really very simple, or at least easy to understand: just to make Kant's theory work. The dissidents know that they 'only' have to make theory and practice agree. In this attempt they behave, as Patočka recommended, with dignity. They will not let themselves be frightened or humiliated.

7

Pavel Kohout:
The chaste centaur
(Havel's Vaněk and Vaněk's Havel)

To Václav Havel on the occasion of his fiftieth birthday

Investigating world drama, a theatre criminologist would be bound to discover a great many instances of theft of character, some of which have even had to be settled in court as plagiarism. To list all the appropriations from authors who, long dead, left their characters to be dealt with at will by their heirs, would prove a nigh impossible task. Except for Ferdinand Vaněk, however, I do not know of any figure playwrights have borrowed with the kind approval of the hero's original father.

I was sitting in Václav Havel's hillside cottage that summer day when, for the 'entertainment of friends', as he remarked with characteristic modesty, he read his one-act play, *Audience*. In it he used the character of Vaněk as a means of describing to us the lot of a brewery worker – his own. With characteristic immodesty, I note that it was I who, after the reading, drew his attention to the fact that he had discovered a vehicle for translating concrete information about concrete people and problems in a concrete period into a dramatic form capable of sustaining life on stage.

The worldwide acclaim received by the play soon proved right both author and listener, the latter – by the same twist of fate that expelled both men from the Czech theatre – also a playwright. And when Vaněk performed equally successfully in a second play, *Private View*, I tentatively asked his creator for permission to use him in recording my own experiences. He agreed not only willingly but actively endorsed the proposal. Out this conversation grew the idea for a jointly composed evening of theatrical entertainment. In the autumn of 1979 the world première of his *Protest* and my *Permit*, collectively named *Tests*, took place in the Akademietheater in Vienna.

By that time Václav Havel was already in jail. As a homage to him I wrote another Vaněk-play, *Morass*, and persuaded our mutual friend, Pavel Landovský, to contribute *Arrest*, yet another play structured around the hero whom we three have come to pass back and forth among us like a challenge cup. This pair we provisionally named *Rests*. Five years later still when, for the first time, I felt the need to reflect in dramatic form the experience of my involuntary stay in the West – a consequence of a trip to Vienna – I added to the sequence my third work, *Safari*.

How can one explain the fact that a writer who has never lacked his own ideas uses a colleague as the basis of a drama – and does so three times? If we disregard my affiliation with a group of authors ruled by the great William and, in our century, presided over by Brecht – both of whom considered the scenic adaptation of the works of others as no less a creative adventure than the treatment of an original theme – I personally see two causes.

Distance in time has confirmed my belief that the initial impulse was generated jointly by the state of society and that of my own life. I was – and feel I still am today, in this other world – a member of a small but amazingly vital community, one forged by far more than the voluntarily chosen and collectively borne lot of exiles in their own country. In this extreme situation people with entirely different personal histories and ideas discovered themselves as well as each other. Without surrendering their own convictions they learned to understand others; without losing the traits of their individuality they found what they have in common.

Although, taken superficially, Václav Havel and I seem almost polar opposites in terms of personality and political inclinations, our friendship has become one of the dominant factors in my life. The nature of our understanding is a topic for another and more important essay, one reflecting on the possibility of a consensus among the whole of Czech society.

The two of us have clearly answered this question in the affirmative, and it appears to me that talking over the character of Ferdinand Vaněk was an expression of my need to meet Václav Havel also in the writer's most intimate sphere – in creation. A Freudian philosopher would probably delight in calling this a manifestation of abnormal sexuality. In fact, through the psychology of his/my hero and with my typewriter as the only tool, I established a much closer and more permanent relationship with my friend than anyone could possibly achieve in bed.

That is why I am certain of the second cause of my attraction to and as yet undiminished relations with the dramatic principle of *Audience*, which has held firm under the threefold pressure added by me. After all, what is the essence of its aesthetics? Vaněk. And what is the essence of Vaněk? Havel. And the essence of Havel?

During the eight long years I have not seen him, half of which he has spent behind bars, the original has surely changed; but the essence is bound to have endured. To describe it as accurately as possible, I must once again resort to intimate vocabulary: chastity. At first, this may sound ridiculous – considering my familiarity with my friend's renaissance personality, his eager penchant for every joy life has to offer. But for a long time I have also known that there is a chastity of a higher order. Both Havel and his fictional twin brother Vaněk have everything that makes a man a man, but they have retained the soul of a child.

Even a child knows how to do wrong, how to hurt, pretend and lie, but to the child these actions are dictated by instant need or emotion, not moral corruption, which is acquired only later. When a child tries to deceive or, more still, to harm, it usually does so with guileless awkwardness, eliciting compassion. A man with the soul of a child does not always elicit compassion in human conflicts, but neither does he forfeit the sympathy of others. Furthermore, in key confrontations such as the one presently taking place in Czechoslovakia, he unconsciously irritates both the bureaucratic (equals police) apparatus as well as the mass of his fellow citizens.

Omnipotent authority is faced with a shy, polite, even obliging intellectual of a visibly non-athletic cast, the like of which it has come to deal with expeditiously, if he be furnished with the soul of an ordinary man – commonly a mixture of cowardice and cynicism – and therefore amenable to a bargain. But when authority enters, this man does not rant and rave; he neither quarrels nor exchanges blows; he doesn't even lie. At the most, he is silent, if the truth might hurt someone other than himself. When authority displays its candies of all flavours and whips of all sizes, it at first misses his quiet 'No', and when it finally hears it, it does not believe. It shows him its instruments; it uses them.

Before his trial ever began, Václav Havel was offered *laissez passer* to New York. The fury he unleashed by his persistence in saying No brought down on him a (for such a delicate man astronomical) term of four and a half years in prison. Only slightly before the term expired was he released, a seriously ill man they feared might die in prison. Ferdinand Vaněk has inherited his disposition.

To once critical intellectuals, the overwhelming majority of whom have by now come to an arrangement with authority, he poses no less of a problem. To them he is an inconvenience greater than authority itself, since he proves them guilty of a life-sized lie: guilty in front of the world, their families and even themselves. Whereas authority knows his momentary powerlessness, to this group of despondents Václav Havel is a very real danger, because the future threatens to prove him right, and that will necessarily mean a condemnation of them. They hate him but at the same time, just to be sure, they obsequiously curry favour with him, only to slander and denounce him the next moment.

As Havel at times in real life, Vaněk is a 'reagent' on stage. His mere appearance whips them on to fervent activity and elicits cascades of words that are supposed to habilitate or rehabilitate them, to convince or convict him. The less they tolerate him, the more they invite him; the fewer questions he asks, the more answers they provide; the less he blames them, the more stubbornly they defend themselves; the more he calms them, the more agitated they get; the more magnanimous he is, the more aggressive they become, and yet – the more they try to hold him back when at last he wants to remove his irritant self from their presence. It is precisely his departure they obviously fear most, the maltster in *Audience*, the couple in *Private View*, and the writer Staněk in *Protest* as well. As if departing together with him were their secret hope – that through him the world might once again become a more decent place, and they more decent people.

No matter how different the life and style of the authors who have appropriated Vaněk so far, each of their Ferdinands preserves symptomatic traits of his spiritual father. Invariably, each and every one of them is in essence Havel portrayed by different painters, including himself.

A good portrait or self-portrait is never as descriptive as a photograph but can present a more truthful depiction and, by eliminating secondary ornaments and focusing only on essentials, reveal the immutable centre of the subject's personality. It is in this sense that Ferdinand Vaněk is an artistic artefact, a skilfully crafted *dramatis persona* escaping the fluidity of life and functioning in accordance with the laws of the theatre. The transposition of Havel's chastity from life to drama via this prototype in all three original plays is proof of an artistic blessing of the highest degree. This is precisely where Havel–Vaněk is the most truthful embodiment of Vaněk–Havel, something of a popular reincarnation of the centaur, Cheiron.

My last piece, *Safari*, summons him on a first investigation of Western society. At the end of the play I, honest debtor that I am, return him to the country of his original owner. He cannot cross over to me a second time, I can only rejoin him. This I hope for; but I also believe that he will not wait, that he will, shyly yet without hesitation, enter into further plays which, in turn, will chart the features of our time on the blank map of contemporary Czech theatre.

Vienna
April 1986

This text was written for an anthology of Vaněk's plays, entitled The Playwright as Non-Person *edited by Marketa Goetz-Stankiewicz and published by the University of British Columbia, Vancouver, Canada.*

8

Iva Kotrlá: Conversations 36

Any consideration of the power of literature in this century must lead us to look at the behaviour which quietly testifies to its influence. On 7 May 1915, when neutral America's liner, the *Lusitania*, was torpedoed by the German submarine U–20, one Albert Bestic, an officer on the sinking ship, recorded the following scene in the first-class dining hall. Alfred Vanderbilt and the theatrical producer, Carl Frohman, were calmly fastening life-jackets to the 'Moses baskets' in which most of the infants on board were having their afternoon nap in the ship's crèche. When Bestic tried to alert the two men to their own peril, Vanderbilt shrugged his shoulders while Carl Frohman quoted the young hero of Barrie's *Peter Pan*: 'Death is an awfully big adventure!' At this point a surge of water swept Bestic out through the door, over the deck rails and into the sea. Swimming on his back, he could hear the cries of the children as they floated around in their wicker cradles. The hurriedly attached life-jackets were useless in the maelstrom that rose up when the ship went down with all hands. (See Colin Simpson's *Lusitania*, London 1972.)

I live in a country whose formation at around this same time was being promoted, at risk to his own life, by a prominent Czech philosopher. As head of the new state he chose for it the moving motto 'Truth prevails', and this is inscribed on the banner that flies above the castle of Prague, my country's capital. In this state, piloted by the same philosopher, another Czech philosopher was to grow up who likewise wrote his works both in Czech and German, albeit the Germans had tried to rock the state's very foundations. He sought to abjure hatred – with his whole life.

That was why, forty years after Thomas Masaryk's death, he risked his own life in Czechoslovakia to help form the Charter 77 movement – an association of people persecuted for their very loyalty to the motto on the presidential flag still flying above the castle. As a spokesman for this citizen group he chose as a motto for their imaginary flag that old and very humane injunction: 'Live in truth!'. (This philosopher, Jan Patočka, was to die in the shadow of the presidential flag, after an exhausting series of interrogations by the state police, still on the fortieth anniversary of the death of the state's founder.) 'The truth prevails for those who live in truth' is the saving message that might well be inscribed on the 'Moses baskets' of every nation's babies.

But would that philosopher with his tradition of humane ideas have called his own death on his own soil 'an awfully big adventure'? In our own days, do not *raisons d'état* only too often take the same lethal course as the U–20, calmly programmed to 'Take aim!' and destroy even babes in arms? What surge of hate and anti-humanism was it that swept the philosopher, Jan Patočka, through the gangway of life into the sea of total, artificial oblivion, where any mention of his name, or of the founder–president's, in their native land is utterly prohibited? One prohibition after another issues from the castle whose banner flutters so wildly in the Prague winds that one can scarcely read the words 'Truth prevails'.

When the Czech king Louis Jagiellon held sway in the castle, one man who defended Czech political interests *vis-à-vis* the Germans was the east European Erasmus, a figure familiar to the whole cultural, and hence the whole political, community of his day. His speeches and pronouncements before the great men of that world used to appear in print in many cities of Christendom, despite his humble background. When this same Erasmus Ciolek, after studying from 1485 at Cracow and Rome, was in the 1490s appointed as a secretary to the Polish king Alexander Jagiellon by the canon of Cracow, the authorities started an investigation of his origins that went on till 1502. It only ended when, in the following year, now an envoy of the Polish crown, he was ordained in Rome by papal edict as Bishop of Plock. Later, in 1518, King Sigismond Jagiellon despatched Erasmus to the Augsburg Diet of the German Empire to urge the assembled princes to defend all Europe from the eastern menace – the Turks. Though they found his address very moving they did not accede to his pleas. Eight years later the Czech king Louis died fighting the Turks on the field of Mohacs, and the recovery of their lost lands in Europe was to cost the blood of many Germans, imperial princes included, over a span of more than 250 years thereafter.

In 1522, when Erasmus Ciolek died, the castle of Prague was of course enjoying a year of glory. On 23 May, Louis Jagiellon's wife, Mary, was crowned Queen of Bohemia. Later, now a widow and regent of the Low Countries, Mary invited to her court Erasmus' namesake of Rotterdam. (He tried to comply with the summons, which was prestigious even in 1535, but died before he could reach the court.)

The works of this other Erasmus – a priest of the Catholic church since 1492, a counsellor to the emperor Charles V since 1516 etc., for whom even as a child Rudolf Agricola had prophesied a great future – proved spellbinding for those Czechs who were more interested in culture than in the defence of political interests. The east European Erasmus Ciolek, who by contrast always subordinated his utterances to the interests of the state, though he was better known to his contemporaries and reached a higher rank in the Church, is now forgotten in the annals of Europe. But Erasmus of Rotterdam found a lasting place in Europe's mental map because in the main he subordinated his writings to the interests of the spirit, the interests of humanism, which in Europe, alas, have so often conflicted with those of the authorities. However, truth prevails.

At this point it would be worthwhile to enumerate the works of Erasmus of Rotterdam translated and printed by Czechs in the course of the sixteenth century. It is a list that testifies to the civilization and humanism of the Czechs in an age when their country was hard pressed by the Turkish menace from the east. This did not deter Czechs from studying with quite feverish interest the thoughts of that great humanist as rendered into their own language. The following is not an exhaustive account:

The Praise of Folly, translated by Zikmund Hrubý z Jelení, 1513
Handbook of a Christian Knight, translated by Oldřich Velenský, Bělá, 1519
Paternoster, a commentary, translated by Ondřej Strojek, Plzeň, 1526
Children's Discourse, Prague, 1534, and:
Children's Manner, Prague, 1537, again in Kralice, and with the Latin original in Prostějov, *circa* 1567, translated by Jan Petřík z Benešova
The New Testament, Erasmus' text translated by Beneš Opát and Petr Czel, Náměstí nad Oslavou, 1533
Dicta Graeciae sapientum, published by Pavel Vorličný, Olomouc, 1558, and Prague, 1562, 1567, 1570, 1573, 1575, 1576, 1578, 1580, 1580, 1585, 1597, 1599
St Mark's Gospel, with a commentary by Erasmus, translated by Jan Vartovtovský z Varty, Litoměřice, 1542
'The immense mercy of God', a sermon, Prostějov, 1558, and Prague, 1573
Preparation to Death, translated by Jan z Lobkovic, one of the leading figures of the Czech nobility, Prague, 1563 and 1564
Cato's Distichs, published by Pavel Vorličný, 1558
The Christian Widow, translated by Jan Kherner, Prague, 1595

Not to be disregarded above all is Erasmus' friend, Jan Šlechta ze Všehrd, who corresponded with him in the early sixteenth century with no interference from state censors. Some of the letters are extant. So much for the Czechs and Erasmus of Rotterdam . . .

But look at it all from the standpoint of 1986, now that the writings of contemporary west European philosophers and humanists, Guardini, Ratzinger and many others are, in contrast to those times, only circulated in privately-made copies. (The same is true of the works of Thomas Masaryk, of Jan Patočka and others too numerous to mention.) Erasmus of Rotterdam and Czechs! Czechs and Czechs!

It is more than two centuries since the appearance in Leipzig of Herder's folksong collection *Stimmen der Völker* (1778) gave its impulse to the Czech revival. Herder also stimulated the collection of Slav folksongs in general; it was the Slavs, he believed, who had a worldwide mission to promote popular humanism. His assertions that 'Russia will assume the leadership in culture and bless Europe with a second renaissance', and that 'Village art will refresh that of the upper classes and purge it of its artificiality' became watchwords for the Czech intelligentsia throughout much of the nineteenth century. But it was the Czech philosopher, Masaryk, who felt impelled to write a book on Russia and Europe, asking whether Herder had not gone too far in those prophecies that so impressed the Czechs. Herder had foreseen a special role for the Ukraine, for example, as a second Hellas. But as an ancient European nation the Czechs cannot survive intellectually on a diet of visionary claims: they need to live in truth.

So when, as a result of power-shifts in Europe, the Czechs were incorporated into an east European system and their state became for the first time a neighbour of the Ukraine, many Czechoslovak citizens found themselves living right under the shadow of that new Hellas. And in their culture they became copiers of books, poems, plays and philosophical essays – even of prayers!

Whenever, then, over the past forty years, a Czech has wanted to read some essay that the censor has padlocked and prohibited from publication in his own country, he has had to resort to pen or typewriter and copy out the lines that have taken his fancy, a procedure quite unnecessary in Erasmus' day. In many cases such activity can cost him his liberty and his property both being liable to confiscation in the public interest.

The thoughts themselves, however, cannot be confiscated. This is something that Erasmus of Rotterdam did for Bohemia. One only needs to recite, in 1986, the title of one of his books:

An Instruction for Everyone on Preparing Himself for Death – on living in truth, Erasmus might have said.

European thought – a broad range to be sure! Around the time when Geert Geertz, prince of Dutch humanists, was nearing death, Spanish noblewomen and other ladies of the imperial aristocracy were embarking on the practice, for cosmetic reasons, of eating little scented cubes of clay. For this was the era when Theophrastus Bombastus von Hohenheim, Erasmus' contemporary, better known as Paracelsus, was teaching that every primary particle was soluble in its own element; those of the human body, for example, dissolved in clay.

A political system that assumes the solubility in clay not only of the human body but of unwritten, unprinted thoughts cannot be classified as humane. So in the face of all the censorship of written and printed words young people in Prague, Brno and elsewhere have had to start writing out their own thoughts by hand and offering them for exchange. Sometimes there is an artistic point in this, encapsulated in the oldest, mid-fourteenth-century Czech version of the Bible with its reference to 'serpents and things that creep on the earth' (Acts X, 12).

Many such writers, of course, have met with little understanding on the part of the authorities and have ended up spending ten years or more in the Czech underworld, risking their lives in the uranium mines. But while some were confined, others – students and working men – were duplicating and exchanging their own manuscripts or handwritten translations of west European books of ideas. And so it goes on today.

It is an apt moment, so it happens, to recall one such do-it-yourself publishing group of young Bohemian and Moravian workers and students which sprang up several decades ago. They came together in late 1953 and held a meeting in Moravia early the following year. The literary texts they had copied out with typewriters and carbon sheets were assembled under the title *Conversations 36 (Rozhovory 36)*, chosen because the participants had all been born around 1936 when the whole world was commemorating the quatercentenary of Erasmus' death. Intellectual oppression was a thriving business in their country by this time. The place where they gathered in Moravia was called Havlov u Tišnova and their host was the seventeen-year-old worker, Václav Havel. He had managed to set up links between quite a few of his contemporaries. From Brno came the students Pavel Švanda, Marie Langrová, Jiří Paukert, Petr Wurm, Viola Fischerová, Alena Vagnerová. A number of young workers came from Prague – Radim Kopecký, the son of a former associate of President Beneš, Ivan Koreček, Milan Dus, Jan Škoda, Jiří Frágner and others. They agreed to put out further typewritten issues and a *Verse Anthology* (*Sborník poezie*), subsequently compiled in Prague. These activities continued until police headquarters in Prague's Bartolomějská Street began to intervene and interrogate. Who today would be capable of putting together volumes of verse and prose with no equipment other than a few battered typewriters?

So I think it only fair that at least one member of that informal group of long ago – all young people fired with belief in the liberating power of literature – should despite all dangers now achieve recognition by the international cultural community. In Europe there should always be some way of hauling up above ground, if only by proxy, those who long to fly in the light of day – over the clay of their native soil!

9

Milan Kundera: Candide had to be destroyed

I

With the defeat of the Prague Spring in 1968, a giant was able to deprive its small neighbour of the last vestige of sovereignty and draw nearer to its strategic objectives in a short period of time. One of these objectives is the cultural domination of its own bloc. It is not simply a question of political subservience – politics is only one component of culture. In Czechoslovakia, it is culture *as a whole* in the largest sense of the word that is at stake: lifestyles, customs, artistic traditions, taste, collective memory and daily morality. A communist system also exists in Yugoslavia. But to the extent that it is a communist system *outside* the Russian sphere, day-to-day life for a Yugoslav resembles much more that of a Frenchman than that of a Soviet citizen. We have acquired the habit in recent times of exaggerating the importance of the political system (it is part of the vulgarized heritage of Marxism that, curiously enough, has been adopted on the right as well as the left), and have ceased to understand what culture is.

In other words, the situation in Czechoslovakia since the pro-Soviet coup of 1948 can be interpreted as a conflict between the imported political system and the entire culture of a country. As the years passed (and with a marked acceleration during the 1960s) the native culture strived to appropriate the system, to mould it and reduce it to a simple form with the aim of imposing its own essence on the foreign system. If considered from a historical perspective, all this can be seen also as a conflict between Western civilization and Russian civilization which, in its communist transformation, is more powerful than ever, striving to roll its borders further and further westward. From this point of view, the process of liberalization in the 1960s appears as an attempt to 'Westernize' socialism and the Russian invasion as an effort at the definitive 'cultural colonization' of a Western country.

Thus, the drama unfolding in Prague is not of the *local* order (a family quarrel in the Soviet house) but reflects with focused intensity *European* fate. Now playing in Prague is the great tragedy of European illusions and erring ways; the possible ruin of Europe is anticipated in Prague. That is why the least Czech is more stubbornly European that any Frenchman or Dane. He sees 'Europe die' every day, with his own eyes, and he is compelled, every day, to defend the 'Europe in himself'. The moral and cultural solidarity of Western countries represents for him an immediate, naive necessity. When he sees that Europe is paralysed by a 'guilt complex', when he hears its voice weaken, he has the impression that his death sentence has again been signed and this time for good.

II

Václav Havel made his début on the Czech public scene during those famous 1960s when Czech society was surmounting and transforming with joy and enthusiasm the imported system. He worked in a small Prague theatre, Na Zábradlí, which has become one of the symbols of the happy atmosphere during those years, a centre of the period's avant-garde. First in collaboration with Ivan Vyskčil (a remarkable author of absurd short stories), he then wrote, alone, two plays without which one cannot imagine the 1960s in Bohemia: *Garden Party* and *Memorandum*.

These two plays are openly inspired by the theatre known as the Absurd, started by Eugene Ionesco. I would like to point out in this respect something little known in France: no contemporary foreign writer had for us at that time such a liberating sense as Ionesco. We were suffocating under art conceived as educational, moral or political. *The Bald Prima Donna*, *The Chairs*, *L'avenir est dans les oeufs* – all these plays fascinated us by their radically anti-ideological nature. They returned autonomy to art and beckoned it to take again the path of freedom and creativity. Therefore, it was not by accident that Havel's theatre, Na Zábradlí, showed its direction right from the beginning by putting on *The Bald Prima Donna* and *The Lesson* in an unforgettable production.

One cannot conceive of Havel without the example of Ionesco yet he is not an epigone. His plays are an original and irreplaceable development within what is called the 'Theatre of the Absurd'. Moreover, they were understood as such by everyone at the time: if Ionesco's absurdity finds its inspiration in the depths of the irrational, Havel is fascinated by the absurdity of the rational. And if Ionesco's theatre is a critique of language, the totalitarian regime has made such a parody of language that Havel's *general* critique of language became at once a demystification of *concrete* social relations.

III

Ideology and juridical order in fascist regimes express overtly the thoughts and desires of those in power. Under Russian totalitarianism ideology and juridical order have, to the contrary, a mystifying quality. The vocabulary continues to exert a hypnotic influence on Western leftists who, even today, remain ready to believe that 'Soviet ideology is fine', but that current practice 'deforms' it and, therefore, one need only 'correct' the practice. They do not understand that the opposition between what one declares and what one does is not a *fault* that can be corrected but rather it is the *foundation* of Russian totalitarianism which is built on this opposition and could not exist without it.

Western man is still arguing solemnly over the legitimacy or non-legitimacy of the Soviet concept of egalitarian, classless society, whereas Soviet society itself has never been based on any sort of equality. Still debated is the Russian conception of internationalism even though it is nothing more than a screen behind which hides one of the most expansionist nationalisms that has ever existed. (It is true that the screen works brilliantly: half a century ago, under its aegis, the brutal Russification of forty million Ukrainians took place without the rest of the world even taking note.) A false vocabulary systematically places the debate on false ground and makes it practically impossible to analyse the concrete reality.

The real sense of Havel's 'absurd' plays from the 1960s was precisely the *radical demystification* of the vocabulary. These plays show a world where words have no meaning, or meanings different from accepted sense, or still again are screens behind which reality has disappeared. After 1968, when he was driven out of the theatre and forbidden to continue his literary critique of language, he transformed his own life into a magnificent demystification of language: He became one of the principal movers behind, creators of, and spokesmen for Charter 77.

Following the example of his plays from the 1960s, the Charter represents neither a revolutionary programme nor any kind of political programme whatsoever; it is not a critic of the 'regime's foundations' and it is not a plan for a 'better world'. The several hundred people who have signed the Charter call only for the valid juridical order and humanitarian principles officially proclaimed by the authorities. They do not engage in polemics but they do take words at the letter. Since the constitution guarantees the freedom of speech, they naively draw all the consequences. Since the constitution mentions the same right to education for all, Chartists are shocked when children whose parents are persecuted cannot pursue their studies. They conduct themselves as if words really mean what they are supposed to mean. They do not seek to demonstrate that the authorities' ideology is a bad thing, but their candid regard systematically reveals the gigantic sham for what it is.

It is in this sense that, despite its modesty and fastidious legalism, the Charter attacks the very foundation of the regime to the extent that it is precisely a grandiose mystifica-

tion of language that, without a doubt, has never known its
equal in the history of humanity. Thus Candide had to be
destroyed. Such is the meaning of the trial of Václav Havel,
sentenced in autumn 1979 to four and a half years in prison.

*This text, written following the trial and sentence of Václav Havel,
in October 1979, was published in French by* le Nouvel Obser-
vateur *and reprinted by Editions Gallimard as a preface to*
Audience. Vernissage. Pétition *by V. Havel, Paris 1980.*

10

Arthur Miller: I think about you a great deal

The WRITER *enters. Wears shirt and trousers. Carrying a bundle of mail. Sits, goes through letter after letter; of a dozen he removes two of importance, the rest he – after an instant of hesitation – drops into his wastebasket. Instantly, the* IMPRISONED ONE *enters, in his forties, wearing rumpled gray clothing. He sits. The* WRITER *does not face him directly.*

WRITER: Yes.

[*Slight pause*]

Amazing, how often I think of you even though we've barely met. And that was so long ago.

[*Reaches into the waste basket, retrieves the letters he dropped in.*]

I suppose it happens whenever I get a load of this kind of stuff. Must get fifty pounds of it a month. I'm on the master list, obviously. Look at this . . . [*Reads off the senders' names.*]
'Ban the Bomb', 'Planned Parenthood', 'Save the Children', 'American Indian Fund', 'Friends of the Arts', 'National Organization for Women', 'Fight the Klu Klux Klan', 'Amnesty International', 'Central Park Conservancy', – whatever that is, 'Save the Animals', 'Save Africa', 'Save the Rain Forests', save, save, save, save. The mind simply cannot take all this seriously. Things just can't be this bad.

[*Slight pause*]

I must say, though – it does remind me of you. Your situation seems worse than all the others, though . . . I'm not sure why. Maybe it's the immense investment so many of us have made in socialism. That people who even call themselves socialist should imprison the imagination . . . That's really what it is, isn't it – the war on the imagination.

And maybe, too, because your prison is probably further west than Vienna. You are almost within range of the sound of our voices. You can almost hear us. I suppose. In effect. Whatever the reason, I really do think about you a great deal.

[*Slight pause*]

Reminds me of another writer I knew many years ago in New York. Quite talented, we all thought. Poet and playwright. Lot of promise. But he had an active case of claustrophobia. Couldn't bear to enter an elevator. And they had no money so he and his wife lived in this tiny room which drove him crazy – used to walk the streets half the night. (It was a lot safer to walk the streets at night in those days.) Anyway . . . in desperation he took a job writing advertising copy for . . . I think it was General Motors. Which allowed him to move into a larger apartment, and eased his anxieties. Years passed and I met him again and naturally I was curious about what he was working on. But the poetry had died, the plays too; what he wanted to show me was this thick file of ads he had written. In fact, he was such a favourite, the company had given him a special office on the ground floor of their skyscraper so he could avoid the elevator. He was middle-aged by this time, and it was quite . . . moving, actually . . . to see how proud he had become of these works in praise of General Motors. In fact, he showed me his different drafts, and pointed out how he had shifted various ideas around until the whole conception was perfected. And I kept watching the look of triumph on his face. And you couldn't help being happy for him – that he had earned so much space around himself. He obviously no longer lived in his old anxiety. Seemed really satisfied with life now, with a solid feeling of accomplishment. His was clearly a successful life . . . that had substituted itself for a poet.

[*Slight pause*]

I thought about you, then. They have taken away your space, haven't they – because you have refused to write their ads. Amazing how, more than anything, power loves

praise. But there are fifty other conclusions one could draw
from this and none of them change anything for you. So I
suppose we must raise it all to the moral level. The moral
level is where nothing gets changed. Yet it exists, doesn't
it; just as my thinking so often of you exists. In fact, it joins
us together, in a way. In some indescribable way we are
each other's continuation . . . you in that darkness where
they claw and pound at your imagination, and I out here in
this space where I think about you . . . a great deal.
[*He drops the clump of appeals into the basket.*]
There will be another clump tomorrow. And the next day
and the next. [*Slight pause*] Imagine . . . if they stopped! Is
that possible? Of course not. As long as mornings continue
to arrive, the mail will bring these acts of goodness
demanding to be done. And they will be done. Somehow.
And so we hold your space open for you, dear friend.
The WRITER *goes to his typewriter and writes. The* IMPRISONED
ONE, *after a moment, rises and walks out. The* WRITER *continues to
write.*

*This monologue was written as an expression of solidarity with
Václav Havel, for performance at the International Theatre Festival
in Avignon on 21 July 1982.*

11

Zdena Salivarová: When I was still living in Prague

While I was still living in Prague, I did not really know the man I call Mr Václav, only because he persists in calling me 'Mrs Zdena'. But our crazy times, which drove me out of the city of my birth and set me down in this beehive of skyscrapers, none of which is more than twenty years old, and turned a one-time cabaret and folk singer into a publisher – these crazy and fascinating times also brought me, on that day in June 1982, to the Convocation Hall of York University in Toronto. There, an academic gown was put on my still slender figure, a quadrangular mortar-board cap set on my fresh perm, and I was asked to give a talk about Mr Václav. This not so ancient but pleasant university had decided to bestow an honorary degree of 'Doctor of Letters' on the playwright *in absentia* – but where in fact was he at that time? In Czechoslovakia, certainly, but where exactly? In Bytýz? In the Svornost? No, I knew those sinister names from my brother, who spent ten of the best years of his life at hard labour in those forgotten holes of central Europe in the 1950s. Mr Václav, was somewhere else, in abodes not much more comfortable, I am sure, than the old uranium mines during the years under Stalin. In any case, that was why he could not be present in Toronto, where a group of professors at York University, among them Václav Táborský, one of his old friends from Prague, had persuaded the university authorities that this man in far-off Czechoslovakia was worthy of the honour.

And since neither he, nor his wife, nor any other relative could come to accept the diploma, the University had chosen me to represent Mr Václav, because I am his original publisher. All over the Western world, of course, many houses bring out his plays, and many theatres stage them. But he writes them in Czech, and that language has been banned in Czechoslovakia and replaced by *Ptidepe*. Since Mr Václav has no talent for learning foreign languages, and thus never mastered *Ptidepe* which otherwise, judging from the books I occasionally read from Prague, has been easily acquired by most of his colleagues, he continued writing in Czech even after the introduction of mandatory *Ptidepe* in 1969, and has published the plays he wrote during this period with Sixty-Eight Publishers Corporation in Toronto, of which I am the head. That is how I became Mr Václav's original publisher, rather than Rowohlt in Hamburg, and that is why I was asked to accept the diploma – his first honorary degree – on his behalf, and give that speech.

I lost the speech, and it wasn't much of a speech anyway. I could probably make a living as a speechwriter for Mr Husák, for I managed to speak for some time without uttering a memorable thought or phrase. So you missed nothing, Mr Václav, by not hearing me or not reading my speech now.

But there was something else you did miss that I think was memorable. Among the men in gowns and caps who were to be honoured that day, there was a large and very black man of imposing proportions whose face seemed somewhat familiar. I realized who he was only when they called him to the rostrum to accept his diploma – Mr Oscar Peterson. I am sure the name will mean more to you than it did to me; unlike my husband I have never been a jazz buff, but the black man's fame has transcended the boundaries of his genre and I knew that he was, in his profession, like a Tennessee Williams, say, in yours. So as you can see, you were in good company. Or rather I was, on your behalf.

It did not end there, however. After I had stumbled through my speech, to which the black man was listening attentively, and returned to my seat, he leaned over to me and whispered in my ear: 'Tell Mr Havel that I am with him all the way!'

I thought you might be pleased by that whisper.

12

Milan Šimečka:
The sorrowful satisfaction of the powerless

Eleven years ago, in 1975, Václav Havel wrote a lengthy letter to Dr Husák, the General Secretary of the Communist Party of Czechoslovakia (and future President of the republic). He chose to address him as 'Dear Dr Husák'. Maybe because of the economy of the style of address, or for other reasons inherent in the nature of relations between the powerful and the powerless, Havel never received a reply to his letter. In this manner it ceased being a matter between himself and the General Secretary and a copy of the letter even found its way to me. By then it was elegantly bound and bore on the fly-leaf a note to the effect that Ludvík Vaculík had had the letter reproduced for the benefit of his friends. When I'd read it, what I envied Havel most was that he had not been influenced by the thought of how futile such approaches to politicians are, and had set down everything that was also troubling me and, no doubt, millions of other despairing and powerless people in this country.

The letter was not a complaint about personal slights and persecution. It was first and foremost a complaint about the state of our common homeland. It objected to the way a good old central European country was being treated, to the lies its people were being fed insultingly day in day out, to the way stagnation and apathy were infiltrating what had been a dynamic and inventive society, and to the harassment of Czech and Slovak culture and its representatives. Another inherent factor of relations between the powerful and the powerless is that the former do not reply to letters of this sort. What stands a better chance of a response is a complaint about a personal injustice, which seems not to call into question their responsibility for the state of the country we live in. When I was in prison, my wife complained to the self-same General Secretary that my letters to her were being stolen. She received a reply and a promise that the situation would be remedied. And even in those countries where citizens receive much more civil treatment than here, it seems that politicians just cannot endure it when powerless citizens – writers, say – get too worked up over issues of general concern and when they start creating the impression that almost anyone with their wits about them is capable of appreciating what's afoot in the political arena. They treat such judgements as inadmissible trespassing on their own private bailiwick by busybody amateurs from cloud-cuckoo-land lacking any understanding for all the complexities involved in the arduous tasks of power which it is theirs to shoulder. I have even heard politicians actually speak in such terms – though only when there were not too many around to hear them, of course. Such attitudes derive from ignorance of human realities and failure to keep sight of the human dimension – but this has been a failing of politics since time immemorial.

However it has been obvious, also since time immemorial, that a position of powerlessness provides the best vantage point for getting a true view of society. In the aforementioned letter and in subsequent articles, powerlessness was elevated by Havel into a virtue. He demonstrated anew what people had long suspected: namely that, within the structures of power, ideas degenerate and the wits are blunted. Ossified political rituals even lead to the distortion and decline of language which gives way to the absurd and incomprehensible blather of resolutions and government decrees. The only qualification that people need in order to perceive more clearly the dangers of 'big-lie' politics is to be powerless. They do not have to be philosophers, writers, scholars or priests. I have come across clear-minded thinkers among powerless labourers, farmers and craftspeople. By and large, the powerless are not given to writing; they stick to verbal debate, and consequently nothing remains in later years to prove how much more right they were than the politicians. The powerless often have a much better idea of what sort of people are likely to succumb to greed or vengefulness in positions of power. They have a more reliable notion which paths in politics are fraught with danger and usually lead to violence and bloodshed, and realize that the 'easy' wars that politicians promise to win, have a tendency to end in catastrophic defeat. In most cases, the powerless do not even gain any satisfaction: when at long last their predictions come true, they are either dead or in their dotage, nodding their heads ruefully as they raise their tea-cups to their lips with trembling hands.

In writing his letter to the General Secretary, Havel was driven by the thought that the powerless must put pen to paper and speak out publicly in defence of the truth. They need no instructions, no institutional backing. It is something that people have to do for themselves if we are not to go on crying over historical spilt milk as has always been the case in the past. Eleven years on, it is apparent to me that – slowly but surely – the reply to his letter is gradually arriving. Changing social realities and, of course, the changes happening to the east of us have ensured that Havel has by now had a response to about a third of his complaints. Wrapped up within a welter of jargon, one can detect a vindication of Havel when they admit to the existence of a sort of stagnation here and assert that rigid thinking is an obstacle, while also noting a lack of boldness and creative verve, and lamenting the sorry moral state of our society. There is a rash of unsigned editorials with clarion calls in favour of new thinking and emboldened officials are beginning to hawk our old dissident concerns as new inventions under their own label. It's all hot air of course, but even so, it's nice to see how ideas which were booted out the back door in an ideological flurry are swarming back in through the window.

I tell my sceptical friends sitting around the table: 'Be glad!' 'What more can you want?' The ideas of the powerless are asserting themselves far quicker than they used to. These days it is taking as few as forty, thirty, twenty, or even eleven years. The fact that our truths are having to be acknowledged by those who bitterly oppose them is far greater cause for rejoicing than a medal or a state pension. And that is the only satisfaction that History can ever offer the powerless.

But, of course, I also share the feelings of futility and dejection which temper such satisfaction. We are all capable of calculating the losses this country has suffered at every possible level: in terms of production quality, authentic culture, initiative, pride in achievement; all the people who have gone elsewhere, not to mention the blood sacrifices. And all because the powerless were silenced and no one paid heed to their warnings. We should be used to it by now, but even familiarity fails to extirpate our grief. It has been going on for more than three generations already. We once had a state that was the envy of Europe, and even those who enjoyed its freedom and security were unwilling to give heed to the poets and writers who warned against selling off its attributes cheaply. By and large, writers in our country have never gained anything but sorrowful satisfaction. I personally have read countless warnings, predicting disasters, lawlessness and the extinction of the nation's spirit. Many authors of powerless writings have now passed on without anyone admitting publicly that they were right. But who was to do so? The politicians?

The satisfaction of being right is a sorrowful one because it is mostly a lonely pleasure. It will never be brought to you on a plate. People have short memories and when an author's words prove true, they begrudge them the credit. None the less I cannot help feeling that Havel and all the other powerless citizens of our country whose fragile words alone have served to establish an accepted degree of awareness here from which it has not been possible to retreat – those who stuck to their guns and their determination to 'call things by their proper names' (as today's favourite Soviet slogan goes) – are better off than their predecessors of former generations who managed to survive the worst and in the end could only draw satisfaction through gritted teeth from the faint signs that the lies were abating. Now that the tempo of civilizing processes is hotting up alongside a growing awareness of the dangers threatening us and of the impossibility of continuing down the same false paths decade after decade, more and more often do the powerless have cause for sorrowful satisfaction. The satisfaction is neither complete nor euphoric, obviously. But however betrayed, sceptical or suspicious we might be, it ought none the less to be a matter of sorrowful satisfaction for us, Václav, to see all the paraphrases of positions we have long defended cropping up all over the place nowadays in our part of the world. What difference does it make that our words are beginning to be repeated by those who once gave us a drubbing for them? We have to be philosophical about it, which is the only way for people in our geographical circumstances. There is no reason for us to make a song and dance about copyright.

This is why I listen unbegrudgingly to the new Soviet leader on the radio talking about the need for truthfulness, reconstruction, revolution, new attitudes, public accountability, and so on and, in so doing, repeating the words of dissidents who have been living abroad in exile for twenty years, or died of despair in the meantime. It is unlikely he uses the words with the same intent as those who wasted away their years in the camps, but it makes good listening, all the same. Of course I'm not philosophical enough to swallow all my bitterness. When I heard another leader at the Soviet congress ask himself in a fit of frankness why it was that he had not spoken out so openly five years before, and when he replied for himself that it was because he then lacked the maturity and courage, it crossed my mind that in my reading I had come to know a whole series of powerless Russians who had had both the maturity and the courage, for which they were reviled and ridiculed, imprisoned and exiled and never an apology have they ever received. Who knows? Maybe they too draw pleasure from their sorrowful satisfaction. As Václav Havel has already pointed out, life has taught us modesty and made us resistant to pathos, whether of the negative or the positive variety. Our sense of humour and our wary scepticism help save us from falling prey to the sorrow that tempers our satisfaction. We all know that conscience and truth – to which the powerless have clung for years – are categories one does not come across too frequently in politics. Most important, though, it has been proven yet again that predictions of future developments and looming perils increase in accuracy the further from the frontiers of power they emerge, and that the most accurate forecasts come from the realms of the utterly powerless.

We are going to be seeing more and more frequent tentative responses to Václav Havel's fateful letter to the Doctor as time goes on. If I know Václav correctly, he won't be too surprised, after what he's been through, that the replies are not addressed to him personally. All that is needed for this particular historical episode to have a happy end is for the greatest possible number of the powerless to realize that even if one lives in a state of powerlessness, one can still assert maturity and courage, and that satisfaction is satisfaction even when it is sorrowful.

August 1986

13

Josef Škvorecký: I saw Václav Havel for the last time

I saw Václav Havel for the last time at the American embassy in Prague. It was late January 1969, a day or two after Jan Palach had immolated himself. (Palach is forgotten now, his grave moved to an unknown location.) I had come to get transit visas for the flight to Toronto via New York, he to attend to some matter relating to his Ford Foundation grant to do research in the States. 'Great!' I said. 'Why don't we fly together?' 'When are you going?' Havel asked. 'The day after tomorrow', I said. He thought for a brief moment, then replied: 'Too soon. I think I'll wait at least until the first anniversary of the invasion. It should be – ' a hesitation, 'interesting.' We shook hands, parted, and since then I've seen him only in photographs – as a brewery worker, a hollow-cheeked political prisoner just out of jail, a godfather to Marta Kubišová's baby girl with a big pascal candle in hand, a mourner at his father's funeral which, thanks to the magnanimity of the party and the government, he was permitted to attend although still in jail at the time.

Many years later, with the help of friends at the University of Toronto, I arranged to have him invited to be the university's writer in residence. That was after four years in prison, and we thought a year in lovely, free Toronto might do him good. While he was still behind bars, in 1982, he received his first honorary doctorate from York University in Toronto, and by that time he was pretty well known to Ontario theatregoers. Over the past fifteen years or so, many of his plays have been staged in the city, some more than once, and he was even given a world première here, the

English version of his *Beggar's Opera*, translated by his one-time compatriot Michal Schonberg. The local New Czech Theatre had produced his one-acters – a series of three short plays with the diffident writer-turned-labourer Vaněk as protagonist – with remarkable success, so we thought he would feel at home in this Czech metropolis on Lake Ontario.

Perhaps he would have – I am certain he would – but he was more concerned about his real, original home. Yes, I would like to come, he wrote, it would be wonderful to see old friends, North America, perhaps to take part in a production of one of my plays (for there is no greater joy for a playwright, and he has been denied that joy since 1968). But then he referred to a few well-known cases of nonconformist Czech writers who had been allowed to leave the country for a few months and then, when they tried to return, were refused entry. Among them were Václav's close friends Jiří Gruša and Pavel Kohout. 'And for better or worse, I want to live here, in Bohemia.'

Is it, in this day and age, really for better or for worse?

Every coin has two sides. The old, old debate between Henry James and H. G. Wells about 'saturation' *versus* 'selection', about narrow but deep *versus* wide but shallow experience; the old, old comparison of two lives in one of Gellner's old, old poems; and – oldest of all – the dichotomy between Ovid, who dies of nostalgia far from beloved Rome, and Józef Korzeniowski who, as Joseph Conrad, becomes more British than most, without ceasing to be a patriotic Pole.

There is really no dichotomy, as long as by 'exile' one means people like Hemingway, Pound, Henry Miller, Gertrude Stein, Chester Himes – men and women who left their country of their own free will – while others – like Frost, Faulkner, O'Neill, Bellow – stayed behind. Not behind bars, however, whether you call them the Iron Curtain or the Berlin Wall or something else. Some of these exiles wanted to see the big, wide world; some yearned to become imbued with the atmosphere of immortal Paris, where one is 'closer to heaven', as Jaroslav Seifert once wrote; others wanted to live surrounded by a foreign tongue so that their own language would become more precious to them and reveal beauties and possibilities obscured by daily usage. Most never ceased to write about home or, at least, about people like themselves: strangers in paradise. After all, they could refresh their memories of the old place whenever they wanted, they could live alternately in Florida and in Madrid; given the speed and accessibility of modern means of transport, they could commute. Just think of our golden girl of tennis, Martina Navrátilová, who loses a match in Paris, gets depressed, boards a Concorde to enjoy a few hours of sunshine on her favourite American beach, then boards the Concorde again, and is in Paris in time for another match which, refreshed by her hop across the ocean, she wins. That, however, is one of the less important wonders of the Western world.

With all such wonders, neither you, Václav, nor I can travel freely between Prague and Toronto, and that has an effect on what we write. I have often been asked, by people who think that writing means knowing the alphabet, to write a real muck-raking piece exposing the true nature of the corrupted regime under which you live. Naturally, I would never dare. In seventeen years, hard-line regimes like Dr Husák's can change the country beyond recognition, though scarcely for the better. I am sure that you, too, would not give thought to the proposition of writing a scathing satire about Czech exiles in Canada. At most I have attempted lighthearted pieces like the Derek MacHane farce called *Trip do Česka (A trip to Bohemia)* written entirely on the basis of reports of the travellers to that unlucky country, and there my inspiration was the language: that funny North American dialect of Czech. You would have to know that dialect if you were ever tempted to write something about my adopted country, but I am sure such a crazy idea would never occur to you. You might end up like that writer in Jan Křesadlo's novel *Fuga trium* (read him, if you can: a unique talent on the foreign fields of Czech literature), who sets his story in Bohemia where he has never been, and so has palm trees adorning Chod villages, and a brothel bouncer named Masaryk, because that's one of the few Czech names a non-Czech can find in an encyclopedia.

Well, this is all beside the point, although I have recently read a manuscript from Prague with Křesadlo-like effects: a story about life in New York based on a one-week trip the poor authoress made once to that city, back in the hopeful sixties. If Ivan Klíma thinks that Philip Roth's Prague in *Prague Orgy* is more like New York, then this mind-travellers's New York is more like Kocourkov, the Bohemian equivalent of Hicksville.

But that is really beside the point. In your seventeen years under Soviet occupation you have created a body of work that tells those of us in exile and our non-Czech friends here, in a truly Jamesian manner, more about the essence of living under such conditions than lengthy political, sociological or cultural tracts, not to mention bulky realistic novels. You have also become a symbol, whether you like it or not (and I have an inkling you do not like it very much), of the noble resistance of the human spirit to the 'big insult', as I call it, a situation where intelligent people have to listen to bunkum and talk bunk, fully aware that it is bunk, because otherwise they would have 'themselves to blame for the consequences', as that classic phrase of *Ptidepe* – your own version of newspeak – goes.

Such a life, my dear Václav, cannot be easy. In fact, as far as I can see, it is a lousy, difficult and dangerous life. Sometimes I think of the Good Book which says: 'For everything there is a season, and a time for every matter under heaven.' At other times I remember Božena Němcova's letter to Josef Lešikar in Texas (his descendants still live in that blessed land): 'Home is everywhere where people live who speak the same language and share the same moral principles and aims.' You have done more than most for our people who live in servitude. I only hope we shall be worthy of you here among the Czechs who still live in liberty.

14

Tom Stoppard: Introduction (to *The Memorandum*)

Václav Havel's career as a playwright has been brief in his own country. It began with *The Garden Party* in 1963, and was suspended in 1968 by the Husák regime which took power in the wake of the Soviet invasion a few months after Havel's third play, *The Increased Difficulty of Concentration*, had opened in Prague. *The Memorandum* is the play that came between those two, in 1965.

Despite the ban on performances of his work in Czechoslovakia, Havel has continued to write, and latterly has produced a *Doppelgänger*, a playwright and *persona non grata* named Ferdinand Vaněk whose adventures are sardonically recalled, so far, in three short plays, *Audience*, *Private View*, and *Protest*. Even so, *The Memorandum* possibly remains his most widely performed play, and the one which best shows off the hallmarks of his gift: the fascination with language; the invention of an absurd society raised only a notch or two above the normal world of state bureaucracy; the absurdities pushed to absurdity compounded by absurdity and yet saved from mere nonsense by their internal logic; and, not least, the playfulness with which it is done, the almost gentle refusal to indulge a sense of grievance, the utter lack of righteousness or petulance or bile – the same quality, in fact, which was to distinguish the Vaněk plays ten years later, by which time Havel might have been forgiven for writing with bitterness.

For let it be said that while this edition of *The Memorandum* was being prepared for the press (April 1980), its author was entering the sixth month of a four-and-a-half-year prison sentence meted out for crimes which have no counterpart in a free society.

Havel's first spell in prison was in 1977. He had been arrested in January soon after the appearance of Charter 77, a document calling upon the Czech government to abide by its own laws. Havel, as one of three designated spokesmen for the Charter and the best known, was kept in prison for four months and ultimately given a suspended sentence of fourteen months. Despite his extreme vulnerability, he associated himself the following year with the Committee for the Defence of the Unjustly Persecuted (VONS in the Czech acronym). Eleven members of VONS were arrested in March 1979 and six of these, including Havel, were brought to trial in October, when the very existence of VONS was defined as act of subversion. A proper account of those proceedings and a proper recognition of the other defendants would be in order, but to a prospective reader of *The Memorandum* the most pertinent echo from that trial is that of the words spoken by Havel to his judges before he was sentenced. Needless to say, no official record exists and the quotation does not claim to be verbatim, but nevertheless this is what the author of this play had to say:

The system is based on an *a priori* assumption that the state can do no wrong. The decision of a court is regarded as being infallible in principle. I want to stress that this assumption of infallibility is very dangerous. Anyone who questions it is automatically defined as an enemy and everything he does is qualified as hostile. If the institutions of the state can never be in error, then anybody criticizing their actions is logically engaging in slander, vilification, and so on. And why should somebody vilify? Naturally, out of hostility. And if out of hostility, then, naturally, in collusion with a foreign, hostile and anti-socialist power. The indictment does not mention what should be the crucial issue – the contents of the VONS statements. The prosecution cannot allow any consideration of what VONS actually said, because to allow that would be tantamount to conceding the possibility of the state's fallibility. . . . If you write that student X copied a piece by Václav Havel and gave it to his fellow students to read, it does not sound nearly so serious as it does when you write that 'Student X duplicated and distributed in an illegal manner an anti-socialist pamphlet by a right-wing exponent.' There are certain words which recur continually in the indictment and which one would describe as loaded, words like subversion, lies, malice, illegal organizations, anti-communist centres, vilification, hatred, and so on. However, when one looks closely at these words, one finds that there is nothing behind them.

If, as nowadays, one might easily suppose the proper study of Literary Man is the intersection of a writer's work and his experience, what a gift that statement seems to offer: here is a play about words, infallibility, logic and the system.

Yet to make too much of that would be to distract attention from the inventiveness of *The Memorandum*. We are introduced to a new official language, *Ptidepe*, designed to banish the confusions of natural, unscientific language, and based on maximizing the difference between words so that no word can conceivably be mistaken for another, the length of a word being proportional to the frequency of use (the word for wombat has 319 letters). Alas, *Ptidepe* begins to assume some of the characteristics of a natural language, emotional overtones, ambiguities, and so on, and is therefore replaced by a new language, *Chorukor*, whose principle is to maximize the resemblance between words, so that Monday becomes 'Ilopagar', Tuesday 'Ilopager', etc, and the worst that can happen is that the right things will occur on the wrong day of the week.

In the lifelike encounters of the Vaněk plays, experience does indeed provide a template for art, but here one relishes the joyous freedom of Havel's imagination. In 1965 joy and freedom seemed possible.

Written as introduction to The Memorandum *by Václav Havel, translated by Vera Blackwell, New York: Grove Press, 1980.*

15

Zdeněk Urbánek: Letter to a prisoner

The following text was written in the spring of 1982. It was intended as a letter to Václav Havel, then spending his third year in jail, having been unjustly sentenced to four and a half years' imprisonment in October 1979. In Czechoslovakia these days, only close relatives are allowed to write to prisoners, and so my letter could not be delivered to him as a whole. I was determined to keep up at least occasional contact with Václav Havel by means of correspondence, and that I was able to do so, despite the regulations, I owe to his wife, Olga, and his brother, Ivan, who would kindly include in *their* letters some of my responses to the incredibly consistent series of his own letters to members of his family, which have since been published under the title *Letters to Olga*. It is a unique book, not only thanks to the circumstances which gave rise to it and the wide range of topics it touches on, but in particular by what I have already referred to as its utter consistency. It is also a highly optimistic and encouraging book in the way it turns a dark reality into illuminating reading, to light being provided by the author's sharp and penetrating mind. Not even while incarcerated behind prison walls did Havel allow his friends and acquaintances to rest.

My text came about as an attempt to comment on the opening of his series of letters, in which he explained how he came to be a dramatist and then went on to deal with his attitude to the theatre. In my very first paragraphs I react to his statement that his finding his *métier* in the theatre was 'to a large extent the result of several fortunate coincidences'. I responded to this by saying that there is no such thing as 'coincidence', and Olga Havel included this in her letter to Václav. His reply was unambiguous and not long in coming. Just about that time, 'convict Havel' fell ill and was transferred to the prison hospital. He had no difficulty in decoding the letter from his wife and discovering who it was that was denying the existence of coincidence. As it happened, he just then picked up a book at random from among a pile of reading matter left there for the patients. The book he found himself holding was a novel called *In Search of Don Quixote* – whose author, in the 1940s, was none other than the man who was trying to persuade Havel that coincidence did not occur. And Havel, then, in his typical, concise but emphatic way ridiculed Olga's (that is, my) argument. Several letters later he wrote, almost too kindly it seemed to me, how much he had enjoyed my book, which he had discovered by chance after we had been friends for twenty years. Coincidence? Even so, I was none too happy – there is so little one can do for a friend in prison.

April 1986

1 Right at the beginning of your letters on the theatre you write that you started to work in the theatre thanks to 'several fortunate coincidences'. Fortunate, I agree. But your very attitude to the theatre and your reflections on it would seem to show that your theory that this was all due to 'coincidence' is, to say the least, highly inaccurate.

2 'Coincidence' is, as often as not, resorted to as an ersatz term, necessitated by the brevity of human life and the lack of personal and collective 'computers' where our human organism is concerned. It is to be regretted that what is probably the result of complicated chain reactions caused by a variety of causes is simply ascribed by us to 'coincidence'. I could quote you a whole galaxy of examples, since every one of us frequently encounters something in his or her life which he, for the want of a better term, defines as 'coincidence'.

3 Let me quote one fortunate and one unfortunate coinci-

dence, as these phenomena are too glibly described. Both cases contain the two basic elements which determine our human condition: on the one hand, there is the hidden – or perhaps for the time being not sufficiently researched – energy of natural processes and phenomena, which our mind dismisses as irrational. On the other hand, there is the relatively much more rational (although motivated by irrational instincts and intuition) human endeavour to attain certain goals. It is said that Fleming 'by chance' allowed a certain kind of mould to grow. But this 'chance' oversight was doubtless caused by something that decided that this was to be a 'fortunate coincidence' for all those suffering from TB and other ailments – by the erudite and painstaking, and inevitably on occasion absent-minded, attention devoted by Fleming's laboratory to a whole range of moulds and the possibility of their therapeutic use. Coincidence? No, I would rather say it was a discovery that owed its existence to many different causes. In its consequences, the 'unfortunate coincidence' that led to the doom of the Peru expedition can be said to be a similar discovery. At the cost of the lost human lives it was again ascertained that, for reasons which are partly rational and partly irrational, people desire knowledge, and that the site of human habitation is determined by irrational events deep below the surface. However, the meaning of this discovery, in a morally rational sense, can also be that people have to be protected against these and other irrationalities. The answer can hardly be a prohibition of expeditions to dangerous parts of the world. That would be to inhibit learning. It is conceivable though that, by making proper use of our human intelligence potential for humanitarian purposes, we could arrive at some early warning system where earthquakes are concerned, as has already been done in the case of certain climatic phenomena, or that it should become the rule rather than the exception that, in places where earth tremors are to be expected, buildings should be erected which will not come tumbling down around their inhabitants. The same potential, if adequately utilized and backed up by a strong moral sense, could be harnessed to prevent other catastrophes, caused by other kinds of irrationality. It is doubtless one of the conditions of such a utilization that 'coincidence' – if by this we mean some unforeseeable, motiveless phenomenon or event – should be excluded from the vocabulary of meaningful terms or concepts.

4 It is certainly no 'coincidence' – in its invalid sense – that I should be put in mind of the surrealists. In his perspicacity, Bréton did not presumably believe that 'coincidence' was devoid of causality, yet for the purpose of the somewhat closed system of his 'pure aesthetics' he found it convenient to ignore the causes of 'coincidence'. And in its pure, motiveless and thus intellectually faulty guise, he mythologized it and promoted it to the position of an aesthetic principle. He vied with his colleagues in describing the magic qualities of 'chance encounters'. These texts of his retain to this day their tempting and enriching properties, but who knows if this simplified denuding of 'coincidences' of their causal links did not play a part in giving this art form, so energetic and rich in marvellously talented individuals, such a relatively short span of life. The Czech poet, Vítězslav Nezval, in his *The Prague Pedestrian*, written at a time when he was still a surrealist, revealed the true origin of 'magical coincidence'. Outside the *Lidové noviny* editorial office he bumped into Josef Čapek, and having greeted him, continued on his way towards the Powder Tower. *En route* he encountered the same gentleman three more times. He writes charmingly of this 'chain of fortune' – and which one of us today would not envy him? But then, with a touching guilelessness that is highly unorthodox for a surrealist point of view, he tells us what gave rise to those coincidences: Josef Čapek was that day issued with a monthly tram pass by his paper, and so it cost him nothing to get off a tram, take a short walk and then board another, only to repeat the exercise a station further on. He was indulging himself in this way and thus giving pleasure to Nezval by their 'chance' encounters. Nezval extended his repertoire to include the drama. Although he was by this time free of his earlier surrealist norms and preoccupations, his lyrical-rhetorical

nature continued to be influenced by surrealism for some time, and this prevented him from truly making his mark in the theatre. While the surrealists did make a contribution to dramatic art, providing many important plays with their distinctive nuances, they never created their own theatre. No doubt this has something to do with their radical attitude that totally ignored the causality of coincidence. Even where films are concerned, they have produced only the exceptional, undoubtedly interesting but not unique or innovatory work. Drama is based on the partly spontaneous, partly conscious effort to discover the causes and interplay of events – the surrealists chose to concentrate on the sensual and emotional consequences of events and their interplay, thus disowning their cherished patron, Freud. But that is another, very long story. Some other time.

5 Of even shorter duration than surrealism were 'happenings', which of course, unlike surrealism, were meant to be something of a new attempt at *Gesamtkunst*, as well as a substitute for conventional, obsolete, bourgeois 'consumer' theatre. The intention was radically to cancel the division between the stage and the auditorium; all those present were to be 'actors' and 'spectators' at one and the same time. Happenings thus played their part in resurrecting some important findings about the conditions necessary for people to understand each other and their position in the world, the circumstances enabling them to be drawn into the mystery or again to come to terms with the elemental energies in themselves, the world, and the universe: all this depended not so much on a unified sensual and emotional upsurge but, rather, on the conscious and controlled conflicts in people and between groups of people. While this goes for other areas of communication and creation, of creating 'worlds within worlds', it applies to the theatre in particular. If we are to experience real involvement with what is going on on the stage, we have to resist doing so with at least a part of our consciousness. A spectator can be drawn into the play and become its living participant only if he is truly reacting to it, that is, responding by half accepting and half rejecting the

entire climate of the stage as well as the individual speeches and situations. The actor will be the more effective, the more actively he experiences the inevitable dichotomy between his own individuality and that of the character he is portraying (the so-called 'identification' method is not so much acting as pretending). Again and again, acquired knowledge is invariably the result as well as the cause of a number of conflict situations: most of us have no wish to have our views or moral precepts changed, yet we are exposed to whole series of events which demand such a change, for otherwise it all 'doesn't make sense'. All good plays, all good theatre, repeatedly put our views and precepts to the test. The play of Arthur Miller's which was here given the colourless title of *The Witches of Salem* was called *The Crucible* in the original. But of course a literal Czech translation would have looked odd on the posters. On the other hand, I know of no more appropriate title for a play – perhaps all the better theatres should be called that. Alas, there exist tougher and more severe tests of human minds and characters, but among the more humane ones the theatre comes top in the arts as a 'crucible' sensitively revealing what kind of metal we are made of. Both on stage and in the auditorium. Bearing in mind the ratio of population and the number of amphitheatres in their day, the ancient Greeks, it would seem, underwent this testing *en masse*. Who can dare claim that he knows something about their psyche? And yet, the texts of the plays give us some idea. It is well nigh unbelievable that they would have gathered in their thousands merely out of some masochistic desire to hear the gods' cruel prophecies about the fate of men. There must have been those among them who came to dispute them. The theatre has, I suppose, always been either the place where many-sided arguments were conducted, where confrontations and tests took place, or it sank to the level of mere spectacle. In a way, the organizers of happenings accepted this lowering of standards as their starting point. They, too, found coincidence handy as something that has no cause. The greatest freedom in self-revelation and self-recognition, they felt, was to be found when the reaction, movements, manner of action and of speech were entrusted to a conglomeration of allegedly 'chance' encounters with other allegedly 'liberated' people, their gestures, speeches and random creations. Of course, this could be, and sometimes doubtless was, amusing and exciting. In a world in which the conscious, motivated and power-supported intentions – even the most humane ones – either end in catastrophe or at the very least turn out quite different from the original aim, happenings undoubtedly had their justification. And yet they failed as a process that would be attractively stimulating and self-revealing at one and the same time. Human spontaneity is either controlled by ready wit, character and erudition, or it turns us back into a particle of some precognitive human protoplasm. It would not take as many half-truths as some other prophecies about the ultimate goals of mankind to theorize that it is our destiny to return to such a state. If only we allow our attention to wander from the overall meaning of the plays of the ancient Greeks, we can easily arrive at such a theory on the basis of some of their features, characters and situations, according to which human beings may well appear to be nothing more than putty in the omnipotent fingers of the gods. But we can also find in these plays other features, characters and situations, which show that people were well aware of this, and ready to resist it and bring about a change in those relationships. Whether for better or worse, it is difficult to say. Unlike the Greeks, Shakespeare considered man to be the author of his own destiny. But is it really so? Who knows? Yet we have made advances in our knowledge. The organizers of happenings have rejected the conflict between mind and spontaneity. But no enthralling drama was born. And a certain kind of knowledge only came from without. If we rely on chance, we shall not learn very much about mankind and its condition. Happenings have gone the way of all flesh, even those organized under the most liberated conditions; the theatre, even under the most adverse of circumstances, survives, neither is it always futile.

6 If it is true that there is no such thing as random

coincidence, then it must also be true that each moment of a human life is decisive in some way and to some degree. We cannot, for instance, relax for even a moment without it being reflected in the whole structure of our life. Even retroactively, because that which follows alters the meaning of that which went before. By taking that short rest, we may miss an appointment. With all kinds of consequences for us and others. Apart from which, we may get used to such moments and the habit will be paid to our good resolutions. Or, on the other hand, having rested we may be better able to fulfil them. Everything will depend on the general situation – and being linked to both the immediate and more distant world environment, these personal situations are inevitably determined by the nature, the stage of development, the permanent as well as momentary dispositions of the entire organism of each individual. It is, and probably will always remain, uncertain whether it is the external or internal factors which predominate. What is important is that their mutual interdependence persists – it only keeps changing with time. Given this, and taking into account both local and universal circumstances of the world we live in, it is at least possible to state, negatively, that nothing happens to anyone that would not befit them. To the shame of many and the honour of a few. But that is probably too rash a moral judgement. In any case, we are not dealing with this area at the moment. Rather, we see that character is not only fate in its entirety, but also the way we realize ourselves in the world, the way we find, or fail to find, a certain rapport with our fellow humans. And in each of those irrevocably fleeting decisive moments our character either facilitates or prevents our making a choice. Which brings us back at long last to that conglomeration of 'fortunate coincidences'. If we accept this term, then we find that there are probably immeasurably more of them in our life than we are able to register and turn into something truly 'fortunate'. Some things we have been born with, others we have managed to achieve thanks to what had been given to us at the start, and if one of these achievements is the ability to distinguish between various kinds of self-realization, creation, communication, or simply possibilities of realization which might give meaning to our existence, we shall find ourselves face to face – from one moment to the next – with the necessity to choose, it being the more daunting the more of these chances we recognize. We stand in tense or desperate helplessness in front of this shop window of possibilities on offer even at a time when we dimly begin to become aware that we have reached an advanced stage of ontogenesis of one or another kind of discovery and communication with mankind. And even if, these days, everything is made all the more problematical by all the external interference, which is frequently insensitive, to say the least, I doubt if even today there exists a poet, lathe operator, mathematician, agriculturist, bridge builder, sociologist, current affairs commentator, or playwright who would be completely devoid of the ability consciously to assist the completion of that process of growth and maturing within himself. Should the choice be consistent with the character or the interests and energy of the chooser, then it is undoubtedly fortunate for him and for those around him, but to dub this 'coincidence' is somewhat ungrateful where the many predecessors in the history of his profession are concerned, and it also deprives us of the history behind the causes that led to one of the most felicitous encounters between a very concrete individual and a very concrete and highly demanding discipline. This, too, is to be found in your reflections, but less so than at least one of your readers would like. And if circumstances are unfavourable to the writing of a play, why not describe how the playwright matured?

7 It is, I believe, more important for us to know the dramatist's birth and growth – thus being given a glimpse of the birth and growth of the drama and the theatre – than would be similar information regarding other disciplines. Theatre dates back to the time when man first began to see himself also from the outside – and it was then that its perhaps not great but, nevertheless, by no means negligible, influence on man and his doings began. I have no idea how it was in your case, for I have never examined you on this

subject, but I should think that if dramatists worthy of the name agreed to be examined on questions pertaining to the history of the theatre, they would not get top marks. Given the nature of theatre, which is far more closely linked to the present than are other arts, they have other things to worry about. And, since they are usually the brightest of people, they would no doubt seek to avoid questions of historical fact. Shaw, I think, would say, only half in jest, that the history of the theatre had just begun with him. Beckett would ask if by theatre you mean that huge hen-coop where he was lured the other day to sit among a multitude of coughers and throat-clearers, who were answered from the other side by a small number of gesticulating and garrulous people; he could only speak with any authority about what was happening inside him in relation to the outside world. Shakespeare would, likely as not, invite the members of the examination board to the Globe: unless it rains too much or the Puritan city fathers declare a plague alert in order to close down the theatres, they will be able to see *Henry IV Part I*, so that if they want to know about the history of the drama and the theatre *from him*, there they will see it. In these and similar terms would they speak of the history of the theatre and about themselves, doing it more honestly and more truthfully than if they tried to convey any number of facts about the origins and development of their profession. They experienced the genesis of the theatre and of drama in their own, individual genesis and growth. There, deep within themselves, they discovered many unforeseen phenomena, which they then put to good use in their plays – but there were, in their development, no random coincidences. They were no wild beasts intent on self-preservation and whipped on by instinct, but rather partly spontaneous, partly highly conscious observers and recorders of men's characters and their position in the world.

As I write this at three in the morning, I am reminded of someone very close to me. Cheers.

Yours,

Z.

16

Ludvík Vaculík: On the house

There was a time when I regarded wealth as a character defect, or fault even: 'property is theft' was the catch-phrase someone once invented. This was an opinion I held long before I encountered Marxism, when I was a youngster in Brumov, where the popular view was that the richer you were the more you an outsider – and wicked to boot. It came to me as a relief when I later realized that the wealthy play a useful social role: in provisionally administering part of the people's property. This idea reconciled me to meeting rich people – had I known any! And since the aforementioned rich people of Brumov were not wealthy anyway, Václav Havel was the first real-life moneybags I ever met.

This particular rich man is someone I like both for his looks and his character. He regards the Havel family property, which is currently administered by someone outside the family, as a valuable experience, something akin to his time in prison. I am of the view that those whose wealth has come to an end painlessly have greater self-assurance thereafter, which can less easily be said of those who leave poverty behind. And since prison – again so long as no harm is done – also tends to strengthen people's character, one might well say that Václav Havel has cornered for himself both of these extreme advantages. 'I'm a wealthy man', I've heard him declare, 'I'm a writer who has the good fortune to be world famous. There is always someone putting on a play of mine somewhere, so I'm earning my living,' he states with more vehemence, 'and the fact that I get involved in political activity in addition is because I feel a moral compulsion to do so and I spurn all attempts to assign base, material motives to me,' he declares in now resolute tones and, one might say, in terms fit for an affidavit. That's rich people for you: they're not ashamed of their wealth. When someone comes into a bit of money after a lifetime's poverty they'd sooner deny the fact.

We are sitting in the underground Lucerna Palace built during the years 1906–1917 by Václav Havel, architect. Above us there are several floors accommodating every sort of activity, including a picture palace from 1914, the Rokoko Theatre of 1915 and the large hall of 1920. There are eight of us: the rich can be relied on to attract a motley entourage. Outside it is a sunny late afternoon; in here it is air-conditioned twilight dotted with lights above the tables. Tomorrow is St Wenceslas' Day and our own particular Wenceslas – Václav Havel – has already ordered several bottles of Hungarian white wine for starters before declaring: 'For the first time in years I've received a piece of good news from the authorities; they sent me a letter saying I've been amnestied by the Czechoslovak President.' The letter is handed round the table and we all congratulate the President on his positive – albeit five-year belated – decision. 'But why are there only Hungarian dishes on the menu?' Karel Pecka asks in surprise.

'To explain', says Václav's brother, Ivan, 'I ought to tell you that this restaurant was originally called Yokohama, though I can't tell you why . . .'

'But we don't remember any of that', interjects brother Václav, 'because it was before we were born . . .'

'If you don't mind I'll tell the story properly', says brother Ivan, and continues: 'during the thirties it was renamed the Black Horse, and kept that name till not long ago . . .'

'Yes, and these seats', Václav jumps up, 'even had little horseshoes on their back legs!' After an indulgent silence, brother Ivan declares: 'What will be of greater interest to our friends, I'm sure, is that in the hall above us, all the pre-war communist congresses were held . . .'

'. . . because when no one else would have them, Mr Gottwald came to see my father and he accommodated him.' Zdeněk points out: 'He *happily* accommodated him, you ought to say – but that doesn't explain why these days you serve stuffed sirloin under the name of Gyulai.'

'That's because it's now the Budapest Restaurant and we're even in for a spot of Hungarian music in a moment', Ivan replies. 'Which is very bad, by the way', Václav adds.

'Go on and tell them', Mrs Olga Havlová urges husband Václav, 'how you used to come here for your lunches . . .'

'Absolutely: and even after 1948 our parents used to bring us here for Sunday lunch, and it's interesting how the staff continued to treat us with what was an almost inexplicable deference, though they weren't supposed to, of course.' After trying for several moments to get a word in, Lenka Prochazková finally joins in the reminiscent chorus with: 'In that hall upstairs my dad managed to ruin his suit at an Ella Fitzgerald concert, and at some ball or other I got engaged to a bloke, though there was nothing going on between us at the time. He called me up the next day to talk about it, but I'd forgotten it ever happened. His name was Foot and he had three fingers missing from one hand, so we called him Handy Pandy.'

'Pity', I say, and Olga chips in: 'I should think everyone in Prague must have come to a ball here at some time, but I've got a wartime photo of myself with my mother in a hat eating ice-cream on the Barrandov Terraces.' Across the table-top Dáša is explaining the Hungarian names of the dishes to Zdeněk in Slovak and Pecka asks across them: 'Who was in the hat?' Zdeněk – most likely because nobody has ever seen him in a hat – looks up to ask: 'In what hat?' Pecka gestures exasperatedly at him: 'Never you mind! Was Olga wearing the hat, or her mother?' Václav Havel says: 'Brousek always was . . .' – I failed to catch precisely what. 'He's not a wicked fellow, he's out to shock, that's all; he just can't help', Václav's voice rises to a crescendo, 'breaking everyone's tacit consensus! Brousek!' Beneath the hands of the serving waiters in their would-be Hungarian attire we discuss what could have led exiled poet Antonín Brousek to divulge what must have been obvious to everyone, namely, that Jaroslav Seifert had not written his Stockholm speech unaided. We are all sore about it, but apart from the inappropriateness of Brousek's action we have no cause to be, though it is a feeling that the poet in exile would seem to be incapable of appreciating. I decide to change the subject.

'Friends!' I cry. 'I read in *Rude právo* that on the river Vashka near the small town of Erton in the Autonomous Soviet Socialist Republic of Komi . . .'

'Commies?' asks Zdeněk.

'. . . they've found a lump of metal alloy which apparently can only have come from some alien artificial body. What do you think?' In response to the universal silence, I say, 'In the light of our experience of the universe and the country in question, my guess is that the river Vashka might well not exist, that the small town of Erton certainly doesn't exist, and that nothing in fact was found in the republic of Komi.'

Václav Havel says, 'Thank you, friends, for accepting the invitation . . .'

'Which you were provoked into extending', says Zdeněk.

'. . . to these surroundings so dear to us.' At this moment the waiter present him with the bill on a salver. Zdeněk seizes the bill, looks at it and tosses it back with a grimace, but Václav says: 'Quite the contrary! I'm surprised how reasonable it is! You can't complain about that! I was expecting it to come to twice as much. Goodness knows when we'll get another chance of spending such a pleasant couple of hours together.'

As we are saying our muted goodbyes upstairs in the Lucerna Arcade, Zdeněk says: 'In the words of Fučík: "Don't weep, don't weep".'

October 1985

A short bio-bibliography of Václav Havel

The following is based on the detailed chronology by Vilém Prečan in Václav Havel, *In Search of Human Identity (O lidskou identitu)*. London: Rozmluvy, 1984.

Those dates shown below in italics relate to Havel's writings.

October 1936
Birth of Václav, son of civil engineer, Václav Havel and Božena née Vavrečková.

1951
The young Havel completes his compulsory schooling but is repeatedly frustrated for 'class' or 'political profile' reasons in obtaining higher education.

1951–1955
He works as an apprentice and, later, laboratory technician at Prague's Czech Technical High School, while attending an evening grammar school course and taking his passing out exam in 1955.

1955
Havel publishes his first articles and continues till 1969 to write for a number of periodicals, mainly literary and theatrical.

Autumn 1956
He makes his first public appearance with a highly critical address at a working party of new authors at the Dobříš Writers' Home near Prague.

1955–1957
Several applications to university humanities departments

having been turned down, Havel takes an economics course
at the Czech Technical High School in Prague.

1957
Having failed to obtain a place in the Film Faculty of Prague's
Performing Arts Academy (AMU), Havel is unable to
continue his studies and starts his two-year military service.

1959–1960
Refused a place in the Drama Faculty of AMU, he obtains
work as a stage technician at Prague's ABC Theatre.

1960
Havel joins the Na zábradlí Theatre, initially as a stage hand,
finally becoming its literary adviser. He contributes scripts to
a number of stage shows, serving simultaneously as assistant
to the prominent Czech producer, Alfred Radok, for the
Prague City Theatre group.

3 December 1963 – The Garden Party
Première at the Na zábradlí Theatre of Havel's first play *The
Garden Party* (*Zahradní slavnost*), which later appears in print
in:

Czech: *Zahradní slavnost*, in *Protokoly* (see 1966)
English: *The Garden Party*. Translated and adapted by Vera
         Blackwell. London: Cape, 1969
German: *Das Gartenfest*, in *Das Gartenfest. Die Benachrich-
         tigung. Zwei Dramen. Essays. Antikoden.* Translated
         by August Scholtis, Evan Berkmann and Franz
         Peter Künzel. Reinbek bei Hamburg: Rowohlt, 1967
            Das Gartenfest. Spiel. Translated by August Schol-
         tis. Reinbek bei Hamburg: Rowohlt, 1970
French: *La fête en plein air*. Translated by François Kérel.
         Paris: Gallimard, 1969
Italian etc.

9 July 1964
Civil marriage with Olga Šplíchalová.

1964 – Anticodes
Havel completes his collection of 'typograms', *Anticodes*
(*Antikódy*), later published in:

Czech: *Antikódy*, in *Protokoly* (see *1966*)

German: *Antikoden*, in *Das Gartenfest. Die Benachrichtigung* etc. (see *3 December 1963*)

1965

Havel joins the editorial staff of the contentious monthly, *Tvář*, and becomes chairman of the working party of young writers in the Czechoslovak Writers' Association. *Tvář* is then closed down by its own staff, who refuse to accept instructions from officials of the Communist Party and the Writers' Association.

May 1965

At a conference of the Czechoslovak Writers' Association on the twentieth anniversary of the liberation of the country, Havel criticizes the activities of the Association and unfair treatment of certain writers.

26 July 1965 – The Memorandum

Première at the Na zábradlí Theatre of Havel's second play *The Memorandum* (*Vyrozumění*), later appearing in:

Czech: *Vyrozumění*, in *Protokoly* (see *1966*)

English: *The Memorandum*. Translated by Vera Blackwell. Introduction by Tom Stoppard. New York: Grove Press, 1980

German: *Die Benachrichtigung*, in *Das Gartenfest. Die Benachrichtigung* etc. (see *3 December 1963*)

        Die Benachrichtigung, Eine satirische Komödie, in *Drei Stücke. Audienz. Vernissage. Die Benachrichtigung*. 'Offener Brief an Gustáv Husák'. Postface by Gabriel Laub. Reinbek bei Hamburg: Rowohlt, 1977

Italian, Norwegian, Polish etc.

1966 – Minutes

Havel's first book, *Minutes* (*Protokoly*), is published by Mladá fronta, Prague. This contains the two plays, *The Garden Party* (*Zahradní slavnost*, 1963) and *The Memorandum* (*Vyrozumění*, 1965), the collection of 'typograms' *Anticodes* (*Antikódy*, 1964), and two essays, 'On dialectical metaphysics' (*O dialektické metafyzice*, 1964) and 'Anatomy of the gag' (*Anatomie gagu*, 1963), with a foreword by Jan Grossman. Later published in

German as *Das Gartenfest. Die Benachrichtigung. Zwei Dramen. Essays. Antikoden* (see *3 December 1963*).

1966–1967
Havel completes his external studies in the Drama Faculty of AMU.

28 June 1967
In a speech at the Fourth Congress of the Czechoslovak Writers' Association, Havel attacks undemocratic procedures within the Association and, under pressure of Communist Party officials, is struck off the list of candidates for the Association's Central Committee, together with Ivan Klíma, Pavel Kohout and Ludvík Vaculík.

March 1968
Havel signs a proclamation by twenty writers on the establishment of an Independent Writers' Circle within the Czechoslovak Writers' Association. This circle of writers and translators not belonging to the Communist Party had, initially, fifty-eight members. In April 1968, it elected a seven-member committee, of which Havel became chairman, and continued to function until the whole Writers' Association broke up in 1970.

At the end of the month he signs an open letter to the Communist Party Central Committee, in which 150 writers and cultural figures commented on the current state of the 'democratization progress' under the Dubček regime.

4 April 1968 – 'On the subject of opposition'
The weekly *Literární listy* publishes his article, 'On the subject of opposition' (*Na téma opozice*), advocating a two-party system and the creation of a democratic party based on Czechoslovak humanitarian traditions.

11 April 1968 – The Increased Difficulty of Concentration
Première at the Na zábradlí Theatre of Havel's third play, *The Increased Difficulty of Concentration* (*Ztížená možnost soustředění*), appearing later in:

Czech: *Ztížená možnost soustředění*, with postscript by Josef Šafařík. Prague: Orbis, 1969

English: *The Increased Difficulty of Concentration*. Translated
          by Vera Blackwell. London: Cape, 1972
              The Increased Difficulty of Concentration. Translated
          by Vera Blackwell. New York, London etc.: French,
          1976
German: *Erschwerte Möglichkeit der Koncentration, Stück in zwei
          Akten*. Translated by Franz Peter Künzel. Reinbek
          bei Hamburg: Rowohlt
Italian etc.

May–June 1968
Havel spends six weeks in the USA on the occasion of the
American première of his play, *The Memorandum*, at the New
York Shakespeare Festival. The play is a great success and
wins him the prestigious Obie Prize.

June 1968
Havel signs a statement by some thirty cultural figures
advocating the revival of the Social Democratic Party.

Summer 1968
He resigns as literary adviser of the Na zábradlí Theatre.

21–27 August 1968
During the first week of Soviet occupation of the country he
takes part in the Free Czechoslovak Radio broadcasts from
the town of Liberec, contributing a daily commentary on the
situation.

September 1968
The Soviet-sponsored *White Book* (*Bílá kniha*) on Czechoslovak
developments attacks his April article 'On the subject of
opposition' (see *4 April 1968*).

Autumn 1968
He becomes a member of the Czechoslovak Writers' Association Central Committee, till its dissolution in 1970, and
chairman of the editorial staff of the revived monthly *Tvář* till
its final closure in June 1969.

1968
Awarded the Austrian State Prize for European Literature.

February 1969 – 'The Czech destiny?'

Under the title 'The Czech destiny?' (*Český úděl?*), the monthly *Tvář* publishes his reply to Milan Kundera's article 'The Czech destiny'.

March 1969
Havel discovers a bugging device placed in his Prague flat by the state police.

21 August 1969
With nine others he signs a declaration, 'Ten points' (*Deset bodů*), condemning the post-Dubček policy of 'normalization' and addressed to the government, parliament, Party Central Committee etc. He is consequently interrogated during the autumn along with the other signatories and finally charged with subverting the republic. A full trial of all ten was set for 15–16 October 1970, but later postponed indefinitely.

1969 – *Similes 2*
The Prague publishing house, Československý spisovatel, publishes, with a foreword by Havel, the collective volume *Similes 2* (*Podoby 2*) containing contributions by eighteen authors, all of whom are banned in the subsequent 'normalization' process.

December 1970
Havel is singled out for attack in the party document, 'Lessons from the crisis-ridden developments in the party and society after the 13th Congress of the C.C.P.' (*Poučení z krizového vývoje ve straně a společnosti po XIII. sjezdu KSČ*).

1970
Havel is awarded the American Obie Prize a second time following the success of his *The Increased Difficulty of Concentration* at New York's Off-Broadway Theatre.

1970 – *The Conspirators*
Havel writes his play, *The Conspirators* (*Spiklenci*), which only circulates privately in Czechoslovakia as No. 86 in the typewritten series, *Edice Expedice*, 1979. It has its première in Germany, in the Theater der Stadt Baden-Baden, on 8 February 1974. Later printed in:

Czech: *Spiklenci*, in *Hry 1970–1976* (see *August 1977*)

German: *Die Retter*. Translated by Franz Peter Künzel. Reinbek bei Hamburg: Rowohlt, 1972

Italian etc.

1971–1972

Listed in confidential official circulars among authors whose books have been withdrawn from school, local, and all other public libraries.

31 May 1972

Together with other banned authors, Havel is attacked at the founding congress of the new 'normalized' Writers' Association from which most major Czech authors are excluded.

4 December 1972

He is one of thirty-five Czech writers who address a petition to the president for all Czechoslovak political prisoners to be granted amnesty.

1974

Havel spends nine months working in the Trutnov brewery in north-east Bohemia.

25 February 1975 – A Butterfly on the Aerial

His television play, *A Butterfly on the Aerial* (*Motýl na anténě*), written in the sixties, is first broadcast by the German Norddeutscher Rundfunk under the title *Fledermaus auf der Antenne*.

8 April 1975 – 'Letter to Dr Gustáv Husák'

Havel signs his 'Letter to Dr Gustav Husák' (*Dopis Dr Gustávu Husákovi*), copies of which circulate privately in Czechoslovakia. It appears in:

English: 'Letter to Dr Gustav Husák, General Secretary of the Czechoslovak Communist Party', in *Survey*, 21/3, Summer 1975

German: *Offener Brief an Gustáv Husák*, in *Drei Stücke* (see 26 July 1965)

French: *De l'entropie en politique. Lettre ouverte à Gustáv Husák*, in *Istina*, XXII/2, 1977

Italian etc.

Late 1975

Havel launches the typewritten series, *Edice Expedice*, in which a total of fifty-one items appear up to April 1979. After Havel's imprisonment, his wife Olga continues this work.

1975 – The Beggar's Opera

He finishes *The Beggar's Opera* (*Žebrácká opera*), based on the play by John Gay. In Czechoslovakia this is only circulated privately as No. 49 in the typewritten *Edice Petlice*, 1975, and as No. 10 in the *Edice Expedice*, 1976. The only stage performance in Czechoslovakia was an amateur one in Horní Počernice, just outside Prague, on 1 November 1976. It was used as a pretext for a major police drive against the author, actors, and some spectators. The play had its première abroad, at the Teatro Stabile in Trieste on 4 March 1976. It was printed in:

Czech: *Žebrácká opera*, in *Hry 1970–1976* (see *August 1977*)
German: *Die Gauneroper, nach John Gay*. Translated by Franz
          Peter Künzel. Reinbek bei Hamburg: Rowohlt, 1975
Italian etc.

1975 – Audience

Havel completes the one-act play *Audience* (*Audience*), which only circulates privately in Czechoslovakia as No. 47 in the *Edice Petlice*, 1975 and, together with *Private View* (*Vernisáž*), under the title *Two One-Act Plays* (*Dvě aktovky*), as No. 3 in the *Edice Expedice*, 1975. It has its première, with *Private View*, in Vienna's Burgtheater on 7 October 1976. It is printed in:

Czech: *Audience*, in *Hry 1970–1976* (see *August 1977*)
English: *Conversation: a One-Act Play*. Translated by George
          Theiner, in *Index on Censorship*, 5/3, Autumn 1976
              Sorry: Two plays (*Audience. Private View*). Trans-
          lated and adapted by Vera Blackwell. London:
          Methuen, 1978
German: *Audienz*, in *Drei Stücke* (see *26 July 1965*)
French: *Audience*. Paris: L'Avant-scène, 1979
              Audience. Vernissage. Pétition. Translated by Mar-
          cel Aymonin and Stephan Meldegg, with a preface
          by Milan Kundera. Paris: Gallimard, 1980
Italian, Swedish, Polish etc.

1975 – Private View
Havel writes the one-act play *Private View* (*Vernisáž*), which only circulates privately in Czechoslovakia as No. 51 in the *Edice Petlice*, 1975 and, together with *Audience*, in No. 3 of the *Edice Expedice*, 1975. For its Vienna première, see *1975 – Audience* (above). It is printed in:

Czech: *Vernisáž*, in *Hry 1970–1976*, (see *August 1977*)
English: *Private View*, in *Sorry: Two Plays* (see *1975 – Audience*, above)
German: *Vernissage*, in *Drei Stücke* (see *26 July 1976*)
French: *Vernissage*, in *Audience. Vernissage. Pétition* (see *1975 – Audience*, above)
Italian etc.

16 September 1976 – 'The trial'
With six other Czechoslovak writers and philosophers Havel signs a letter to Heinrich Böll appealing for solidarity with the young pop groups on trial for their dissident performances, and continues to help organize protests against the persecution of these musicians. He writes an article, 'The trial' (*Proces*), on the trial of these young people.

Late September 1976
Havel is invited by the Austrian Minister of Education to the première of his plays, *Audience* and *Private View*, but is not allowed to travel to Vienna because, as the Czechoslovak Foreign Ministry puts it, he 'is not a representative of Czech culture'.

1976 – A Hotel in the Hills
Havel completes his play, *A Hotel in the Hills* (*Horský hotel*), circulated in Czechoslovakia privately in the *Edice Petlice*, No. 62, 1976, and in the *Edice Expedice*, No. 10, 1976. It receives its première in Vienna at the Burgtheater on 23 May 1981. Printed in:

Czech: *Horský hotel*, in *Hry 1970–1976* (see *August 1977*)
German: *Das Berghotel*. Translated by Gabriel Laub. Reinbek bei Hamburg: Rowohlt, 1976
Italian etc.

Late 1976

He takes part in discussions leading to the foundation of the Charter 77 movement and to its 'Declaration' of 1 January 1977. After the Charter 77 announcement, Václav Havel, the philosopher Jan Patočka and the former Foreign Minister Jiří Hájek form the first trio of Charter spokesmen. In the course of delivering the 'Declaration' with its list of signatories to the government, parliament and the Czechoslovak Press Agency Havel is detained along with the actor Pavel Landovský and the writer Ludvík Vaculík, and all three are subjected to interrogation, house searches, TV scrutiny etc. The announcement of Charter 77 gave rise to a large-scale repressive action directed at its spokesmen as well as against most of the original signatories.

14 January 1977

Havel is taken for interrogation, held in detention till 20 May, and charged with subversion of the republic as the author of the 'Letter to Dr Gustáv Husák' and as the principal begetter and organizer of Charter 77.

August 1977 – Plays 1970–1976

The *émigré* Sixty-Eight Publishers in Toronto publish in Czech a collection of Havel's plays 'from the prohibition years' under the title *Plays 1970–1976* (*Hry 1970–1976*). This includes *The Conspirators* (*Spiklenci*, 1970), *The Beggar's Opera* (*Žebrácká opera*, 1975), *A Hotel in the Hills* (*Horský hotel*, 1976), *Audience* (*Audience*, 1975), *Private View* (*Vernisáž*, 1975) and a 'Postscript by the author' (*Dovětek autora*, December 1976). Jiří Voskovec contributes a preface.

17–18 October 1977

Criminal proceedings against Ota Ornest, Jiří Lederer, František Pavlíček and Václav Havel culminate in a trial before the bench of the Prague City Court, where Havel is sentenced to fourteen months' imprisonment, conditionally deferred for three years, for attempting to damage the interests of the republic.

December 1977

Havel signs an open letter from thirteen Czech writers,

addressed to their colleagues abroad, asking them, in connection with the Belgrade meeting of the signatory states to the Helsinki Agreement, to demand more explicit formulation of the principle of free exchange of information and recognition of the right to publish prohibited works.

28 January 1978 – 'Report on my case'
With a number of friends, Havel is detained by the police on arrival at the railwaymen's ball, held for investigation until 13 March, and accused of obstructing an official in the exercise of his duty, and of assaulting an official. Criminal proceedings were halted on 21 April 1979. Havel describes the circumstances of his arrest and imprisonment in his 'Report on my case' (*Zpráva o mém případu*), dated 20 March 1978.

21 March 1978
Havel signs a petition to parliament by 298 citizens urging abolition of the death penalty.

7 April 1978
With twenty-three other signatories of Charter 77, he signs the statement 'A hundred years of Czech socialism' (*Sto let českého socialismu*), for the centenary of the Constituent Congress of the Czech Social Democratic Party.

27 April 1978
The Committee for the Defence of the Unjustly Prosecuted (*Výbor na obranu nespravedlivě stíhaných*, VONS) is set up, with Havel among its eighteen members. He continues actively to support it until his arrest on 29 May 1979.

August–September 1978
Havel attends two joint meetings of representatives of the Polish KOR (Committee for Citizens' Self-Defence) and of Charter 77 on the Polish frontier. A third meeting, on 1 October, is broken up by the co-ordinated action of Czechoslovak and Polish police.

October 1978 – 'The power of the powerless'
He signs his essay, 'The power of the powerless' (*Moc bezmocných*), which only circulates privately in Czechoslovakia as No. 149 in *Edice Petlice*, 1979. Discussions of this essay

among Charter 77 signatories issued under the title *Freedom and Power* (*O svobodě a moci*) in a volume only privately circulated in Czechoslovakia. They were later published in:

Czech: *O svobodě a moci*. Cologne: Index, 1980
English: *The power of the powerless. Citizens against the state in central-eastern Europe*. Introduction by Stephen Lukes. Edited by John Keane. London: Hutchinson, 1986
German: *Versuch in der Wahrheit zu leben: von der Macht der Ohnmächtigen*. With a foreword by Hans Peter Riese. Translated by Gabriel Laub. Reinbek bei Hamburg: Rowohlt, 1980.

6 November 1978
Havel resumes his function as a Charter 77 spokesman and continues to exercise it until 8 February 1979.

7 November 1978 – 'Reports on my house arrest'
The security police start shadowing Havel continuously and, from December 1978, keep permanent watch over both his Prague flat and his country house in Hrádeček, near Trutnov in north-east Bohemia. Havel writes about this in January and March 1979 in his two 'Reports on my house arrest and attendant circumstances' (*Zprávy o mém domácím vězení a jevech s ním souvisejících*). On 3 March 1979, he writes to the Federal Ministry of the Interior protesting against this illegal restriction of his movements.

1979 – Protest
Havel completes the one-act play, *Protest* (*Protest*), circulating only privately in Czechoslovakia in the *Edice Expedice*, No. 89, 1979. It receives its première on 17 November 1979 in Vienna's Burgtheater together with Pavel Kohout's one-act play *The Pedigree Certificate* (*Atest*). Printed in:

German: *Protest, Ein Einakter*. Translated by Gabriel Laub. Reinbek bei Hamburg: Rowohlt, 1978
French: *Pétition*, in *Audience. Vernissage. Pétition* (see *1975 – Audience*, above)
Italian etc.

27 February 1979
He writes to the Austrian president, Rudolf Kirschläger, asking him to make use of his visit to Czechoslovakia to intervene on behalf of Czechoslovak political prisoners.

29 May 1979
The security police start a large-scale drive against the VONS Committee, carrying out a number of house searches and arresting fifteen of the committee members. Ten of these, including Havel, are taken into police custody and charged with criminal subversion of the republic. Six appeared in court in October 1979; the remaining four were released without trial on 22 December 1979.

August 1979
A Foreign Ministry official informs Havel while he is in custody that he has been invited to spend a year in New York as a literary adviser on Broadway. Havel refuses to discuss the offer.

22–23 October 1979
The trial takes place in Prague's City Court of Petr Uhl, Jiří Dienstbier, Otka Bednářová, Václav Benda, Dana Němcová and Václav Havel for criminal subversion of the republic by virtue of their activity in the VONS Committee. Havel is sentenced to four and a half years in prison.

19 December 1979
On the initiative of AIDA (Association internationale de défense des artistes victimes de la répression dans le monde), the Cartoucherie Theatre in Paris presents a dramatic reconstruction of the trial of the six VONS members in Prague. This was also performed in German on 9 February 1980, in Munich, and in English at the Greenwich House Theatre in New York on 12 November 1982. The German version was shown on television in Austria and Switzerland, as well as Germany.

7 January 1980
Havel is taken from his Prague prison to the prison camp at Heřmanice near Ostrava.

24 March 1981
The Paris Théâtre des Mathurins gives a performance of
Havel's *Protest*, together with Sartre's *Huis clos*, in aid of the
VONS Committee and particularly of its members in prison.

18 June 1981
In a resolution dealing with Czechoslovaks arrested and
imprisoned for political reasons, the European Parliament
calls for the release of Václav Havel among others.

July 1981
After spending a week at a prison hospital in Prague, Havel is
transferred to the prison at Plzeň-Bory, where he remains till
January 1983.

21 November 1981
The Warsaw theatre, Mala Scena Teatru Powszechniego, puts
on three of Havel's short plays – *Audience*, *Private View* and
Protest – which continue running until 13 December.

8 December 1981
The Plzeň District Court rejects Havel's request for conditional release after serving half his sentence.

17 February 1982
The International Committee for the Defence of Charter 77
confers the Jan Palach Prize on Havel for his literary works
and his selfless defence of human rights.

10 June 1982
York University, Toronto, confers the honorary degree of
Doctor of Letters on Havel *in absentia* in recognition of his
literary achievement and as a gesture of solidarity with the
silenced and imprisoned author.

21 July 1982
The 36th International Theatre Festival at Avignon includes a
six-hour 'Night for Václav Havel', featuring Samuel Beckett's
Catastrophe and Arthur Miller's *I think about you a great deal*.

17 August 1982
Toulouse University confers an honorary doctorate on Havel.
The actual ceremony takes place in February 1984 (see
February 1984).

December 1982
Shortly before President Husák's visit to Austria, Interior Ministry officials suggest to Havel, in prison, that he request a presidential pardon. Havel declines the suggestion.

January 1983 – Letters to Olga
Between June 1979 and September 1982, while under police detention and then in prison, Havel wrote to his wife – and through her to many of his friends – a large number of letters, some of which were confiscated. A total of 144 letters, however, reached her and these were from the start circulated in private copies. In January 1983, they were collected and issued under the title *Letters to Olga* (Dopisy Olze) in the *Edice Petlice*, No. 260, 1983, and in the *Edice Expedice*, No. 166, 1983. They were later printed in:

Czech: *Dopisy Olze*. Postface by Jiří Dienstbier. Editorial note by Jan Lopatka. Toronto: Sixty-Eight Publishers, 1985

German: *Briefe an Olga, Identität und Existenz. Betrachtungen aus dem Gefängnis*. Postface by Jiří Dienstbier. Translated by Joachim Bruss. Reinbeck bei Hamburg: Rowohlt, 1984

23 January 1983
Havel suddenly develops serious pneumonia and is transferred, handcuffed, from Plzeň-Bory to a prison hospital in Prague. There, on 7 February, he is handed the City Court's decision to suspend his sentence for health reasons, and is moved forthwith to the public hospital, Pod Petřínem, in Prague.

4 March 1983
He is released from hospital for home treatment and the remainder of his sentence is waived, in September 1985, under the amnesty commemorating the fortieth anniversary of the liberation. On regaining his freedom, Havel resumes his part in drawing up important Charter 77 documents.

3 April 1983
Havel gives his first interview since leaving prison to the

French journalist, Antoine Spire; this was published in *Le Monde*, 10/11 April 1983.

May 1983 – Mistake
He writes a one-act play, *Mistake* (*Omyl*), for the 'Evening of solidarity' with Havel and Charter 77, put on by the Stockholm Stadsteater on 29 October of that year, together with *Catastrophe*, dedicated to Havel by Samuel Beckett. It appeared later in:
English: *Mistake*. Translated by George Theiner. In *Index on Censorship*, 13/1, February 1984
Polish etc.

15 October 1983 – 'Responsibility as destiny
Havel signs his essay, 'Responsibility as destiny' (*Odpovědnost jako osud*), as the foreword to English and French versions of Ludvík Vaculík's novel, *The Czech Dreambook*; in Czechoslovakia this essay only circulates in private copies.

February 1984 – 'Politics and conscience'
Havel completes his essay, 'Politics and conscience' (*Politika a svědomí*), written for the conferment ceremony of his honorary doctorate of Toulouse University. In Czechoslovakia it only circulates in private copies. It appeared in:

English: in *The Salisbury Review*, 3/2, January 1985.

11 August 1984 – 'Six asides about culture'
He writes his essay, 'Six asides about culture' (*Šest poznámek o kultuře*), as a contribution to discussion of the 'first' (official) and 'second' (unofficial) cultures existing in Czechoslovakia; known only from privately circulated copies, but later published in:

English: 'Six asides about culture'. Translated by Erazim Kohák, in *A Besieged Culture. Czechoslovakia Ten Years after Helsinki*. Stockholm–Vienna: The Charter 77 Foundation, 1986.

August 1984 – Largo Desolato
Havel completes his play, *Largo Desolato* (*Largo desolato*), circulated in Czechoslovakia only privately as No. 185 in the

Edice Expedice, 1984. It receives its première at the Vienna Burgtheater on 14 April 1985. Printed in:

Czech: *Largo desolato*. Munich: Obrys/Kontur, 1985

German: *Largo desolato*. Preface by Siegfried Lenz. Translated by Joachim Bruss. Reinbek bei Hamburg: Rowohlt, 1985

French: *Largo desolato*. Translated by Erika Abrams and Stephan Meldegg. Paris: Gallimard, 1986

Italian etc.

September 1984 – In Search of Human Identity
The London *émigré* publishers, Rozmluvy, issue in Czech a collected edition of Havel's essays, articles, protests, polemics and declarations from the years 1969–1979 under the title *In Search of Human Identity (O lidskou identitu)*, edited by Vilém Prečan and Alexander Tomský.

November 1984 – 'Thriller'
Havel completes his essay, 'Thriller' (*Thriller*), for a radio series on myths in modern life, broadcast by German station Hessischer Rundfunk; only circulated privately in Czechoslovakia. It was published in:

English: 'Thriller'. Translated by Paul Wilson, in *Idler*, June/July 1985.

3 January 1985
Havel is held in police custody for forty-eight hours in connection with the nomination of new Charter 77 spokesmen.

April 1985 – 'An anatomy of reticence'
Havel writes his essay, 'An anatomy of reticence' (*Anatomie jedné zdrženlivosti*), 'intended for the Peace Congress in Amsterdam'. Known in Czechoslovakia only from privately circulated copies. Later published in:

English: 'An antatomy of reticence'. Translated by Erazim Kohák. Stockholm: The Charter 77 Foundation, 1986
         'An anatomy of reticence'. Translated by Erazim Kohák, in *Cross Currents. A Yearbook of Central European Culture*. No. 5, Ann Arbor, 1986

German: *Euer Frieden und unsrer – Anatomie einer Zurückhal-
      tung*. Translated by Joachim Bruss, in *Kursbuch 81*,
      September 1985.

August 1985
Havel is twice held by the police for forty-eight hour periods,
first in Prague on 9 August, then in Bratislava on 16 August,
in connection with the drafting of a Charter 77 statement on
the anniversary of the Soviet invasion in 1968.

October 1985 – Temptation
He completes his play, *Temptation* (*Pokoušení*), circulating only
privately in Czechoslovakia as No. 223 in the *Edice Expedice*,
1985. It receives its première at the Vienna Burgtheater on 22
May 1986, under the title *Die Versuchung*. Printed in:

Czech: *Pokoušení*. Munich: Obrys/Kontur, 1986.

1985 – Symposium
Havel edits for private circulation, and writes an introduction
to, *Symposium* (*Hostina*), a collection of essays by over twenty
Czech philosophers living in Czechoslovakia or in exile.

January 1986
Havel is awarded the Erasmus Prize by the Erasmus Prize
Foundation in Amsterdam.

Contributors

Samuel Beckett (1906): Irish writer, poet, novelist and playwright, living in Paris and writing both in English and French. Nobel Prize 1969.

Heinrich Böll (1917–1985): novelist, essayist and playwright, one of the best-known German authors of the post-Second World War period. Nobel Prize 1972.

Timothy Garton Ash (1955): English author, journalist and essayist; he is well known for his writing about central and east European themes. His book, *The Polish Revolution: Solidarity*, won the Somerset Maugham Award 1984.

Jiří Gruša (1938): Czech poet, critic and novelist, signatory of the Charter 77. In 1978, he was held several months in custody in connection with the *samizdat* publication of his novel, *The Questionnaire*. After a stay in the USA and Germany, he was stripped of his Czechoslovak citizenship in 1981; he now lives in Bonn. His writings are blacklisted in his own country, but published abroad in Czech as well as in German, French, English etc.

Ladislav Hejdánek (1927): Czech philosopher and essayist, one of the leading Charter 77 spokesmen and organizer of unofficial philosophy seminars. Constantly harassed by the police, he lives in Prague and works as a stoker. His writings are banned, but circulate in *samizdat* editions.

Harry Järv (1921): Swedish writer, critic, essayist and bibliographer, Deputy National Librarian and director of several important literary reviews. He is especially concerned with central and east European culture.

Pavel Kohout (1928): Czech poet, novelist, playwright and theatre producer, signatory of Charter 77. After a one-year stay in Austria in 1978, he was stripped of his Czechoslovak citizenship; he now lives in Vienna. His novels and plays are banned in his country, but widely published and produced abroad.

Iva Kotrlá (1947): Czech poet, critic and essayist, expelled from university in 1970 and harassed by the police since then. She lives in Moravia; her writings are blacklisted in Czechoslovakia, but circulate in *samizdat* editions or books published abroad.

Milan Kundera (1929): Czech novelist, essayist and playwright, professor at the École des Hautes Études en Sciences Sociales, Paris. He has lived in France since 1975 and was stripped of his Czechoslovak citizenship in 1979. His writings are banned in his country, but widely published abroad.

Arthur Miller (1915): playwright and essayist, one of the most important in the post-Second World War generation of American dramatists.

Zdena Salivarová (1933): Czech novelist, screenwriter and translator. Since 1969 she has lived in exile in Toronto, Canada, where – together with her husband, Josef Škvorecký –she founded the well-known Czech publishing house, Sixty-Eight Publishers, which has also issued Václav Havel's writings.

Milan Šimečka (1930): Czech philosopher, essayist and publicist, writing both in Czech and in Slovak; banned from the Bratislava University and constantly harassed by the police since 1970. Signatory of Charter 77, he lives in Bratislava. His writings are blacklisted in his country but circulate in *samizdat* editions and books published abroad; several were translated into English, German, French etc.

Josef Škvorecký (1924): Czech novelist, essayist, playwright and translator, author of several novels translated into

English, French etc. Exiled in 1969, he founded – together with his wife, Zdena Salivarová – the *émigré* publishing house, Sixty-Eight Publishers. His writings are banned in Czechoslovakia, but successfully published abroad.

Tom Stoppard (1937): English novelist and well-known playwright. One of his successful comedies, *Professional Foul*, is located in Prague and dedicated to Václav Havel.

Zdeněk Urbánek (1917): Czech novelist, essayist and translator of English and American literature. Signatory of Charter 77, he lives in Prague. His writings are banned, but circulate in *samizdat* editions.

Ludvík Vaculík (1926): Czech journalist, author of the famous 1968 'Two thousand words manifesto', and one of the most important novelists of his generation. Signatory of Charter 77 and founder of the well-known typewritten series, *Edice Petlice* (Padlock Publications), he is constantly harassed by the police. He lives in Prague; his writings are banned in Czechoslovakia, but widely published abroad.

Jan Vladislav (1923): Czech poet, essayist and translator, signatory of Charter 77 and founder of the typewritten series, *Kvart* (Quarto). Harassed by the police, he was forced into exile in 1981. He now lives in France; his writings are blacklisted in Czechoslovakia, but circulate in *samizdat* editions and books published abroad.